TEACHING ASIAN AMERICA

Pacific Formations
Arif Dirlik, Series Editor

TEACHING ASIAN AMERICA

Diversity and the Problem of Community

Edited by
LANE RYO HIRABAYASHI

ROWMAN & LITTLEFIELD PUBLISHERS, INC.
Lanham • Boulder • New York • Oxford

"The term 'Asian American' defines no particular group, rather it is an umbrella phrase that covers or encompasses an incredible diversity of groups and individuals with their own specific origins, cultures, and identities. Here, two Chinese American students study photographs of an Asian American neighborhood as they attempt to delineate the varied character of that locale for an introductory course on Asians in America."

ROWMAN & LITTLEFIELD PUBLISHERS, INC.

Published in the United States of America
by Rowman & Littlefield Publishers, Inc.
4720 Boston Way, Lanham, Maryland 20706

12 Hid's Copse Road
Cumnor Hill, Oxford OX2 9JJ, England

British Library Cataloguing in Publication Information Available

Library of Congress Cataloging-in-Publication Data

Teaching Asian America : diversity and the problem of community /
    edited by Lane Ryo Hirabayashi.
        p.   cm.—(Pacific formations)
    Includes bibliographic references and index.
    ISBN 0-8476-8734-1 (cloth).—ISBN 0-8476-8735-X (paper)
    1. Asian Americans—Study and teaching.   2. Pluralism (Social
sciences)—Study and teaching—United States.   I. Hirabayashi, Lane
Ryo.   II. Series.
E184.06T43   1998
305.895'073—dc21   97-35604
                                                                              CIP

ISBN 0-8476-8734-1 (cloth : alk. paper)
ISBN 0-8476-8735-X (pbk. : alk. paper)

Printed in the United States of America

∞ ™ The paper used in this publication meets the minimum requirements of American National Standard for Information Sciences—Permanence of Paper for Printed Library Materials, ANSI Z39.48–1984.

*We dedicate this anthology to the students
who put themselves on the line
to build the field of
Asian American and Ethnic studies*

Contents

PART II: RECONSIDERING COMMUNITIES

Acknowledgments

My deepest thanks go to the authors who took the time and made the effort to write up their chapters. Each of their contributions conveys the dedication to teaching that still characterizes Asian American studies at the end of the twentieth century.

Professor Evelyn Hu-DeHart, chair of the Department of Ethnic Studies at the University of Colorado, Boulder, (CUB), provided key support which helped me to complete this project. I would also like to acknowledge the assistance of the staff of the Department of Ethnic Studies—Steven Medina, Karen Moreira, and Anna Sheffield. Dean Albert Ramirez, who then directed CUB's IMPART (Implementation of Multicultural Perspectives and Approaches in Research and Teaching) program provided a generous grant. Among other things, it enabled me to hire two talented undergraduates, Tina Le and Brian E. Coleman, who helped me enormously with logistical and production tasks. The opportunity to affiliate with UCLA's Asian American Studies Center as a fellow of the "Endowed Chair in Japanese and Asian American Studies," 1996, provided an opportunity to research a range of pedagogical issues. I'd like to thank the Center's faculty and staff—especially its director, Professor Don T. Nakanishi—for this.

Franklin Ng, Wendy Ng, and Linda Revilla, made valuable suggestions early on. Similarly, Marilyn C. Alquizola, Kenyon Chan, Edward Guerrero, Alice Y. Hom, Yen Le Espiritu, Gary Y. Okihiro, and Alvina Quintana gave me advice during the difficult moments that this project entailed.

Professor Arif Dirlik, editor of Rowman & Littlefield's Pacific Formations series, was instrumental in sharpening the penultimate version of this work. I am grateful for his thoughtful comments and suggestions, as well as those of senior editor Susan McEachern and, finally, those proffered through the process of anonymous review.

1

Introduction

LANE RYO HIRABAYASHI

There is, necessarily, an intimate relationship between the *content* of an academic field and its *pedagogy*; that is, the philosophies, methodological approaches, and techniques entailed in teaching it. Yet while there have been various attempts to specify the focus of Asian American studies (AAS),[1] to delineate the evolution of Asian American studies programs on specific campuses,[2] as well as to document the different educational issues which face Asian American students,[3] no book-length volume exists which focuses specifically on pedagogy. *Teaching Asian America* redresses that gap. This anthology features twenty accounts by university professors based on their first-hand experiences. Each simultaneously sheds light on key issues in AAS, and illustrates creative responses to the challenges of diversity as we approach the millennium. Furthermore, a number of chapters discuss courses and topics that have seldom been addressed in the literature, such as Asian American men's issues (Chan), teaching AAS in the community colleges (Ling), Vietnamese American studies (Chung), and resistance to AAS on the part of "middle-class Caucasian students in 'East of California' " campus settings (Ma). This is clearly only a beginning; still we hope that this anthology will serve as an invitation to colleagues to write about additional topics and to share other ideas about how we can be maximally effective as teachers.[4]

I solicited the chapters which make up this volume on the basis of two questions which intrigued me. First, I asked colleagues to consider what is, and what should be, taught in AAS as we approach the millennium. Second, how are course content and pedagogies influenced by contemporary intellectual and political developments in cultural studies, postmodernism, queer theory, and transnational/diaspora studies, among other areas? The variegated responses can be read at a number of different levels. The lead chapters in Parts I and II present theorized accounts of how knowledge in AAS is "produced, negotiated, transformed, and realized,"[5] very much in the spirit of Lusted's observation that pedagogy

1

entails an interaction between a teacher and a learner, and thus is "insep-arable from what is being taught and, crucially, how one learns."[6] In this sense, David L. Eng's fascinating analysis of interpellative processes—which juxtaposes the pedagogies of AAS, queer studies, and the core cur-riculum at Columbia University—is a milestone which deserves careful consideration. While other chapters reflect more of a disciplinary ap-proach to teaching AAS, insofar as the influence of fields such as history, psychology, literature, and composition are significant, Eng's and Kang's chapters, especially, exemplify the inter- and multidisciplinary nature of the Studies, whether critique or social action is the immediate objective.

Collectively, and most importantly, all of the chapters provide timely and insightful responses to key challenges as we move into the twenty-first century, especially in regard to the contributions of ethnic studies to our educational system, and the broadening of knowledge about the roles and contributions of people of color in the United States. I outline these challenges below in order to create a larger context for my colleagues' contributions which make up this volume.

A Current Impasse?

In a 1995 special issue of UCLA's *Amerasia Journal*, "Thinking Theory," the sociologists Michael Omi and Dana Takagi propose that there is an intellectual divide in AAS. In their view, there are scholars who prioritize the study of history and social structure, as opposed to those for whom analyses of discursive practices are central.[7] According to Omi and Ta-kagi, this division also entails a split with, on one hand, those who are "practice" oriented and who see Asian American studies as a vehicle to promote solidarity and the construction of new, progressive communi-ties. On the other, those who prioritize rereading Asian American issues in terms of postmodernist theories seem to believe that deconstruction itself, if assiduously applied, is deeply and sufficiently political in and of itself.[8]

This might appear, at first glance, to present an impasse;[9] certainly some authors such as Robert Ji-Song Ku question whether AAS has lost sight of its original mission, turning its collective back on the needs of working-class students in pursuit of academic respectability. The full im-plications of either position, however, as well as new possibilities for rap-prochement, are revealed in a timely and useful fashion through a close study of how those who *teach* Asian American studies conceptualize and implement their courses.

Critical Perspectives

It is a difficult, often problematic, time to reassess how we teach Asian American studies. This is because initial assumptions about subject construction (including such topics as identity and subjectivity), time (including history versus the current globalization of mass media and instantaneous communications), place (especially in terms of conceptions of home and community), and power (vis-à-vis oppression, resistance, and emancipatory politics) are in flux. In this sense, the 1980s was a period when the original vision of Asian American studies, as well as what might be called its "moral economy,"[10] was buffeted by shifting political and intellectual terrains. Feminist as well as the gay liberation movements raised and heightened contradictions around gender and sexuality (as noted herein by Okihiro, Kang, Sakurai, Fujino, Eng, Chan, and Wat). Postmodern/poststructural theories, with their call for the deconstruction of master narratives, and critiques of identity politics, as well as essentialized subjects—individual and collective, alike—presented another set of challenges which have problematized many of the foundational assumptions undergirding AAS (Eng, Kang, Sakurai, and Chan).[11]

My sense is that while we might try to run, we can't hide from these challenges. Concomitantly, our pedagogies must respond to these shifting terrains. Some of the possible issues as well as implications, in terms of pedagogy in and of the Studies, can be outlined as follows.

Asian Origins/U.S. Placements

It is widely known that the 1965 Immigration Act profoundly altered the demographic composition of peoples of Asian descent in the United States. Changes have manifested themselves at virtually all levels and can be seen in the plethora of nationalities, regions of origin, class levels, changing gender ratios, forms of family composition, and so on.[12] Within the Japanese American population, those who are American-born constitute more than 70 percent of the total. In all other groups, new Asian immigrants predominate. This shapes not only linguistic and cultural practices; new Asian immigrants have commitments and ties to place(s) of origin in Asia that are more immediate and certainly more complex than those held by the second, third, and fourth (etc.) generations.

At a pedagogical level, we may ask: How does the above impact the content and strategies of teaching the Studies? Except for a pioneering article by Sau-ling Wong, there is virtually no discussion of the selection and use of Asian language literature in Asian American studies courses.[13] While there is more literature available about the special learning needs of, say, Vietnamese and other Southeast Asians, one has the definite impression that these strategies are of primary concern only at certain levels of the educational system (K–8) or in English as a Second Language— ESL—pitched curriculum.[14] There is much work to be done. Still, a number of authors herein address the broader philosophical issues involved in teaching AAS to a generation that has a wide range of cultural, familial, and regional ties to Asia, which were not as characteristic of the largely American-born students of Asian descent who initiated the Studies. In this sense, the authors herein belong to a generation of educators who believe that effective multicultural curricular change revolves around "*incorporating* into the subject matter *minority perspectives that give voice and agency to the groups being studied* (my emphasis)."[15]

Embracing Diversities

Much discussion has been directed at the implications of the above for the topic of subject formation. Who is, in other words, an "Asian American?"[16] Under the influence of postmodernist frameworks, some theorists propose that "identity" is not given; it is not an essence, but rather a matter of construction, negotiation, and discipline. In terms of pedagogy, a new agenda has emerged: that we, as professors, need to develop materials, lectures, and assignments that attune students to the diversity, heterogeneity, and hybridity that presently characterizes peoples of Asian and part-Asian descent in America (Kang). Some authorities have taken this task to the limit, boldly proclaiming that the designation "Asian American" is outmoded and actually impedes progressive organizing and change. Others suggest that, should we deconstruct and abandon the idea of the "Asian American" subject, new, more realistic, and more constructive alliances can emerge: biracial/multiracial, and multiethnic coalitions, for example, that transcend (and thus do not reinscribe) race in the popular consciousness and in grass-roots organizations.

As promising as this might sound, in my view this critique elides two substantive facts. First, looking at a number of chapters (Chung, Lawsin, Rocher, and Khandelwal), there is tangible evidence that Vietnamese, Filipino, and South Asian Americans want to have the opportunity to have their histories, experiences, and communities highlighted within the AAS curriculum. This is an issue of parity, since the Studies has offered many opportunities along these lines for those of Chinese or Japanese descent. As the chapters cited above indicate, new Asian immigrants also want to have the opportunity to enjoy the varied benefits that an ethnic-specific focus can generate (although one would hope that these groups might avoid the biases and limitations that cultural nationalism clearly generates). And as Khandelwal argues, putting South Asians in the United

INTRODUCTION 5

States at the center of the Studies offers a cross-check on too-narrowly formulated hypotheses and representations. I cannot and do not disagree with this thesis. Second, the term "Asian American" was and is a *political*, and not psychological, designation.[17] Thus, practices that the term invokes are strategic in nature, which does not belie the fact that persons of Korean or Thai descent, for example, may feel ties of "kinship" and solidarity on an intragroup level—as well as with, say, Japanese and Chinese Americans—based on common experiences here in the United States.

Reconsidering Community

Similar concerns mark the way that AAS professors approach the foundational topic of "community/communities." Once the watchword, and even the *raison d'être* of the Studies, communities have been refigured by some as essentialized constructs as well.[18] Here critics—within Ethnic Studies and from other vantage points—charge that "internal differences," revolving around class, minority status, gender, and sexual interests, may be submerged, even elided, because "race" and racial oppression are deployed as the central variable for analysis and for organizing in the Studies.[19]

Others, however, believe that what is at stake is not altered by these charges and concerns. As so effectively articulated by Laura Hyun Yi Kang, many in the academy (Osajima, Fong, Wat, Liem, and Lawsin among others) think that engagement via *practice* is a key dimension of learning in AAS. Lawsin's contribution demonstrates that praxis also mediates the interaction between student and teacher in a way that is profoundly different from the usual classroom *modus operandi* of the traditional academic disciplines, a point that is also emphasized in many of the chapters in Part II. In this sense, practice, especially in regard to community-building, has always been, and remains, an integral part of pedagogical formulations in the Studies. The task in the twenty-first century, then, is how to build myriad connections and levels of consensus, but to reconsider the benefits and weigh the possible costs.[20] As Kobashigawa and Ling point out, for example, AAS must attend more carefully and systematically to the growing class heterogeneity that has resulted from the immigration reforms of 1965, as this has implications for both politics and pedagogy.

Time/Place

More broadly speaking, the issues of diversity, identity, and community are linked to related issues, such as how we have conceptualized time, place, and home in the Studies.

In a recent essay, Elaine Kim proposes that the practitioners of AAS have always had a fascination with history, perhaps in an effort to dig up their "buried pasts."[21] She also notes that pre–World War II levels of prejudice and discrimination were so pervasive, so similarly manifested in terms of processes of racialization and institutional discrimination, that the project of creating both ethnic-specific as well as "Asian American" subjects was greatly facilitated from an experiential point of view. (Lawsin's chapter illustrates some of the same points, in terms of the uses of history and culture in teaching about the Filipina/o American experience.)

While this is certainly true, an examination of current pedagogies indicates that new agendas have been taking shape in the AAS classroom. As Gary Y. Okihiro argues, herein, our conceptions of time and place (via "home" and "community") in the Studies have been either left implicit, or fairly narrowly conceived. In a striking essay, Okihiro delineates the ways that our views of Asian American history necessarily shift in response to how we conceived of where and what the "center" is—in terms of time and place—and also *who* is at the center, in terms of subject formation. The resulting pedagogy based on this vision is rich, not only in terms of expanding students' horizons, but also in terms allowing the imbrication of new interpretations of ethnic-specific and pan-Asian American histories and experiences.

We would do well to expand upon Okihiro's contribution. Doing so would enable us to be more reflexive about how and why time and space have been both racialized and sexualized in our own, and in other, accounts. This emphasis also segues into the question of how we might best teach about these epistemological issues in a creative and engaging fashion.

Critical Theories/Oppositional Practices

In short, readers will find that each chapter that follows offers constructive insights into the tensions between "diversity" and "community," and into the different dimensions of pedagogy in AAS, including substantive content, methods, and learning processes. As such, this anthology also offers unique insights into how ethnic studies can contribute to a broader and certainly richer set of rejoinders to debates over who is an American, and what this entails at multiple levels.

Specifically, each author illustrates how AAS involves the creation of special kinds of knowledges which are at once critical as well as potentially oppositional (in terms of the practices that critique often engenders). By "critical," I mean that the varied pedagogies presented below promote critique and critical awareness in a systematic effort to unmask the construction of material and symbolic oppression—whether manifest in terms of the larger social order, interpersonal social relations, or within the Studies (by which I mean the field of Asian American studies) itself.[22] By "oppositional practices" I suggest that for many, although not all, professors of AAS, theory and critique are not enough in and of themselves. Many of the authors below are concerned with developing tangible strategies and practices that would serve to counter hegemonic constructions at representational, *and* interpersonal and institutional levels.

It bears emphasis that "oppositional practices" are not merely reactive or negative; they may actually be quite positive and constructive insofar as "culture building" (that is, developing knowledges, practices, and institutions that are liberating and life-enhancing) remains a major goal of the Studies.[23] Indeed, this is why most of the chapters in Part II are explicitly concerned with the issue of building "community." Historically speaking, community formation has been a collective resource for racialized minorities in the United States, especially for first-generation immigrants. Thus the gap between the Constitution, and its ideals of equal access and protection, and the actual experience of people of color in this society, guarantees the perpetual regeneration of community even as we reach the millennium.

Beyond this, the chapters herein clearly indicate that Asian American studies has extended its initial discussion beyond "race" per se, especially in terms of an exclusive emphasis on the racial oppression of Asian Americans (Kang, Sakurai, Fong).[24] Rather, authors speak of racial formation, and the dialectic between ethnic-specific and pan-Asian dimensions of Asian American identity (Okihiro, Wat, Rocher). Contemporary practitioners of the Studies are also more sensitive to Asian Americans' own potentially oppressive practices around issues of race, class, gender, and sexual diversity, both inside the classroom and out (Eng, Fujino, Ma, and others).[25]

Conclusion

This anthology offers readers a unique opportunity to examine the wide range of approaches and emphases in terms of teaching Asian American studies that have always distinguished, and still presently characterize, the field.[26] As is true of the earliest AAS courses, most of the chapter's authors privilege "insiders' " points of view, highlighting the ethnic group's histories and experiences *as these are lived and perceived by the members of that group.* Most authors prioritize and confront the key concepts of ethnicity and race. Still, pedagogy in Asian American studies remains profoundly broad and multidisciplinary. This would appear to be one of the permanent strengths of the Studies: it strives for a holistic approach and, at the same time, it promotes a productive cross-fertilization among the disciplines (Eng, Kang, Liem, and others). These same processes have also created tensions, to be sure but, to date, these have been stimulating and often productive in nature.

In sum, the chapters in this anthology indicate that a great deal of cross-fertilization between the so-called "structural" and "discursive" camps has actually occurred, at least in terms of the pedagogy of the Studies and current practices in the classroom—certainly more so than theoretically pitched expositions might imply. As Eng's and Kang's lead essays exemplify, and this anthology as a whole indicates, there is clearly something to be gained for all involved should the strengths of each broad current be used to critique and refashion the overall field of Asian American studies as it continues to evolve.

Those emphasizing techniques of deconstruction and close analyses of discursive constructions have much to offer. We *do* need closer readings of what constructions of identity and community entail, especially in regard to the silences and elisions that result, because when boundaries are drawn we may not always clearly see who is excluded, let alone systematically marginalized. Concomitantly, those whose concerns revolve around practice exhort us to work collectively to expose, challenge, and change "enforced inequalities" in the interest of promoting social justice. Unfortunately, this goal seems as relevant as ever. Nonetheless, it is precisely our examination of the role of pedagogy in Asian American studies, and our mutual efforts to transform practices in the university and beyond, which brings the promise of greater synthesis to light.

Notes

1. A good overview of the field of Asian American studies (AAS), although with a "West Coast" emphasis, is presented by Sucheng Chan and Ling-Chi Wang, "Racism and the Model Minority: Asian-Americans in Higher Education," in *The Racial Crisis in Higher Education*, Philip G. Altbach and Kofi Lomotey, eds. (New York: SUNY Press, 1991), 43–68. As for positioning AAS within the larger context of ethnic studies, see Evelyn Hu-DeHart, "Ethnic Studies in U.S. Higher Education," in *Handbook of Research on Multicultural Education*, James A. Banks and Cherry Banks, eds. (New York: Simon and Schuster, 1995), 696–707.

2. For example, Don T. Nakanishi and Russell Leong, "Toward the Second Decade: A National Survey of Asian American Studies Programs in 1978," *Amerasia Journal* 5, no. 3 (1978): 1–19. For more recent developments on the East

Coast, *East of California: New Perspectives in Asian American Studies,* Gary Y. Okihiro and Lee C. Lee, eds. (Ithaca: Asian American Studies Program, Cornell University, 1992), offers an interesting overview.

3. Don T. Nakanishi and Tina Yamano Nishida, eds. *The Asian American Educational Experience* (New York: Routledge, 1995); Bob H. Suzuki, "Higher Education Issues in the Asian American Community," in *Minorities in Higher Education,* Manuel J. Justiz, et al., eds. (Phoenix: Oryx Press, 1994), 258–85.

4. There are many more chapters which could have been included in this anthology had there been room. There seems to be a virtual absence of commentary on what, or how, to teach about many of the smaller populations of Asian descent (for example, Thai Americans), or about Asian American Muslims. Except for a fascinating article by Sucheng Chan, "On the Ethnic Studies Requirement, Part I: Pedagogical Implications," *Amerasia Journal* 15, no. 1 (1989): 267–80, we lack commentary on how to teach AAS effectively to students who are *not* of Asian descent. I have avoided, here, the thorny issue of whether or not Pacific Islanders are or should be included within the Asian American studies rubric; this is still very much under debate, and I hold no special knowledge that would help to resolve this question one way or the other. Finally, we also need more discussion on issues like the pros and cons of "team-teaching," the use of World Wide Web technology, or even how the products of Asian American youth culture—such as hip-hop music or "'zines" like *Giant Robot*—might be used to good effect in the classroom.

5. Jane Kenway and Helen Modra, "Feminist Pedagogies and Emancipatory Possibilities," in *Understanding Curriculum as Racial Text: Representations of Identity and Difference in Education,* Louis A. Castenell Jr., and William F. Pinar, eds. (Albany: State University of New York Press, 1993), 140.

6. David Lusted, "Why Pedagogy," *Screen* 27, no. 5 (October, 1986): 2–14.

7. Michael Omi and Dana Takagi, "Thinking Theory in Asian American Studies," *Amerasia Journal* 21, nos. 1 and 2 (1995): xi–xv.

8. Dorinne Kondo, "Poststructuralist Theory as Political Necessity," *Amerasia Journal* 21, nos. 1 and 2 (1995): 95–100.

9. As David L. Eng notes, herein, many times these positions are represented as antinomies which then wind up generating rather sterile "either/or" debates.

10. Marilyn C. Alquizola and I outline the "moral economy" of AAS at San Francisco State in our article, "Asian American Studies: Reevaluating for the 1990s," in *The State of Asian America,* Karin Aguilar San-Juan, ed. (Boston: South End Press, 1994), especially 356–57. Interested readers can also see our chapter, "Asian American Studies: Knowledge Production and Institutional Autonomy," in *Color Line to Borderlands: Ethnic Studies in Higher Education,* Johnnella E. Butler, ed. (Seattle: University of Washington Press, forthcoming).

11. A useful overview is Pauline Marie Rosenau, *Post-Modernism and the Social Sciences: Insights, Inroads, and Intrusions* (Princeton, N.J.: Princeton University Press, 1992). An application of such approaches, specifically addressing the concepts of ethnicity and race, is Ali Rattansi, " 'Western' Racisms, Ethnicities and Identities in a 'Postmodern' Frame" in *Racism, Modernity and Identity on the Western Front,* Ali Rattansi and Sallie Westwood, eds. (New York: Polity,

1994). While global restructuring has produced changes which have undermined foundational concepts, we must assiduously query the role of universities and scholars in the production of postmodern theory; see Arif Dirlik, *After the Revolution: Waking to Global Capitalism* (Hanover, N.H.: Wesleyan University Press, 1994); and, Masao Miyoshi, "Sites of Resistance in the Global Economy," *Boundary 2* 22, no. 1 (1995): 61–84.

12. See William P. O'Hare and Judy C. Felt, *Asian Americans: America's Fastest Growing Minority Group* (Washington, D.C.: Population Reference Bureau, February, 1991); and Paul Ong, et al., "The Political Economy of Capitalist Restructuring and the New Asian Immigration," in *The New Asian Immigration in Los Angeles and Global Restructuring*, Paul Ong, et al., eds. (Philadelphia: Temple University Press, 1994).

13. Sau-ling Wong, "Teaching Chinese Immigrant Literature: Some Principles of Syllabus Design," in *Reflections on Shattered Windows: Promises and Prospects for Asian American studies*, Gary Y. Okihiro, et al., eds. (Pullman: Washington State University Press, 1988), 126–34.

14. See, for example, Bruce Thowpaou Bliatout, et al., *Handbook for Teaching Hmong-Speaking Students* (Folsom, Calif.: Folsom Cordova Unified School District, Southeast Asian Community Resource Center, 1988).

15. The quote is from Evelyn Hu-DeHart, "Reconceptualizing Liberal Education: The Importance of Ethnic Studies," *Educational Record* 76, nos. 2–3: 22–31. In the same article, Hu-DeHart distinguishes between the kind of multicultural curricular change her quote describes, as opposed to what she calls "the integration, infusion, or transformation method" of curricular reform, typical of educators who merely add bits of new information to their pre-existing lectures and courses. Hu-DeHart discusses related issues in her article, "The Undermining of Ethnic Studies," in *The Chronicle of Higher Education*, "Section 2: Opinion & Arts," 20 October 1995.

16. I discuss various definitions of "Asian Americans" in Lane Ryo Hirabayashi and Malcolm Collier, "Embracing Diversity: A Pedagogy for Introductory Asian American Studies Courses," in *ReViewing Asian America, Locating Diversity*, Wendy L. Ng, et al., eds. (Pullman: Washington State University Press, 1995), 15–31; and "Asian American Studies and Institutional Politics," in *Asian Pacific Americans and the U.S. Southwest*, Thomas K. Nakayama and Carlton F. Yoshioka, eds. (Tempe, Ariz.: Arizona State University, 1997).

17. Glenn Omatsu, "The 'Four Prisons' and the Movements of Liberation," in *The State of Asian America*, 19–69.

18. A discussion of "community," which attends to some of the key points of the postmodern critique of this concept, is presented in my essay, "Back to the Future: Re-Framing Community-Based Research," in *Amerasia Journal* 25, nos. 1 and 2 (1995): 103–18.

19. Iris Young argues this point very effectively in *Justice and the Politics of Difference* (Princeton, N.J.: Princeton University Press, 1990). In a caveat on page 236, however, Young clearly sympathizes with minorities' efforts to build community if it gives them a means to confront "cultural imperialism."

20. Two very useful resources for conceptualizing the pragmatics of multieth-

nic community-based organizing in the 1990s are: *Race, Power and Promise in Los Angeles* (Los Angeles: MultiCultural Collaborative, 1996); and Wilbur C. Rich, ed., *The Politics of Minority Coalitions: Race, Ethnicity, and Shared Uncertainties* (Westport, Conn.: Praeger, 1996).

21. Elaine Kim, "Beyond Railroads and Internment: Comments on the Past, Present, and Future of Asian American Studies," in Gary Y. Okihiro, et al., eds. *Privileging Positions: The Sites of Asian American Studies* (Pullman: Washington State University Press, 1995).

22. Young's discussion of the concept of oppression offers a useful analytic reference point; Young, *Justice and the Politics of Difference*, 9; *passim*.

23. The concept of "culture and community-building" as a tool of resistance is adapted from Mina Davis Caulfield, "Culture and Imperialism: Proposing a New Dialectic," in *Reinventing Anthropology*, Dell Hymes, ed. (New York: Vintage Press, 1962), 182–212.

24. Many of the authors herein agree that Omi and Winant's approach to racial formation theory offers the best means of conceptualizing race; Michael Omi and Howard Winant, *Racial Formation in the United States* (New York: Routledge, 1986.

Incidentally, I disagree with David Mason's claim that such an approach necessarily results in the "conflation of the concepts of race and ethnicity into a theoretical principle by invoking the concept of racialization"; see David Mason, "Themes and Issues in the Teaching of Race and Ethnicity in Sociology," in the special issue, "Race, Ethnicity and the Curriculum," in *Ethnic and Racial Studies* 19, no. 4 (October, 1996): 789–806.

By contrast, one can draw from Aristide R. Zolberg to argue that "ethnicity"— best conceptualized as a type of *cultural* segmentation—is analytically distinct from "race"; see Robert J. Thompson and Joseph R. Rudolph Jr., "Ethnic Politics and Public Policy: A Framework for Cultural Analysis," in *Ethnicity, Politics, and Development*, Dennis L. Thompson and Dov Ronen, eds. (Boulder, Colo.: Lynne Rienner, 1986), 25–63.

25. An insightful and useful literature has emerged in the 1990s that makes substantive and conceptual contributions to the Studies along these lines; for example, see the anthology, edited by David L. Eng and Alice Y. Hom, *Q & A: Queer in Asian America* (Philadelphia: Temple University Press, forthcoming).

26. One example of initial interest in pedagogical issues in the Studies can be found in *Proceedings of the National Asian American Studies Conference II: A Tool of Change or a Tool of Control?*, George Kagiwada, et al., eds. (Davis, Calif.: Asian American Studies, Department of Applied Behavioral Sciences, University of California, Davis, 1973). This important overview of the state of the field in the early 1970s includes a full section on curriculum; many of the other sections, such as those on Asian American women, community, and research, service, and organizing, have pedagogical components.

As for the present, this anthology complements more recently developed resources that are available; see, for example, the two-volume collection of syllabi, presented in *Ethnic Studies: Selected Course Outlines and Reading Lists from American Colleges and Universities*, Volumes I and II, Gary Y. Okihiro, ed. (New

York: Markus Weiner, 1989). Also of interest are resources for conceptualizing and teaching about the multiracial experience; see, for example, Teresa Kay Williams, et al., "Being Different Together in the University Classroom: Multiracial Identity as Transgressive Education" in *The Multiracial Experience: Racial Borders as the New Frontier*, Maria P.P. Root, ed. (Thousand Oaks, Calif.: Sage Publications, 1996), 359–379.

Part I:

Embracing Diversities

2

Queer/Asian American/Canons

DAVID L. ENG

I. Lesson Plan

- How to teach?
- How to teach queer/Asian American/canons?

II. Fully Committed

At Columbia University I am fully committed to teaching courses in both Asian American literary studies and the university Core Curriculum (Homer to Virginia Woolf).[1] As such, my teaching duties challenge the polemic "either/or" argument often underpinning debates on ethnic studies and the canon: support for the former necessarily meaning opposition to the latter, and vice-versa. Structurally, my teaching responsibilities demand a "both/and" approach to mainstream and minority literatures. The following pedagogical meditations focus first on what I regard to be a formal structure of repetition that underwrites all learning experiences. Because I am also fully committed to thinking about the category of queerness in the classes I teach, after establishing this common structure, I will consider the specific issue of teaching queer and Asian American studies together.

III. A Side Note Digression

Given recent student protests across university campuses nationwide (including my own) demanding the establishment of viable Asian American studies programs, it seems particularly urgent for us to (re)think two important and related questions: "What is Asian American studies?" and "What is Asian American identity?" As the role of diaspora has come to anchor debate on the former issue, the role of queerness in relation to the latter will emerge with equal force.[2]

At a recent East of California (EOC) faculty retreat I attended at Cornell University a colleague wondered aloud at the impossibilities of assuming a faculty position for which students had to go on a hunger strike to secure. The difficulties of any one faculty member stepping into such a contested position—to fulfill the multiple and competing expectations of starving Asian Americanists, as well as their detractors—underscores the timeliness of a collection such as this focusing on the teaching of Asian American studies. How do we begin to formulate an effective pedagogy that addresses both the intellectual *and* political lineaments of the two questions above, both inside and outside the classroom?

IV. These Are a Few of My Favorite Things

It is not difficult for the students in my Core Curriculum seminar, "Literature Humanities: Masterpieces of Western Literature and Philosophy," to understand that a work such as Homer's *Iliad* has become a "classic" through a process of repetition. Each time Homer's poem appears on a syllabus, each time it is cited in a student essay, and each time it is critiqued by a figure of authority (even a teacher like me), it accrues a bit more prestige, a bit more history, a bit more citational power. We might summarize this continuous process as "canon formation;" we might also call it the shaping of "western tradition."

What is more difficult for my students to grasp, however, is that this process of repetition—of canon formation—works not just on the level of the object (the work being studied, being repeated) but on the level of the subject (the someone who is reading the work). This act of reading and repeating—of repeated reading—is at one and the same time an interpellative process (the more invisible, the more effective) that, to cite Louis Althusser, "hails" unsuspecting first-year Columbia students in order to stitch them into the ideological quilt of the university.[3]

By reading these books, the Core Curriculum promises, you will be transformed from generic individuals into Columbia scholars, "human beings" in metonymic universalizing parlance.

(From the *Columbia University Bulletin:* "At the heart of the Core Curriculum are four general education courses that attempt to explore what it means to be human and to provide all Columbia students, regardless of their major or concentration, with a lively inheritance of Western literature, philosophy, history, music, and art."[4])

You will join the generational ranks of those impressive Columbia graduates who have preceded and who will most certainly follow you.

(From the *Bulletin* again: "[S]tudents enrolled in this required, year-long course share a common educational experience not only with their class-mates, but in some measure with every student who has gone to the College since 1919."[5])

You will be educated and, in the most broadly interpellative sense, become the privileged guardians of western tradition.

This interpellative structure is a process of certification that is repeated over time: a credentialling of students not just as good citizens for the university, but as good citizens for—and ultimately (this is key, no?) as good custodians of—the nation. This is a reiterative process of interpella-tion that attempts to efface the variable categories of race, gender, sexual-ity, class, religion, and region by which students are differently marked prior to entering the university classroom. In slightly different terms, this is an interpellative process that works to resolve political contradictions, economic stratifications, and cultural inequities through a narrative of individual development that demands from each and every participant an identification with one universalizing aesthetic form.[6] Under such a homogenizing imperative, increasingly heterogeneous, "multicultural" student populations are encouraged to forget their particular material—political, economic, and cultural—histories by the attractive proposition of one all-purpose and unifying *cultural* umbrella dubbed the "western canon." Spread open, this umbrella promises to shade over uneasy social differences. It accomplishes this task through the promise of easy access to the nation; in the growing shade of global capital, it promises the world, too.

V. Social Amnesia(c)s

Althusser tells us that interpellative processes successfully hail their in-tended targets 90 percent of the time.[7] What of the remaining 10 percent? Are these the especially hungry ones? How do we address within the classroom setting their particular concerns, our particular social amne-sia(c)s?

VI. Critically Queer

"The term 'queer'," Judith Butler writes

has operated as one linguistic practice whose purpose has been the shaming of the subject it names or, rather, the producing of a subject *through* that shaming interpellation. "Queer" derives its force precisely through the repeated invocation by which it has become linked to accusation, pathologization, insult. This is an invocation by which a social bond among homophobic communities is formed through time. The interpellation echoes past interpellations, and binds the speakers, as if they spoke in unison across time. In this sense, it is always an imaginary chorus that taunts "queer!"[8]

We must keep in mind, as Butler's observations suggest, that interpellative processes create at once not just laudatory subjects—good citizens for the nation—but also abject subjects of shame. The performative success of a privileged label such as "educated Columbia University graduate well-versed in the western classics," or the performative success of a derogatory term such as "queer/chink/faggot," relies upon a common structure of hailing that accrues its choric efficacy through repetition and over time. In this sense "queer/chink/faggot" is also part and parcel of western culture: it is "traditional" insofar as it has been canonized by the mainstream through repetition and over time as a locus of shame. Like "queer," we might note that "Asian American" is "traditional," too, insofar as it has been canonized by the mainstream through repetition and over time as a locus of absence—as dismissible and unimportant, for instance, in the consideration of American identity and nation formation, the Manichean black/white landscape of national race relations, and the development of new intellectual projects within the university.[9]

For those of us in the academy—faculty, students, and administrators—who desire the recognition of queer and Asian American topics as other than "shameful" and "unimportant," we must confront, expose, and debate with deliberate urgency the genealogies and particular citational histories of "queer" and "Asian American studies." The failure of intellectual and political movements on university campuses to acknowledge the performative force of contested terms such as "queer," "Asian American," and "canon" has predictable results: the intransigent refusal to rethink curriculum distributions and requirements.

Our task as queer/Asian American/canon scholars and activists cannot be merely to reject the canon as exclusionary and biased through curt dismissal, as if such swift denunciations would ever result in lasting change. Rather, our pedagogical mission is never to underestimate the performative force of a term such as "canon," but instead to foreground to our students the long citational history of the term's privileged institutionalized status. It is only by helping our students understand the interpellative seductions that such a term offers to the student population at large—"good citizen[s] of the university/nation/world"—that they can appreciate the extreme difficulties we collectively face in our attempts to resignify the term.

As queer/Asian American/canon scholars and activists, we must also understand that to enfranchise "queer" and "Asian American studies" as viable terms within the academy, and as possible categories—objects and subjects—of study is to demand a startling turn against a constitutive history of "shame" and "unimportance" that is by no means easy or simple to counteract. To what extent does our positing of "queer" or "Asian American" reiterate and retain a history of abjection and absence? If these terms are now subject to reappropriation, then, as Butler asks, "what are the conditions and limits of that significant reversal? Does the reversal reiterate the logic of repudiation by which it was spawned? Can the term overcome its constitutive history of injury? Does it present the discursive occasion for a powerful and compelling fantasy of historical reparation?"[10]

Yet we must also emphasize to our students that processes of interpellation are never complete or completable. While they demand a faithfulness to the same, to uniformity, and to predictability, the performative success of interpellations is contingent upon reiterating a set of historically authorized norms.[11] As such, processes of interpellation are finally provisional, guaranteed only insofar as those who are hailed maintain in their own repetitive inscriptions a healthy amount of good faith to the axis of the same.[12]

In psychoanalytic theory the impulse to return to the same old desired object (the same old sexualities, the same old racial categories, and the same old books) is never quite possible, contravened by the law of repression. "Because the backward path ostensibly leading to gratification is blocked, as Freud puts it in *Beyond the Pleasure Principle*," Kaja Silverman notes, "we have no choice but to move forward; repression dictates that the desired object can only be recovered or 'remembered' in the guise of a substitute. There can thus be no return or recollection which is not at the same time a displacement, and which, consequently, does not introduce alterity."[13] This is to say that in addition to sameness, reiterative processes always introduce at one and the same time the possibility of alterity and subjective agency—of difference, deauthorization, and departure from historically authorized norms.

As educators, our pedagogical strategy for teaching queer/Asian American/canons must be not only to discuss explicitly the interpellative structure of the classroom environment but to think collectively of strategies of departure from interpellative norms regulating our impulses to return. Interpellation underwrites all learning processes—a dynamic of which students must become aware and for which students must learn to take responsibility. This is a daunting task of personal responsibility but one, however, we cannot afford to ignore in this age of personal responsibility acts.

VII. Another Side Note Digression

Is Virgil's *Aeneid* the prototype model for thinking personal responsibility acts such as the recently instituted "Personal Responsibility and Work Opportunities Reconciliation Act" and "Illegal Immigration Reform and Immigrant Responsibility Act"?[14] Is Aeneas the precursor of the modern-day deadbeat dad abandoning his modern-day welfare mother and child? Of course not: he is a good *pater*, no question about it (ask loyal heir Ascanius). But there sure are a lot of dead bodies and broken hearts—women's bodies and women's hearts—littering the road to Rome (ask Creusa and Dido). Breaking up is hard to do, but so is nation-building.

VIII. Queer Asian American Studies

What to tell your students in your Asian American literature/studies/ topics courses:

- Racial, sexual, and class formation are not discrete categories for analysis but come into existence only through one another.
- We are never purely or merely racialized subjects. We are, as Norma Alarcón puts it, multiply interpellated.
- Asian American scholars have not adequately considered the ways in which sexuality and, in particular, queerness has underpinned the formation of (multiply interpellated) present and past Asian American subjectivities.

IX. Immigrant Acts[15]

Lisa Lowe's recent *Immigrant Acts* provides an exemplary model for thinking out various social axes of difference that work to produce contemporary and historic versions of Asian American identities. For instance, Lowe notes how nineteenth- and twentieth-century historical processes of immigration exclusion and legal definitions of citizenship link together to form a racialized, gendered Asian American subject before the law:

> Racialization along the legal axis of definitions of citizenship has also ascribed "gender" to the Asian American subject. Up until 1870, American citizenship was granted exclusively to white male persons; in 1870, men of African descent could become naturalized, but the bar to citizenship re-

mained for Asian men until the repeal acts of 1943–1952. Whereas the "masculinity" of the citizen was first inseparable from his "whiteness," as the state extended citizenship to nonwhite male persons, it formally designated these subjects as "male," as well.[16]

Lowe analyzes the juridical mechanisms by which Asian American immigrants were barred at once not only from institutional and social definitions of "maleness," but from normative conceptions of the masculinity legally defined as "white" (e.g., normative heterosexuality, nuclear family formations, entitlement to community). As such, Asian American sexual and racial formation cannot be thought of as separate processes of identity formation restricted in their singular isolation, but as coming into existence only in and through a dynamic relationship to one another. Lowe's work highlights the crucial need for us in Asian American studies to understand that discourses on "deviant" sexuality and queerness affect not merely those contemporary male and female Asian American subjects who readily self-identify as "queer" but a much larger Asian American constituency—gay, straight, or queer.

To think of Asian American identity in this manner is to allow a certain capaciousness to the term "queer." This is a queerness more attuned to form rather than one limited to strict notions of content—sexual identifications and sexual practices. We need to think about queerness in Asian American studies in the broadest possible terms because Asian American history reminds us that our historically disavowed status as citizen-subjects of the U.S. nation-state renders us "queer," perpetually outside conventional boundaries of the "normal," sexuality being only one of many "deviances." This is a persistent queerness tracing its historical roots backwards to shifting twentieth-, nineteenth-, and eighteenth-century legal definitions of "citizenship"; to variable national political, economic, and cultural climates of anti-Asian/American sentiment, and to the punitive, insistent, and continuous national imagining of the U.S. nation-state in terms of "whiteness" and "straightness."

It is imperative for us in Asian American studies to remember that the powerful scholarship thus far produced in our field on bachelor societies and prostitutes, on model minorities and Confucian family values, and on paper sons and picture brides provides critiques not only of racial and class formation, but discourses on queerness, sexuality, and gender at one and the same time.[17] To invoke, for instance, the historical phenomenon of paper sons is to already be discussing implicitly issues that have everything to do with sexuality, homosexuality, homosociality, and queerness; the question of real and imagined paternity; the anxieties of patrilineal transmission; the historical, material, and psychic configurations of juridically procured male communities; the state-impelled displacement of biological filiation to communal affiliation; and the notion of deviant and normative (hetero)sexuality.[18] To raise, as a final and brief example, the issue of Chinatown bachelor societies is to understand immediately that the gendered feminization of Chinese American "old-timers" as exploited and underpaid cooks, waiters, and laundrymen (stereotypical female occupations) is at once a racial, sexual, and economic feminization that clings in this particular instance not to female but male bodies. This is what I would describe as a critically queer understanding.

X. Stonewall Inspiration[19]

That the Stonewall riots were led in part by African American and Latino drag queens is a fact that has been recently noted by historians and cultural critics in various academic fields.[20] However, this important fact is not one that merely needs to be appended to the historical revisions of this event. On the one hand, this is a fact that challenges scholars in queer studies to reconsider altogether how racial difference may have provided a constitutive framework by which the modern gay movement emerged and gained its coherence; on the other hand, this is a fact that insists upon the need for scholars in the areas of African American, Latino, as well as other ethnic studies fields to integrate into their institutional canons what has only hitherto been a watershed event of the modern lesbian/gay movement.

This integration of queerness is one that will undoubtedly have widespread implications on the historiography of both these fields, bringing to bear a number of pressing queries: how, for example, do race and queerness intersect at cross purposes in the articulation of historical events such as Stonewall? How is racial difference sublimated into and masked by questions of sex and sexual difference in the narrating of history, the writing of literature, and the production of subjects and cultural paradigms? How do race and queerness merge—how do they collide—in the fields of the psychic and the material?

Stonewall provides an intellectual caveat for those of us in Asian American as well as queer studies to search for the interrelation of race, sexuality, and class at all times, even in those instances where their separability may at first seem self-evident.

Notes

Author's note. I would like to thank Alice Y. Hom, Catherine Prendergast, Leti Volpp, Lane Hirabayashi, and Judith Goldman for their helpful suggestions and comments for the revision of this essay.

1. The Core Curriculum is a group of mandatory courses that every Columbia student must take in order to graduate. It is structured around two year-long seminars, "Literature Humanities" and "Contemporary Civilization," two semester-long courses, "Art Humanities" and "Music Humanities," and other various distribution requirements. The following description of the Core Curriculum, instituted in 1919, comes from the *Columbia University Bulletin, Columbia College 1996–1997, 46: "The Core Curriculum is Columbia's signature, its intellectual coat of arms. At the heart of the Core Curriculum are four general education courses that attempt to explore what it means to be human and to provide all Columbia students, regardless of their major or concentration, with a lively inheritance of Western literature, philosophy, history, music, and art. But, as justly celebrated as the content of these courses is, the real secret of their success lies in the give and take of the small class experience. Taught in seminars limited to approximately twenty-four students, they ensure that a Columbia College education begins with the active, not passive, use of the mind. As a result, these course are, in the best sense, the most practical that Columbia students take: the skills and habits honed by the Core—observation, analysis, argument, imaginative comparison, respect for ideas and nuances—are nothing less than a rigorous preparation for life as an intelligent citizen in today's world."*

2. For debates on transnationalism, see *Amerasia Journal* 22, no. 3 (1996), a special issue on "Transnationalism, Media & Asian Americans," as well as *Amerasia Journal* 21, no. 1–2 (1995), a special issue on "Thinking Theory in Asian American Studies." For debates on queerness, see *Amerasia Journal* 20, no. 1 (1994), a special issue on "Dimensions of Desire: Other Asian & Pacific American Sexualities: gay, lesbian and bisexual identities and orientations."

3. Louis Althusser, "Ideology and Ideological State Apparatuses (Notes towards an Investigation)" in *Lenin and Philosophy*, Ben Brewster, trans. (New York: Monthly Review Press, 1971), 127–86.

4. *Columbia University Bulletin*, 46.

5. The longer text from the *Columbia University Bulletin* on the "Contemporary Civilizations" requirement, p.p. 46–47, reads: "Although this course has undergone some evolution since its inception in 1919 as a War and Peace issues course, Contemporary Civilization, or 'CC,' has been a central part of the Columbia College core curriculum ever since that time. As a result, students enrolled in this required, year-long course share a common educational experience not only with their classmates, but in some measure with every student who has gone to the College since 1919. The objective of the course—to help students 'to understand the civilization of their own day and to participate effectively in it'—assumes that all College students, regardless of their particular academic and professional interests, should have an opportunity to study and reflect critically upon the major ideas, values, and institutions that have helped shape the contemporary Western World."

6. See Lisa Lowe's second chapter "Canon, Institutionalization, Identity: Asian American Studies" in *Immigrant Acts: On Asian American Cultural Politics* (Durham, N.C.: Duke University Press, 1996). Lowe writes: "In drawing a

distinction between 'major' and 'minor' literatures, David Lloyd has argued that the Anglo-European function of canonization is to unify aesthetic culture as a domain in which material stratifications and differences are reconciled. A 'major' literary canon traditionally performs that reconciliation by means of a selection of works that uphold a narrative of ethical formation in which the individual relinquishes particular differences through an identification with a universalized form of subjectivity; a 'minor' literature may conform to the criteria of the 'major' canon, or it may interrupt the function of reconciliation by challenging the concepts of identity and identification and by voicing antagonisms to the universalizing narrative of development" (43).

7. Althusser, *Lenin and Philosophy*, 174–75.

8. Judith Butler, *Bodies That Matter: On the Discursive Limits of "Sex"* (New York: Routledge, 1993), 226; Butler's emphasis.

9. Different labels have different histories. The history of the "Asian American" (arising in the late 1960s as a term of self-affirmation for the Asian American movement) is relatively new in comparison to "queer," though the idea of Asians in America as "unimportant" is certainly an old one.

10. Butler, *Bodies That Matter*, 223.

11. We are, of course, multiply interpellated subjects. What happens when a laudatory label such as "educated Columbia University graduate well-versed in the western classics" is coupled with a derogatory term such as "queer/chink/faggot"? What types of irreconcilable differences and productive contradictions might arise from a claiming of both terms at once?

12. Of course, unconscious investments in normative interpellations complicate any conscious distancing of oneself from axes of sameness.

13. Kaja Silverman, *The Threshold of the Visible World* (New York: Routledge, 1996), 181.

14. The "Personal Responsibilities and Work Opportunities Reconciliation Act" (PRAWORA), passed in August 1996, makes drastic changes in U.S. government programs affecting low income populations. For instance, the act imposes work requirements on welfare recipients, time limits on receiving benefits, and severe cuts in food stamp funds. It also restricts legal immigrant eligibility for public benefits and sharply reduces the availability of SSI (Supplemental Security Income) to many disabled children. Finally, it eliminates federally guaranteed child care, imposes new cooperation requirements on welfare recipients who must establish paternity claims, and abolishes federally guaranteed cash assistance by repealing AFDC (Aid to Families with Dependent Children) and giving individual states the authority to create and administer their own welfare programs.

The "Illegal Immigration Reform and Immigrant Responsibility Act" (IRAIRA), passed in September 1996, restricts immigrant access to benefits by making it more difficult to seek asylum from persecution, to obtain relief from deportation, to adjust immigrant status, to reunite with family members, and to challenge abuses or errors by the Immigration and Naturalization Service. The law also imposes for the first time an income test on people who try to bring family members from abroad. See Neil A. Lewis, "With Immigration Law in

Effect, Battle Goes On," *The New York Times*, 2 April 1997: A10. I thank Leti Volpp for her clarifications of PRAWORA and IRAIRA.

15. The following analysis of Lowe comes from my recent article, "Out Here and Over There: Queerness and Diaspora in Asian American Studies," *Social Text 52/53* (1997).

16. Lowe, *Immigrant Acts*, 11.

17. Jennifer Ting's "Bachelor Society: Deviant Heterosexuality and Asian American Historiography" in *Privileging Positions: The Sites of Asian American Studies,* Gary Y. Okihiro, Marilyn Alquizola, Dorothy Fujita Rony, and K. Scott Wong, eds. (Pullman: Washington State University Press, 1995), 271–79, provides a convincing critique of the conflating of the sojourner and bachelor community myths to produce a heterosexually deviant Chinatown ghetto.

18. The phenomenon of paper sons was created through the 1906 San Francisco earthquake and fires that burned down city hall and its birth records. As a result, Chinese male immigrants in the country were able to claim both citizenship and "paper sons" who then asserted the right to enter the United States. See Sucheng Chan's *Asian Americans: An Interpretive History* (Boston: Twayne, 1991) and Ronald Takaki's *Strangers From a Different Shore: A History of Asian Americans* (New York: Penguin, 1989) for a more detailed historical analysis of the phenomenon.

19. The following Stonewall analysis comes from the "Introduction" to *Q & A: Queer in Asian America,* David L. Eng and Alice Y. Hom, eds. (Philadelphia: Temple University Press, forthcoming, 1998).

20. There are various historical accounts of the Stonewall riots. It is, however, safe to say that numerous and diverging accounts attest to the fact that there was no one cause or individual who started the riot. African American and Puerto Rican drag queens, street kids, and butch lesbians all had a hand in this moment. See Martin Duberman's *Stonewall* (New York: Plume Book, 1994), Lillian Faderman's *Odd Girls and Twilight Lovers: A History of Lesbian Life in Twentieth Century America* (New York: Columbia University Press, 1991), and John D'Emilio's *Making Trouble: Essays on Gay History, Politics and the University* (New York: Routledge, 1992).

3

Teaching Asian American History

GARY Y. OKIHIRO

My shifting identities and contexts, over the twenty years I have taught Asian American history, have forced me to rethink many of my positions and basic assumptions. Growing up Japanese in Hawaii of working-class parents on a sugar plantation has no doubt influenced my approaches to teaching Asian American history. My gender and sexuality, my students, and the institutions in which I have taught have similarly affected my research and pedagogy. The simple truth of that proposition, that one's location manifests itself in one's teaching and writing, is revealed both in my evolving course syllabi and in Asian American historiography broadly.

We know full well that we foreground California and Chinese and Japanese men in our historical narrative. We tell our students that Asian American history began when the first groups of Chinese men arrived in search of Gold Mountain, and that they formed bachelor societies that were sites of both dissolution (gambling, dope, women's prostitution) and resistance (cultural persistence, quasi-kinship groupings, legal contestations, economic associations) to white racism. Japanese men followed the Chinese first as students in the San Francisco Bay Area, and then as workers mainly in agriculture, displacing and replacing Chinese who were being driven into urban enclaves in San Francisco and Los Angeles.

We have much to say about the causes and conditions of immigration; men's labor; the white, mainly working-class, anti-Asian movement; and the bachelor societies, and have less to say about women who enter our discussion primarily as prostitutes and picture brides but clearly as accessories to men's desires and needs. Koreans, Filipinos, and South Asians trail off toward the end of the quarter or semester as "sort of like" the Chinese and Japanese, and wasn't it unfortunate that we ran out of time.

I must admit that my first introductory Asian American history courses fell into that rut, and that teaching a classroom full of Chinese and Japanese Americans in California, I was hardly challenged to examine my assumptions. And sexism (much less, homophobia), we insisted, was our secret to be kept within our communities, to be whispered about, but not be permitted to distract us from the more pressing concern of white racism. So I continued to teach and think about Asian American history as the story of Chinese and Japanese heterosexual men in California.

Of course I had to cope with the anomaly of transposing my accounts of growing up in Hawaii with the realities of my students who grew up in California, but somehow my jokes elicited laughter and I believed that their nodding heads was an indication of effective communication and not sleep-inducing boredom. Also it seemed to me that my students up until the late 1970s felt themselves to have been a part of the 1960s generation—my kind—and we maintained a bond that seems to have been broken with my students of the 1990s. When I said "the war" during the 1970s, I didn't have to explain which war I was referring to, and the "Panthers" were decidedly black and not gray.

My persistent belief, however, that Hawaii should be a part of my Asian American curriculum induced me to offer a course on Hawaii's past alongside my usual offerings on Chinese and Japanese Americans. I also offered an advanced course on Korean and Filipino Americans. Still, my introductory history of Asian America was mainly reflective of the wider historiography, and my research interest fastened upon the concentration camps because of the times and our search for self in the past. My course on that subject was an outgrowth of my reading and writing.

I suppose what began the process that refigured and reconstituted my courses and their contents was the entry of Whites and gradually Africans and Chicanos into my Asian American studies classes brought about by the university's multicultural general education requirement. Whites were already prominent figures in my version of Asian American history back then, and in fact the White/Asian dyad was (and is) the principal axis of our field, with Chicanos and Africans oddly relegated to the periphery. Within my more racially diverse classroom, I had to articulate to my students a more expansive universe of racial construction and negotiation than I had thereto provided.

The changing ethnicities of my Asian American students and their class, cultural, and political locations have likewise affected my teaching and research agendas. I now barely mention Japanese Americans, and my students will not permit me to end the Asian American story at World War II. History, as far as they are concerned, began after 1965. So America's imperialist war in the Philippines is now for many of them but a warm up act for the main feature, the Vietnam war, and Vincent Chin has come to exemplify the anti-Chinese and Japanese movements of the nineteenth and early twentieth centuries.

Much to my chagrin, a good number of my students today limit their interests to their particular ethnic groups and see, ironically, "Asian American" as an orientalizing, totalizing term and construct. I find myself, accordingly, simultaneously including more readings and discussions on the specific ethnicities of my students—generally Chinese, Korean, South Asian, Filipino, and Vietnamese—and fighting their inclination to pull away, almost bodily, from the pan-Asian and Third World embrace.

I suppose my students are correct in their tightly drawn borders of relevance. Many of their lives are patently transnational, but also closely tied to parents, siblings, relatives, and communities of a single ethnicity and nation. They thus seek identity and authenticity within those confines. The Taiwanese "love boat" goes to Taiwan. But there might also be another, larger dimension to this apparent trend. Divide and rule comes to mind. A logical conclusion to that sort of reasoning became clear to me when a student insisted that Asian American history bore absolutely no relevance to her contemporary life of conspicuous privilege. I couldn't contain my rage.

My move away from California has afforded me a different vantage from which to see the Pacific, which for me now is "the other" shore. And although I must confess that the quintessential "California sound" of the jazz group Hiroshima brings a quickening to my heart especially in the dead of Ithaca's long and dreary winters, I am keenly aware of California's choking grip on the throats of our historical imagination. I am not engaging in California-bashing when I say that places east of California constitute different, but just as typical and authentic sites of Asian America.

My changes, mind you, of my texts and contexts didn't happen overnight nor were they simply given. And my teaching of Asian American history was always struggled over and negotiated with my constantly changing students. Sometimes my designs worked; at other times, the same plans failed miserably. It was improvise, improvise. At one point, I got so situational that I walked into class that first day without a syllabus and tried to map out a course of study that was relevant and of interest to each student enrolled in that class. The students looked at me as if I was a madman, and some doubtlessly marked me down on my course evaluations as hopelessly disorganized. And I wouldn't be telling the whole truth if I failed to admit that my sheer laziness and sometimes exhaustion from the teaching load, committee work, research and writing, community involvement, and sustaining a semblance of a collegium precluded pedagogical innovations, and I know of long stretches when my course syllabi and lectures rarely changed.

While my research agenda and course content have moved, albeit in fits and starts, my educational goals haven't deviated over the two dec-

ades of my career. I still try to ensure that each aspect of the class is
relevant to the lives of my students, that my pedagogy and the course
content empower them, and that the ideas presented work to subvert, to
destabilize the dominating hegemonies and hierarchies both within Asian
American studies and the wider social relations. Needless to say, on the
ground, within the classroom, at the point of engagement, the realities of
teaching and learning aren't always so lofty, but we must be immodest
about the importance of our work and unashamed to lay claim to our
original aim of social transformation. Despite the heralded "discoveries"
of critical theorists of various stripes, the ideas of relevance, vernaculari-
zation, subjectivity, and social change were articulated and debated
within ethnic studies during the 1960s and '70s.

In my present introductory Asian American history course and with
my educational goals in mind, I strive for two outcomes: (1) that students
connect themselves with the Asian American past; and (2) that students
develop their critical abilities and obtain tools with which to deconstruct
the master narratives. The past for many of us seems remote and irrelevant, particularly for most college students who can but recall perhaps a
decade within the confines of growing up, and for postmodern America
generally, especially when discontinuity, situational relations, and the
present and future dominate our thinking and behavior. Coupled with
that alienation from the past is the inclination toward ethnic insularity.
So I spend some time discussing with my students, during the first week
of class, concepts such as the individual and society, social groupings,
and the social constructions of race, ethnicity, gender, class, and sexuality
to show the derivations of and oppositions to collective identities.

I ask students to undertake several projects designed to reveal how
intellectual productions are freighted with assumptions and designs, and
to underscore how history and like labors help to shape our concepts of
self and others. In one exercise, students locate and survey U.S. history
texts for their depictions of Asian Americans. They invariably find that
Asians are widely absent from those pages, and that when included, are
presented mainly as victims, most notably of the nineteenth-century anti-
Chinese movement and the World War II detention of Japanese Americans. Asian contributions to America, if mentioned, include the Chinese
construction of the transcontinental railroad and Asian involvement in
California's agriculture. Students quickly see that both their absence and
presence within those texts advance the marginalization of Asians in
American history and community. In another exercise, students survey
U.S. race relations texts, and in yet another, texts on women's studies.
Finally, students write an essay on "Asian American history and me," to
connect themselves, Asians and non-Asians, to that past.

During the remaining three-fourths of the semester, we examine Asian

American history itself, and use as our master narratives Ron Takaki's *Strangers from a Different Shore* (1989) and Sucheng Chan's *Asian Americans: An Interpretive History* (1991). My students react to those texts quite differently, and although not exhaustive of the range of opinions, many find Takaki's text enjoyable for its stories and appreciate Chan's for its clarity. Besides assigning them for comparative purposes about how historians approach a subject, I use the texts to give students a basic familiarity with the Asian American experience, because they need the names, dates, acts, and deeds upon which to hang their analyses and critiques.

We then proceed to discuss some of the prominent variables that affect the writing and our conception of Asian American history. I begin with the idea of that history, its sources, their purposes, and their legacies. For instance, we talk about the search for roots, for identity among Asian American intellectuals of the 1960s and '70s, but also about the foundational studies of Mary Coolidge, Yamato Ichihashi, and Bruno Lasker on the Chinese, Japanese, and Filipinos. In particular, I narrow upon Mary Coolidge's *Chinese Immigration* (1909) to excavate some of her paradigms that posit the centrality of the anti-Chinese movement, the uniqueness of California and the times, the ignorance and prejudices of Southerners and the white working class, the normality of Chinese bachelor societies and their benign sexualities, and the internationalization of a domestic problem. Those themes, along with Coolidge's overall positioning of the Asian presence in America as a problematic, have come to dominate the received historiography.

We discuss historical periods, their natures and functions, and examine periodization in Asian American history texts. Generally, I believe, our periodization pivots around the fulcrum of race, and specifically around the relations between Asians and Whites. We might characterize Asian American chronology broadly as pre-European and European, or the Asian heritage and its articulation and incorporation. Thus, the deeds of Whites and not Asians demarcate and define our historical times—labor migration typifies and exclusion marks the end of immigration, anti-Asianism prompts Anglo-conformity, acculturation, and resistance, and the 1965 Immigration Act begins the period of postexclusion.

Suppose, in contrast, we delineated a periodization internal to Asian America and not in relation to white America. (Of course historical periods, like other social processes, could never be wholly internal to any single group.) Ethnicity would be a motive force to propel our historical trajectories, and likewise gender and class. If we took gender constructions and contestations, the rise of patriarchy and women's resistance to it, as the primary determinant of history, we would probably foreground the late nineteenth century as pivotal because of the rise of nationalism and feminism in Asia, and the early twentieth century in the United States among mainly Chinese, Japanese, and Korean Americans because of the opportunities and contradictions afforded to women under capitalism.

Or suppose we reconfigured the racial pivot to be the relations between Asians and Africans. Our beginnings would not be found in the trans-Pacific journey of Asians to the Americas, but in the land bridge that connected Africa with Asia and in the maritime traffic on the Indian Ocean. African migrants traveled to and settled in South and Southeast Asia, where they formed some of the earliest societies and where their descendants remain today. Africans are also Asians. And Asian and African ships sailed the Indian Ocean monsoons at least a thousand years before Europeans crossed South Africa's Cape, establishing an Afro-Asian economic system that extended as far east as China and west to Southeast Asia, India, the Arabian peninsula, and down the East African coast to Mozambique. Asians and Africans exchanged material objects, technology, and culture, and Indonesians might have settled on Madagascar during the first centuries of the C.E. Asians are also Africans.

When Europeans entered the Indian Ocean, they impressed Asian and African sailors to man their ships beginning in the early sixteenth century, and seized African and Asian laborers for their plantations in Asia and Africa. The Dutch, for instance, transported Indonesian and East African slaves to their refreshment station at the Cape of Good Hope as early as 1658. Europeans also took African and Asian slaves and indentured workers to their plantations in the Americas. In the Pacific, Filipino sailors, involved in Spain's Manila galleon trade, jumped ship in Mexico, traveled to Louisiana, and likely established the first Asian communities in North America perhaps a decade before America's Revolutionary War. And in the Atlantic, Asian Indians on board European ships landed in cities such as Philadelphia, Boston, and New York, where they took on Anglicized names and possibly married into the local African American communities during the 1780s and '90s.

By shifting the racial dyad from White/Asian to Asian/African, I ask students to rethink several orthodoxies within Asian American history as written and to question some of their own, unstated assumptions. A widespread belief, perhaps desire, among many of my students is that the Asian American experience, seen as a progression from immigration to success story, more closely resembles its European, as opposed to its African, counterpart. I try to rattle that cage with my contention about the kinship of Asians and Africans, but I also attempt to undermine the privileging within Asian American history of East Asians and the West Coast. Southeast and South Asians should be numbered among the founders of

Asian America, and Africa, the Caribbean and U.S. South, and eastern seaboard, remembered as veritable sites of our beginnings.

Assuredly, if we in Asian American studies were to move not only the racial but also ethnic pivot by centering South Asians, as an example, many of our basic categories would tumble in a heap. For starters, the "racing" of our subject would be decidedly altered and made more complex, and Confucian status ethics will no longer explain household and community formations. Africa and the Caribbean will comprise the sources of our traditions, along with Asia, and colonization, diaspora, nationalism, postcolonialism, and subalternity would constitute major subject categories. And numbers alone wouldn't determine a group's importance to Asian America. In truth, though, we needn't foreground any ethnicity to create hierarchies, old or new, but we should engage in exercises such as these to interrogate our positions and clear the debris of decaying presumptions about our subject matter and notions about who we are as a people.

Recentering women, as described under my consideration of chronology, involves more than adding women to the history of white (or Asian) men. I urge students to reconceptualize Asian American history by thinking about the social construction of gender and its consequences, the imposed and oppositional definitions of feminine and masculine, the heavily gendered texts of our historiography and their privileging of men as normative, and the contours of a new history of Asian America formed by the agency of gender relations.

Besides a different chronology, students derive a more expansive notion of our subject's location. Asian men in the United States, they come to understand, weren't outside the bounds of gender relations nor were they innocent of patriarchy's primacy. Asian men were intimately connected to women in Asia; most of them were in America to reproduce the patriarchal family and laboring within the core they contended with ascribed and self-generated notions of themselves as Asians and as men. Thereby women's activities in Asia constitute a correlate of men's activities in the United States along with the deeds of the comparatively few women who made the crossing during the nineteenth century.

Surely we can now say that Asian American history mustn't be circumscribed by our determination to root ourselves firmly within American soil or by American exceptionalism, but should be unapologetically transnational. That recognition is one of the consequences of a gender-based Asian American history. But above all, by recentering women, students gain an appreciation of the field's unalloyed fascination with race and its complicity in maintaining patriarchy, and obtain a powerful explanation for history's movement and an inarguable case for alternate, and at the very least multiple, pivots.

Like our segmentation of race from gender, class has disappeared entirely or shows up as an isolated category in our analyses of history's motive forces and relations of power. Perhaps that slighting of class derives from our tendency to conflate or to see as coterminous race and class among Asian migrants. All Asians were workers in our flattened universe. But we know that merchants were among those seeking Gold Mountain, that they became the leaders of the immigrant communities, and that they were exempted from the full force of exclusion that was directed against the laboring class. Perhaps our lapse comes from our racial politics that homogenizes the white majority on the one hand and the oppressed on the other, or perhaps our master narratives are influenced by the appropriating class within our communities.

Whatever the cause, class seems to dangle like an underdeveloped limb from the body of Asian American scholarship. The characterization isn't entirely fair. From the start, the white working class has been depicted as the villains of the anti-Asian movement by liberal writers, and more recently their involvement in anti-Asianism has been advanced as a manifestation of class struggle by radical intellectuals. We also have community and labor histories that show the multiple and conflicting positions of Asian Americans to the relations of production, and pathbreaking studies that contextualize Asian migration and labor and entrepreneurship within U.S. and global capitalism. The limb is still attached to the body.

But class has never, I believe, been central to our analyses. We persist in our belief in the push-pull (or some variant thereof) hypothesis of Asian migration, we see articulation as a racial encounter, and we present our work and subject matter as yet another aspect of multicultural America. In fact, our original, sharp demand for inclusion when exclusion was the rule has been blunted and domesticated into a normative pluralism that smothers conflicts and contestations within its embrace. We now appreciate cultural diversity, but omit in that consideration the relations of power, domination, and subordination. Our once abrasive agenda of social transformation, inclusive of race, gender, and class, has become a part of the grain. I suppose another aspect and consequence of our failure has been our inability to locate the intersections of the racial, gender, and class formations and to incorporate that into our teaching and writing.

A final aspect of my attempt to equip students with tools and concepts with which to critique our narratives involves geographic regions and sexualities. The grouping of these two variables in the writing of history, unlike the more studied pairing of nationalisms and sexualities, reveals my ignorance and isn't indicative of their importance. I have a bit more to say to my students about the field's penchant for the West and urban spaces over places east of California and rural settings than I have to say about the historiography's take on sexuality and its overriding normative heterosexuality. Needless to say, both the spatial and sexual dimensions, including ideas from identity and cultural geographies, regionalism, gender and space, ecofeminism, and queer theory, have transformative implications for our teaching and writing of Asian American history. But I have only begun to try to understand some of those consequences.

The beauty, I propose, of teaching (and writing) Asian American history is that it is a creative act of constant discoveries. In the end, we needn't install a master narrative or in the words of African American historian Nathan Irving Huggins, "holy history"; we must instead help students understand the subjectivities of history and the pernicious nature of singular symbols and rigid canons. History is much too deep and complex for such slogans. But I also contend that in our rejection of historicism and in our quest for relevance, Asian American history mustn't be reduced to a variation of cultural pluralism in which there is no center, no power, no struggle. Further, we as historians bear responsibility for our work; we don't merely write (or teach) for ourselves. And we will and should be judged by the communities that have given us this privilege. That gift requires us to be brazen in extricating truth from error, for the sakes of those who have gone before and those who are yet to come.

Note

This essay originally appeared as "Reflections," chapter two of *Teaching Asian American History,* by Gary Y. Okihiro (Washington, D.C.: American Historical Association, 1997), and is reprinted here courtesy of the American Historical Association.

4

"Just What Do I Think I'm Doing?" Enactments of Identity and Authority in the Asian American Literature Classroom

PATRICIA A. SAKURAI

I had recommended to a graduating senior (a business major) that he drop by my office to discuss the reading material in order to compensate for some of his absences. Otherwise, his excessive absences would leave me little choice about failing him, as the syllabus for my Asian American literature class clearly stated. When the second-generation German American finally did stop by during the last week of classes, he sat down, smiled, and immediately opened discussion: "So, okay, tell me what it's like to be Asian American." More than a little surprised but trying to maintain a sense of humor, I replied with a smile, "You read the material. You tell me." "No," he clarified, "I mean tell me about your experiences. Like, did you ever experience racism?" Great, I told myself, so he really didn't learn anything from my course.

I begin with this short narrative because it has served as an important wake-up call for me, as someone involved in the teaching of Asian American studies and, more specifically, Asian American literature. As much as my training as a graduate student in an English department enabled me to deconstruct the scene described above, to pick apart essentialist notions of identity, to play with the ironies of the student's questions even, I nonetheless was left angry and resentful, and no amount of analyzing and theorizing could seem to change that. While the student's behavior might have been motivated primarily by his own lack of preparation (it was soon clear he had read only a couple of the books during the quarter), I was upset by the ease with which he felt he could ask me to narrate my own life—his assumption that he could "demand performance," as one colleague recently put it—and by his assumption that such a narration could substitute for the reading material for the course. I had to wonder, would he have behaved the same way if I had been male? And

35

what did this say about his attitude toward Asian American studies, my course, taken only to fulfill the university's ethnicity requirement? Would he have walked into a philosophy professor's office under the same circumstances and asked if he or she ever had any deep philosophical thoughts? "Like, have you ever had a headache?" (Come to think of it, this particular student indeed might have.)

As strange as it might seem, beyond being perturbed by the student's behavior itself, there was a part of me that was genuinely surprised that all the poststructuralist theorizings and reconceptualizations of identity that I had found so enabling and empowering in my own work could do nothing to alleviate my sense of disempowerment and anger at that moment. I could deconstruct and deconstruct, but there it still was—that moment of being categorized, labeled, named. I admit this not to promote binary oppositions between theory and practice, or between the discursive and the "real," but rather to point to my own failure to remain vigilant of precisely such oppositions. I had failed to place the theoretical work I found so invigorating within the context of my experiences, to bring the complexities, the paradoxes and contradictions of my experiences to my theoretical beliefs. Apparently, I had forgotten that there had to be a place for my own experiences in all my theorizings of identity. Otherwise, what exactly did I think I was theorizing? While I had thought I had remained realistic in my applications of theory, my desire to theorize away my anger forced me to realize just how much I had neglected to push the confrontation and potential commerce between my critical practice and my own lived reactions and experiences.

Russell Leong's recent words seem particularly relevant: "For me, theory usually emerged from practice, and not the other way around. . . . [T]he underlying principles and assumptions which drove people to make choices in their daily lives was what I thought of as 'lived theory,' or the theory of living that emerges from work and working with others."[1] His words remind me that the first "theorizings" that spoke to me and helped me understand a bit of the world around me did not come from professional theorists, but from many different people in my life, from the work of writers and artists, and from my own experiences.

As I set out to think about my work in the classroom, then, my aim is not to take an "antitheoretical" position, but rather, to engage more fully some of my theoretical beliefs at the site of the Asian American literature classroom. Certainly we can theorize, but we cannot "theorize away" the experiences, the senses of identity, the interactions, or the emotions evoked in the classroom. The challenge, then, is not merely to explain the interactions of the classroom through various theories, but to try to promote a more fruitful commerce between the two at that particular site.

Do as I Say, Not as I Do: Theorizing Identity in the Classroom

If there was one thing I knew I did not want to do in my Asian American literature courses, it was to play the literary tourist guide. I did not want to present Asian American literature as some finite cultural terrain to be traveled by my students, nor pawn myself off as being "in the know" simply by virtue of my own Asian Americanness. Rather, I wanted to present Asian American literature as an open-ended, historically situated category, richly varied in its content, constantly shifting and redefining itself. Moreover, I wanted to openly question the very notions of identity and cultural production on which my potential role as a tourist guide depended. My course description for my first Asian American literature class (in which "Mr. Tell" of my opening story was enrolled) went as follows:

> Rather than starting with an assumed notion of Asian American literature, we will consider some of the particular issues involved in naming such a literature. How do we define Asian American literature? What criteria do/should we use in defining and discussing these texts? What, exactly, is at stake in this process? We will explore a wide range of Asian American texts in a number of genres and forms, examining common themes as well as each text's uniqueness, keeping in mind the various contexts in which these texts and the above questions might be considered. The goal of this course, then, is not only to introduce students to Asian American writings, but to foster critical frameworks for reading them as well.

Linked to the questions put forth in the above description is the question of what it means to be Asian American in the first place. Grand aspirations, perhaps. But, like many others, I was firmly convinced that "essentializing Asian American identity and suppressing our differences . . . not only . . . underestimate[s] the differences and hybridities among Asians, but it also inadvertently supports the racist discourse that constructs Asians as a homogeneous group."[2] Such finite and fixed definitions of "Asian American" inevitably lead to exclusionary practices ironically parallel to those used to exclude and oppress Asian Americans: Who counts as "really" American? Who does not? I wanted to be sure I did not present the literature in my classroom in a way that promoted and/or solidified prescriptive definitions of "Asian American."[3]

In terms of critical practice, then, I was wary of attempts to broadly theorize the writings of Asian American authors under general formulations of "ethnic literature." Work such as William Boelhower's genre-focused formulations about ethnic autobiography, while thought-provoking and helpful in ways, in the end struck me as too prescriptive of meaning and interpretation.[4] This is not to say I would not present students with such criticism to consider for themselves. I wanted them to be aware of the various critical approaches available to them and to struggle through their own critical terms.

My own approach to the literature tended to stress historical context, as I felt connections between the content and context for many of the texts were important ones. For example, I believed it mattered that the questions of identity posed within Frank Chin's plays were asked in a post–civil rights context. It mattered, as Lawson Inada makes clear, that while most of the stories in Toshio Mori's *Yokohama, California,* were written before World War II, it was only published as a collection in 1949—for reasons not hard to deduce, making the collection seem more a testimony to Japanese American postwar resiliency than the work of a writer setting out to reflect those communities that were later destroyed with the internment.[5]

Certainly, I did not see such an approach to the literature as antithetical to aesthetic concerns. While some were bemoaning the death of literary studies, the drowning of texts in issues of racism, hetero-sexism, class oppression and the like, I found that the works I brought to the classroom were still very much alive for me when viewed under such a lens.[6] Indeed, such concerns made them all the more vibrant and meaningful. As I viewed them, more traditional questions of form, structure, and language clearly had their place in an Asian American literature classroom and were hardly at odds with topical concerns. Shawn Wong's novel *Homebase* and Myung Mi Kim's collection of poetry *Under Flag,* for example, take on the challenges of conveying experience through language (a struggle hardly unique to Asian American literature), breaking up time and place through narrative structure (in Wong's case) and fragmenting grammar, imagery, and voice (in Kim's). The results are beautifully crafted works that create meaning not only through what is said but through the very ways in which life is written. Both texts fuse form and thematic content—Rainsford's struggle for a sense of place in America in *Homebase,* the violence of U.S. occupation and the displacement of relocation in *Under Flag*—content that in turn speaks of and, for me, demands a historical context.[7]

I still approach Asian American literature in this way. But in all my aspirations, I had ignored the crucial gap there might be between what I wanted students to learn in my Asian American literature course and the context of that learning—the dynamics of our discussions and the interactions between people (myself included) sitting in the classroom. For all my abilities to link content and context with the texts I read, I failed to do the same when it came to the content and context of the learning situation in which I myself was involved. I had thought I was promoting a certain interrogation of identity, advocating notions of identity that were not prescriptive but that facilitated an understanding of the "heterogeneity, hybridity, and multiplicity" (Lowe) of the Asian American community. But in what ways did the heterogeneity of the classroom itself play out?

Here I turn to yet another wake-up call. Interviewing for a tenure-track job to teach ethnic literature at a small Midwest liberal arts college last year, I was asked how I dealt with student dynamics in the classroom. In the context of a classroom in which racial issues are a topic of discussion, the interviewer asserted, minority students often take such discussion as an opportunity to attack white students. What would I do to ensure that white students felt comfortable in my classroom? Needless to say, I found the question offensive in its assumptions about and interpretation of minority student behavior. Further, considering the pedagogical benefits of discomfort, why did she assume students needed to be made comfortable? Why assume only white students would be uncomfortable? Still, in what ways had I been guilty of the same type of essentialist thinking? In my eagerness to be sensitive to differences of race, class, gender, and sexuality, what assumptions did I make about who would be concerned about which issues, who would already know what, who would need to learn what? Why was I at all surprised to find that some of the most vigorously antiracist thinkers in my classes included white students and that some of the most conservative and uncritical included students of color when I supposedly already knew to expect such based on both my antiessentialist theoretical musings and my daily interactions with people outside the classroom? How, exactly, did essentialism enter into the classroom? How did I myself conceptualize student dynamics and interactions? How would I need to change these conceptualizations?

Diana Fuss posited at the end of *Essentially Speaking* several years ago: "It may well be that the best way to counteract the negative, often hidden effects of essentialism in the classroom is to bring essentialism to the fore as an explicit topic of debate."[8] Thinking that I had done just that—had made essentialism a primary topic of discussion, I began to suspect that doing *just* that was not enough. Debating and theorizing essentialism does not "theorize away" essentialism, nor does it adequately address strategic uses of essentialism or the "counteressential," more subtle and not-so-subtle ways in which identity impacts the classroom. While certainly Fuss does not make claims that it does, I consider some of my reservations about her arguments in her last chapter, "Essentialism in the Classroom," ironically to pursue the very project she eventually calls for—a rethinking of essentialism and identity in the classroom.[9]

Speaking from Experience: Recovering Authority, Relinquishing Control

Fuss begins her last chapter by critiquing the negative ways in which

> [p]ersonal consciousness, individual oppressions, lived experience—in short identity politics—operate in the classroom both to authorize and de-authorize speech. "Experience" emerges as the essential truth of the individual subject, and personal "identity metamorphoses into knowledge. Who we are becomes what we know; ontology shades into epistemology.[10]

Clearly, I would agree with Fuss that we need to guard against essentializing notions of identity in the classroom that uncritically fuse identity with certain knowledges, authority, and experience, as my own fear of becoming a tourist guide of Asian American writings bears testimony. However, I am disturbed by the means through which she then reinforces her argument. As bell hooks aptly points out in "Essentialism and Experience": "In her [Fuss's] narrative it is always a marginal 'other' who is essentialist. Yet the politics of essentialist exclusion as a means of asserting presence, identity, is a cultural practice that does not emerge solely from marginalized groups."[11] Reminiscent of my interviewer's question above, Fuss's assumption and interpretation of "minority" student behavior itself ironically promotes a certain essentialist assumption. Fuss states: "Problems often begin in the classroom when those 'in the know' commerce only with others 'in the know,' excluding and marginalizing those perceived to be outside the magic circle."[12] Again, as hooks points out, to assert that such problems often *begin* with those who themselves have been marginalized seems an odd assertion indeed:

> a critique of essentialism that challenges only marginalized groups to interrogate their use of identity politics or an essentialist standpoint as a means of exerting coercive power leaves unquestioned the critical practices of other groups who employ the same strategies in different ways and whose exclusionary behavior may be firmly buttressed by institutionalized structures of domination that do not critique or check it.[13]

And beyond such objections to the generalizations on which Fuss bases her argument, and beyond notions of the strategic "positive" uses of essentialism in the classroom noted by Fuss and pursued by hooks, I am bothered by the treatment of students' narratives of experience as necessarily and always expressions of essentialist notions of identity and the dismissal of the fact that such narratives can in fact refute essentialism in profound ways.

While Fuss in the end speaks of the possibility of recovering narratives of experience as useful in the classroom, it is still only as essentialist narratives:

"Essentially speaking," we need to both theorize *essentialist spaces from which we speak* and, simultaneously, to deconstruct these spaces to keep them from solidifying. Such a double gesture involves once again the responsibility to historicize, to examine each *deployment of essence*, each appeal to experience, each claim to identity in the complicated contextual frame in which it is made (emphasis mine).[14]

I would agree that such a strategy would be useful, indeed, necessary when it comes to "essentially speaking." But such an approach as stated by Fuss ignores the possibility that some of the narratives of experience presented by students might be already theorizing and critiquing essentialist notions of identity and experience even before we begin to engage them. Perhaps one of the reasons some students—and in my experience, not only Asian American students—respond so strongly to a text like Maxine Hong Kingston's *The Woman Warrior* is not because it solidifies their sense of what an Asian American is (as some critics fear), but because it makes intelligible the very indeterminacy, the difficulties involved in trying to "name the unspeakable"[15]: "Chinese-Americans, when you try to understand what things in you are Chinese, how do you separate what is peculiar to childhood, to poverty, insanities, one family, your mother who marked your growing with stories, from what is Chinese? What is Chinese tradition and what is the movies?"[16] Significantly, Kingston repeats such questions at the end of the novel, offering no neat solutions: "I continue to sort out what's just my childhood, just my imagination, just my family, just the village, just movies, just living."[17] Rather than seeing themselves neatly represented in such texts, as in a mirror, perhaps some students instead hear echoes of their own questions and experiences, their own sense of indeterminacy. One of my current students, a Korean American woman, has commented in class, "I know they [other Asian Americans] think I'm a banana." Speaking of her interactions with various Asian American student groups on campus, she questions attempts to include or exclude her as an Asian American: "It's just not that simple." It seems to me that if we are to remain vigilant against essentializing identity and experience in the classroom, we also need to be attentive to the ways in which a student speaking "as" an Asian American might in fact be questioning the possibility of speaking "as" an Asian American in the first place. Rather than simply asserting authority based on experience and identity, as Fuss would have it, I argue that students themselves often complicate simplistic notions of identity. To assume that I am the only one in the classroom privy to the pitfalls of essentialism seems a foolish notion indeed.

My point then, is not to say that the situations described by Fuss do not happen, that students—and teachers—do not sometimes assume essentialist positions. My own blind spots are proof enough. Rather, it is to argue that a concern with countering essentialist narratives of experience should not rest on an assumption that reduces all personal narrative to essentialist discourse that needs to be avoided, discouraged, or externally theorized. Perhaps one of the less obvious ways in which essentialism enters the classroom is through the assumption that certain students will "speak essentially" in the first place. "Essentially speaking" cannot be treated as synonymous with speaking from experience. Like hooks, I find narratives of experience, both students' and my own, to be important components of learning and theorizing in the classroom. Indeed, what better place to welcome narratives than in a literature classroom where we are constantly engaging narratives? What better way for students to build on their own theories than to think through and interrogate their own experiences? And if such narratives involve issues of authority, power, and empowerment as Fuss claims they do, and as I too believe they do, then these issues need to be brought to the discussion.

Asserting authority over one's own experiences is not the same as "deauthorizing" others to speak of theirs. And if we are to critique the specific ways in which some students appeal to experience to assert their authority and right to speak in a given classroom, we cannot do so without acknowledging the ways in which "systems of domination already at work in the academy and the classroom silence the voices of individuals from marginalized groups and give space only then on the basis of experience it is demanded,"[18] as hooks makes clear. Moreover, whereas Fuss remarks on the ways in which experiential knowledge is privileged in certain classrooms, more often such knowledge is devalued and dismissed as "just personal experience." Indeed, returning to my exchange with Mr. Tell, part of my dismay was due not only to the all-too-familiar demand to tell about my life "as" an Asian American, but also to his assumption that the only knowledge I had to offer was experiential—the exposure of my own bias against experiential knowledge yet another aspect of that particular wake-up call, a bias not at all uninformed by the challenge of asserting Asian American literature as a "legitimate" field of study.

And speaking of my own particular battles, just where does a teacher fit into all this talk of identity, authority, and experience? While Fuss is clear in her critique of student recourse to "the authority of experience,"[19] less clearly addressed are her assumptions about her own authority in the classroom. Turning again to hook's critique, implicit in Fuss's narrative is a certain privileging of her position as a teacher, as a "transmitter of knowledge,"[20] as someone who might unproblematically control and direct what happens in her classroom. Yet at one point in her essay (and here I diverge from hook's critique), the exercise of her privilege and authority as a teacher is conspicuously absent. As she describes the "oppression scale" she has seen develop in her classroom, she narrates an incident in which one student was silenced by another:

> Recently a student in a class on postcolonialism objected to another student's interest in the social structural forms of non-Western homosexual relations; "what on earth does sexual preference have to do with imperialism?" the angry student charged. The class as a whole had no immediate response to the indictment and so we returned to the "real" issue at hand (race and ethnicity); the gay student was effectively silenced.[21]

My own immediate response is to ask, where exactly was she in "the class as a whole" when this exchange occurred? For all her authority, why would she choose not to intervene in such a silencing? And what of my own impulse to intervene?

Given the type of interrogative discussion I claim to want, I believe it would have been my responsibility to intervene. While a part of me would like to believe in a fully democratic classroom, to believe that I as a teacher can leave my own institutionally granted power and authority at the door, I can only take such aspirations so far. Reluctantly or not, in the end I still hold a certain amount of power as a teacher, at the most basic level indicated in the grading of students' work.[22] Like it or not, contested or not, I am in an institutionally reinforced position to judge what counts as knowing and what questions might be dismissed or overlooked as irrelevant. And clearly such judgments are subjective. While I hardly think of myself as reveling in such authority, I understand that I cannot ignore it either. Indeed, if it weren't for my authority to hand out grades, Mr. Tell would not have set foot in my office in the first place, and I would not have then had the opportunity to challenge Mr. Tell's assumptions in the two-and-a-half-hour discussion that followed our initial exchange (a discussion he in fact pursued, to his credit). For better or worse, my own judgment that he had not learned enough to pass my course resulted in a fruitful discussion after all. All this is not to say that I do not find it important to undermine my own authority in the classroom as well. While I might have read more, spent more hours thinking about it, I am hardly privy to some "truth" about Asian American literature or Asian American identity by any means. Like my students, I can only try to figure it out for myself, to theorize and speculate, strategize and act.

And what of my own identity? Clearly, I had overestimated the amount of control I might have over perceptions of what my identity, my authority might mean. By vigorously critiquing essentialist notions of identity, by eschewing the position of tourist guide, there was an extent to which I thought I could become "identity-less," that somehow I could just talk—a disembodied voice launching critique from nowhere. I thought that I could separate my authority in the classroom from perceptions of my identity. Like Fuss, I thought of myself as a transmitter of information, a trainer of critical thinking without a position of her own that needed critique. As my experience with Mr. Tell made clear, somewhere along the line I had confused an understanding of essentialism with having control over that phenomenon. For all my efforts, he still saw an Asian American woman when he walked into my office. But this "failure" to control perceptions of my identity was not entirely negative. For one, a number of students have told me how significant it has been for them simply to see a woman of color teaching in the humanities or simply hearing someone in a position of authority saying that the experiences and writings of Asian Americans mattered. While I don't mean to oversimplify the complex realm of the politics of representation, I would hardly call their sense of encouragement a negative effect of my "Asian American" and/or "female" presence.

This overlooked "positive" aspect of authority as it is wedded to identity in the classroom has served as a much-needed reminder of what seemed obvious in the reading material—that essentializing labels are hardly a sheer matter of choice, nor are they always a negative in result. The space in which class took place was itself quite neatly categorized within the university's classifications of "ethnic" and implied "nonethnic" courses, housed within an Asian American studies program rather than an English department—essentializing gestures, strictly speaking. At the same time, I would hardly declare such classifications simply essentialist and wrong minded; given the struggles to bring "ethnic" courses more substantially into the curriculum, to create autonomous Asian American studies programs, it would seem misguided simply to call the course's labeling and classification a "bad" thing.

It would seem, then, that not only essentialism (as per Fuss's call), but also strategic essentialism needs to be brought to the fore of class discussion if there is to be "room for paradoxes"[23] and such contradictions. Such a discussion would seem particularly at home in an Asian American literature class that both questioned the notion of Asian American literature as a finite category while at the same time asserting Asian American literature as a rich and meaningful area of study. To borrow from Lisa Lowe,

> The concept of "strategic essentialism" suggests that it is possible to utilize specific signifiers of ethnic identity, such as Asian American, for the purpose of contesting and disrupting the discourses that exclude Asian Americans, while simultaneously revealing the internal contradictions and slippages of Asian American so as to insure that such essentialisms will not be reproduced and proliferated by the very apparatuses we seek to disempower.[24]

Strategic essentialism as a topic of discussion, then, provides an arena in which we might deconstruct essentialist notions of identity, thereby combating their oppressive and prescriptive effects, while at the same time recognizing the very real ways in which such notions continue to manifest themselves—in anti-Asian violence, in stereotypes, in culture, in literature, and, yes, in the classroom itself. Unlike the focus on essentialism alone, addressing strategic essentialism forces the issue of contextualizing and historicizing articulations of identity, a pedagogical strategy indeed very much along the lines of Fuss's call.

All of the above, then, has brought me to an obvious point, but one I needed reminding of when it came to my own teaching practices in an Asian American literature classroom: as much as we might combat essentialist notions of identity in our teaching, no matter how much deconstructed, identity does matter. The identity of Mr. Tell mattered: an Asian American student asking me the same questions would already be moving away from simplistic essentialist notions of identity, the questions themselves implying that we could have had different experiences yet still both be "Asian American," or that "Asian American" implied something beyond mere skin color. Discursive effect, cultural construction, however conceptualized, it does matter who is speaking and in what context "identifications," essentialist or otherwise, occur.

So goes my own narrative of experience, a welcomed chance to hash out some "lived theory" about reconciling theory and experience in the classroom. And it is in the spirit of my own beliefs about the uses of narratives of experience that I offer this narrative to be deconstructed, contested, contextualized, and recontextualized. In doing so, I hope that it might prove useful to others in their various particular situations. Mr. Tell? I'm glad to say he eventually passed.

Notes

1. Indeed, the special issue of *Amerasia*, "Thinking Theory in Asian American Studies," in which Leong's words appear, has proven a valuable catalyst for the reevaluation of my own critical practices; Russell Leong, "Lived Theory (notes on the run)," *Amerasia Journal* 21, nos. 1 and 2 (1995): v–x.

2. Lisa Lowe, "Heterogeneity, Hybridity, Multiplicity: Marking Asian American Differences," *Diaspora* 1, no. 1 (Spring 1991): 30.

3. A discussion of the debates surrounding the work of Frank Chin and Maxine Hong Kingston has proven particularly effective in combating essentialist notions of Asian American identity. See, for example, Merle Woo, "Letter to Ma," in *This Bridge Called My Back: Writings by Radical Women of Color*, Cherrie Moraga and Gloria Anzaldua, eds. (New York: Kitchen Table: Women of Color Press, 1981), 140–47; Elaine Kim, " 'Such Opposite Creatures': Men and

Women in Asian American Literature," *Michigan Quarterly Review* 29, no. 1 (Winter 1990): 68–93; King-Kok Cheung, *"The Woman Warrior* versus *The Chinaman Pacific*: Must a Chinese American Critic Choose between Feminism and Heroism?"* in *Conflicts in Feminism*, Marianne Hirsch and Evelyn Fox Keller, eds. (New York: Routledge, 1990), 234–51.

4. For a response to Boelhower's *Immigrant Autobiography in the United States: Four Versions of the Italian American Self* (Verona, Italy: Essedue Edizioni, 1982), see Sau-ling Wong's "Immigrant Autobiography: Some Questions of Definition and Approach," in *American Autobiography: Retrospect and Prospect,* Paul John Eakin, ed. (Madison: University of Wisconsin Press, 1991), 142–70. Aijaz Ahmad and Frederic Jameson's exchange concerning Third World literature also comes to mind with this topic; see Aijaz Ahmad, "Jameson's Rhetoric of Otherness and the 'National Allegory,' " *Social Text* 17 (Fall 1987): 3–25; and Frederic Jameson, "Third-World Literature in the Era of Multinational Capitalism," *Social Text* 15 (Fall 1986): 65–88.

5. Lawson Inada, "Introduction," *Yokohoma, California*, by Toshio Mori (Seattle: University of Washington Press, 1985), v–xxvii; Frank Chin, *The Chickencoop Chinaman* and *The Year of the Dragon (Seattle:* University of Washington Press, 1981).

6. Harold Bloom, of course, comes to mind as one such critic with his "defense of the aesthetic"; see Liz McMillen, "Literature's Jeremiah Leaps into the Fray" (Interview/Article on Harold Bloom), *The Chronicle of Higher Education*, 7 September 1994, A10–11 +. Also of note is the recently formed Association of Literary Scholars, launched as an alternative to the now "too political" Modern Language Association.

7. Myung Mi Kim, *Under Flag* (Berkeley: Kelsey St. Press, 1991); Shawn Wong, *Homebase* [1979] (New York: Plume, 1991).

8. Diana Fuss, *Essentially Speaking: Feminism, Nature & Difference.* (New York: Routledge, 1989), 119.

9. Clearly, despite my differences with some of her assumptions, I am indebted to Fuss not only for serving as a springboard for my own musings here, but for the insights offered in *Essentially Speaking* as a whole, her deconstruction of construct/essence binaries.

10. Fuss, *Essentially Speaking*, 113.

11. bell hooks, "Essentialism and Experience," *American Literary History* 3, no. l (Spring 1991): 175.

12. Fuss, *Essentially Speaking*, 115

13. hooks, "Essentialism and Experience," 176.

14. Fuss, *Essentially Speaking*, 118.

15. Maxine Hong Kingston, *The Woman Warrior* [l976] (New York: Vintage, 1977), 6.

16. Kingston, *The Woman Warrior*, 6. This is not to say that Kingston's text is not open to essentialist readings by any means. Indeed, as Dorinne Kondo writes, "There can be no act of flawlessly liberatory aesthetic/political intervention. But there are degrees, and those degrees are critical." See her "Poststructuralist Theory as Political Necessity," *Amerasia Journal* 21, nos. 1 and 2 (1995): 97.

17. Kingston, *The Woman Warrior,* 239. For discussions of such indeterminacy in Kingston's text, see Sau-ling C. Wong, "Autobiography as Guided Chinatown Tour? Maxine Hong Kingston's *The Woman Warrior* and the Chinese-American Autobiographical Controversy," *Multicultural Autobiography: American Lives,* James Robert Payne, ed. (Knoxville: University of Tennessee Press, 1992), 248–79; and Deborah Woo's "Maxine Hong Kingston: The Ethnic Writer and the Burden of Dual Authenticity," *Amerasia Journal* 16, no. 1 (1990): 173–200.

18. hooks, "Essentialism and Experience," 175.

19. Fuss, *Essentially Speaking* 113.

20. hooks, "Essentialism and Experience," 187.

21. Fuss, *Essentially Speaking,* 116.

22. Of course there are exceptions and variations, such as UC Santa Cruz, where I understand students are not graded. Still, evaluations are given at the end of the term.

23. Kingston, *Woman Warrior,* 35.

24. Lowe, "Heterogeneity, Hybridity, Multiplicity," 39.

5

The Case for Class: Introduction to the Political Economy of Asian American Communities in the San Francisco Bay Area

BEN KOBASHIGAWA

Frederick Jameson's concept of social-spatial cognitive mapping was the inspiration for this introduction to a systematic analysis of Asian American groups and communities within a political economic framework.[1] Two theoretical schemes provide the conceptual grid: the global restructuring of American capitalism through the 1970s and 1980s and the racially segmented class system. The task or project for the students, who are mostly from the Bay Area, is to situate the different Asian American groups and communities they know within a transformed class structure shaped by the local effects of the global restructuring of capital. The students learn to fill in the Asian American part of the picture, as it were.

However, I would like to situate this discussion of new directions in teaching Asian American studies in a pedagogically concrete way. The course is an upper-division undergraduate course with a prerequisite of at least two other Asian American courses; thus, it is possible to design this course as a theoretically oriented extension of the students' prior learning.[2] This is an important point because of the impracticability of trying to employ a theoretical approach in Asian American studies when one is also having to introduce and motivate the subject matter of Asian American studies *de novo*. At least, that is the way things are in an urban, state university like San Francisco State. The motivation and attitude of Asian American students is also a factor pedagogically. I mostly encounter students from working-class and lower-middle to middle-income families, a majority of whom are of recent immigrant background. They are a hard-working bunch and interested in getting ahead. The result in the teaching situation is limited patience for theoretical discussions and a certain amount of built-in ideological antipathy towards an approach (class system/political economy) that is intentionally politically progres-

49

sive and critical of the system. The course, thus, operates on a terrain of having to prove itself, against the grain for many of the students. In a situation like this I find myself gearing the presentation towards highlighting the "social lessons" revealed by the approach. The payoff is a chance to introduce a broad theoretical framework that generates significant social insights into the situation of being Asian American.

The two theoretical components are taught in an applied theory mode, with background reading, explanation of concepts, and application to Asian American cases. The political/economy aspect is presented through a seventy-page article by the Bay Area Study Group,[3] which gives a rich description of the main regional economic effects of the global capitalist restructuring in the 1970s to 1980s period. The group has organized its presentation in terms of transformations of the regional class structure resulting from deindustrialization, building up a regional center for global corporate and financial capital, erosion of the traditional working class, emergence of high-tech manufacturing, "Third Worldization" of the labor force, and fragmentation of the old-guard ruling elite, to name the most important processes. A spatial mapping of these political economic developments is provided in terms of five principal economic zones in the Bay Area, corresponding to the historical strata of the regional economy. I point out to the students the rather fragmented picture one gets of Asian Americans in this analysis to emphasize the need for a political economy from an Asian American viewpoint.

To provide a language for identifying class locations and discuss capitalist class relations, I make use of Mario Barrera's racially segmented class schema for the second theoretical component.[4] The significant feature of his schema is the representation of race/class relationships by way of a pervasive racial segmentation within American society which posits dominant and subordinate segments within classes. Racial segmentation depends on the extent to which a system of institutionalized discriminatory practices results in a concentration of racial minorities in subordinate positions. Racial barriers are more or less permeable, depending on the historical period.[5] For the class aspect of the schema, Barrera draws on Barbara and John Ehrenreich's four-class approach to modern capitalist society, which includes a position for a "Professional/Managerial Class" in addition to capitalists, workers, and petty bourgeoisie. I deliberately avoid theoretical digression into the Marxist class theory debates of the 1970s to justify the choice of this class schema over others; rather, I simply adopt it for its pedagogical suitability for the course. To operationalize the class categories in a quick, but systematic way, I make use of Eric O. Wright's method of defining "class locations" through plus-and-minus combinations of a select set of criteria.

With this foundation, the course can proceed through a series of topics organized sequentially by location in the class structure. With an Asian American focus for each topic, the end result is a mapping of Asian American locations within the class structure, accounted for historically and in relation to broad changes in the Bay Area political economy. The students wind up the course working on a group project in which they apply what they have learned. They are given a very free choice of topics—"Some significant controversy or issue affecting any of the Asian American communities or groups in the Bay Area"—but are asked to make conceptual links to relevant changes in the political economy in terms of class location as part of their interpretation of what is happening to the community or group.

Meanwhile, incorporated into the topical progression through the class structure is a substantial amount of analysis of empirical data. Students are introduced to the Asian American occupational distribution data from the 1980 and 1990 census. For the purpose of analyzing patterns of racial segmentation, the primary statistic used is occupational concentration (number employed in different occupations as percent of the group's employed population). This statistic is used to indicate areas of high occupational concentration or underrepresentation by comparison to other groups, especially white males in the Bay Area. For example, for white males in the Bay Area, skilled blue-collar work (precision production, craft and repair occupations) is a major source of employment, but is generally an area of underrepresentation for Asian Americans. The students learn how to set up tabular comparisons of this sort by race (Asian, White) X gender X native vs. foreign born as well as by specific Asian groups for the nine-county Bay Area (Consolidated Metropolitan Statistical Area) as a whole or for different geographical sublevels (Primary Metropolitan Statistical Area, county, city). Analysis of occupational data anchors discussion in something that is both more concrete than a purely discursive approach to political economy and more systematic than the students' anecdotal knowledge. It also achieves the additional objective of exposing students to hands-on use of an important data set on Asian Americans.

Part of the special interest of this political economy approach, of course, is the fact that the new Asian immigration coincided with the 1970s–1980s restructuring of the global capitalist economy. Since the effect of restructuring was to convert the Bay Area into a regional center of high economic growth, there were many opportunities for finding a place in the rapidly transforming class structure. Therefore, changes in the structure must become part of the answer to how Asian Americans end up placed in different parts of the class structure and, in particular, how we as a group achieved an "intermediate" position in the racial hierarchy, as found in most socioeconomic indicators.

One of the main changes in the Bay Area emphasized by Dick Walker et al. of the Bay Area Study Group is the upward pull on the class structure resulting from a regional high-growth economic base consisting, especially, of "high-tech manufacturing, high-stakes finance, and high-life recreation." Working as professional, administrative, and managerial employees in the corporate sector or as independent entrepreneurs in new start-up companies, this affluent "new middle class" also made very fluid the boundary in Barrera's schema between the dominant professional/ managerial and capitalist class segments. How did this structural change relate to Asian Americans? One could view it as the political economic underpinning for the "Asian American success" image by generating the reality of the "yuppification" of a segment of the Asian American population. To what extent? is an interesting question, however. On the one hand, we have the fact of a high percentage of Asian Americans appearing in the "managerial and professional specialty occupations" albeit more on the professional than the managerial side. On the other hand, some pretty familiar themes of the critique of the "model minority" stereotype—the glass ceiling, the continuing group-income differentials (a la Cabezas et al.), as well as the differential access of Asian groups (and between men and women)—limit the overall picture of success. However, one "social lesson" of the class-structure approach is to not dismiss the existence of Asian American affluence as atypical, but rather to appreciate it as a real development with possible consequences for Asian Americans as a whole. That middle-classness is, for instance, absolutely transforming the whole classical arts scene in the conservatories and ballet schools in the Bay Area and has the prospect of changing the racial face of some dominant cultural institutions.

Another observation from a political economic viewpoint, relevant to Asian American attitudes on the relative achievement of racial groups, is the element of luck on the Asian American side. I refer to the upward pull of the Bay Area's high demand for professional and technically trained labor on a group which happens to have both a high rate of professional immigration and, for historical reasons, is highly oriented to educational achievement as a means of survival or of getting ahead. However, all this is only one half of the picture as Ng's dual labor market analysis showed comparing Chinese, Black, White, both male and female, workers.[6] The "intermediate" position of Asian Americans in the racial hierarchy is composed of a combination of both high levels of well-paid professional and technical employment as well as highly exploited, low-wage labor.

Analysis of the occupational patterns of the Asian American working class is complicated by past historical experience. As a result, the impact of capitalist restructuring is quite different for Asian Americans than for white workers. For the latter, the 1970s and 1980s has been a period of economic and political decline, but the pain and misery generated by "deindustrialization" in the Bay Area is a relatively insulated thing, obscured by the overall economic growth. Since Asian Americans were historically excluded from the dominant segment of the working class, they ended up underrepresented in the occupations most exposed to the effects of deindustrialization. Only relatively speaking, however, since over one-third of employed adult Asian American males were in blue-collar occupations in 1970. This difference, of course, represents a historical irony which can be illustrated by the fate of the Chinese and Irish. Both arrived at about the same time in the Bay Area in the mid-nineteenth century, both were positioned to rise with the growth of American manufacturing, but each followed different class trajectories after clashing in the Chinese exclusion period.[7] Japanese Americans had a similar history and were similarly underrepresented in the ranks of skilled labor in the 1970s, whereas African Americans, who migrated up from the South during and after World War II and established communities with many blue-collar, middle-income families, were rolled back economically in the 1970s and 1980s. Another comparison further emphasizes the significance of the position of groups within the class structure. The monopoly of white skilled workers in the construction trades in 1970 immunized a significant portion of their group from the decimating effects of the cutback in manufacturing industry, whose skilled positions were relatively more open to non-white workers.

The political economic survey continues with a look at the new immigrant influx into the subordinate layers of the class system. The low-paid jobs which reflect the underside of the shift to a so-called service-oriented economy and high-tech manufacturing turn out to be the only economic opportunities available to many new immigrants. The different Asian ethnic (and other immigrant) concentrations in restaurant (Chinese) and hotel work (Filipino), airport security guards (Filipino), garment industry (Chinese), and computer electronics manufacturing (Vietnamese) in Silicon Valley are generally familiar to the students. This class segmentation of the working class, more pronounced for newer Asian groups compared to earlier ones, is reflected empirically in higher percentages of employment in the machine operator, assembler, and laborer occupational categories compared with skilled blue-collar occupations. That is the reverse of the pattern for white males, for whom skilled blue-collar occupations predominate over the semi- and unskilled manual occupations. The jobs are the dead-end kind described in dual labor market theory, which new immigrants facing racism and other barriers to employment have historically resorted to as entry-level positions in American society. With no place to rise to in most cases, many families look to self-employment as an alternative. They, thus, repeat a historical pattern, which I've labeled an Asian American class trajectory. The personal consequences of these class dynamics include deferment of ambition onto the children and emphasis on the next generation as the main avenue of advancement.

Certain themes regarding the situation of Asian Americans can be highlighted relative to the emergence of the new Asian working class. The phenomenon is often referred to as the "Third Worldization of the labor force" (Asian, Hispanic) from an outsider viewpoint and perceived as a counterpart to deindustrialization and the decline of the American (white) working class. Analysis of the situation in class structural terms makes it easy to show the class dynamics of the envy and hostility directed against Asians (and Hispanics), in the absence of economic competition and labor substitution, amounts to a case of transference of resentments (i.e., classic scapegoating). At the same time, in other quarters, the new immigrant labor is welcomed. There is an appreciation of the benefits of economic revitalization, especially the revival of local manufacturing industry, which has tempered the anti-immigrant reaction up to now. Perhaps, this ambivalence accounts for the tendency to split off undocumented immigrants as the public target of recent scapegoating. In contrast, Asian American preoccupations are differently constituted by the racially segmented class structure. Exploitative as the jobs may be, they are also definitely felt to be an indispensable resource from the point of view of the economic opportunity for immigration. This function became even more important with the shift to family-based immigration in the 1980s, which brought many ordinary working-class families in need of immediate employment. Yet, disillusionment with the American dream is also experienced because of the dead-end character of these opportunities, especially for those with qualifications for middle-class occupations in their home country who are trapped in these jobs.

The rapid formation of an Asian small-business class reflects distinct movements from different points in the class structure into self-employment, which is often lumped together in the popular press as single Asian (immigrant) propensity for entrepreneurship. The different avenues into self-employment reflect very different class dynamics, giving rise to a very heterogeneous petit bourgeois or small producer class. One is the direct transplantation of immigrant capital on both a small scale (perhaps accounting for most of the Asian entrepreneurship in the garment industry) and a larger scale, giving direct entrée economically, if not socially, into the Bay Area's capitalist class. Another reflects the capitalization of professional and technical expertise and skill. This seizes the mainstream small capitalist/petit bourgeois business opportunities which arose from corporate capital's postfordist shift to the flexible labor force through subcontracting, outsourcing, leasing, consultancies, and reliance on temporary employment agencies. The most visible avenue are the ethnic concentrations in small family owned businesses in specialized areas. As many of the students know from their own backgrounds, these are characteristically high-risk, labor-intensive, and often marginally profitable means of escape from the dead-end situation of low-wage unskilled labor. An especially interesting case study, which can be used to illustrate many aspects of the impact of class location on Asian American life, is the Asian Indian concentration in residential hotels in San Francisco's South of Market area. Incidentally, comparison of this case with Turner and Bonacich's (1980) general model of the Middle Man Minority turns up an important difference in the Asian American situation.[8]

More generally, discussion of the class dynamics associated with the different avenues of movement into self-employment shows the importance of continuities in personal situation despite the mobility between class locations. In a racially segmented class structure, ethnic enterprise as an alternative to low-paid immigrant labor depends on extremely limited possibilities for accumulating sufficient savings of capital for investment. This situation imposes a family strategy requiring multiple wage earners before shifting into self-employment. Self-employment's drawbacks, however, are the long hours (auto-exploitation of labor) and the unpaid family labor needed to maintain a family business. Moreover, relying on capital pooled from friends and relatives to start a business generates another counterpart to the conditions of low-wage labor because profits must be divided and loans repaid. However, the sacrifices can pay off economically. Asian American success in this arena has had an impact on the larger political economy by economically revitalizing urban spaces long given up for dead. Not so visible to the general public, however, is the high business turnover rate, which represents a hidden dimension of the cost borne on the Asian American side to produce that effect.

When the movement of some into the ethnic small business category (typically, petit bourgeois class, subordinate segment) involves hiring others with the same ethnic background as employees, the result is one example of class differentiation within the Asian American community. The Chinese enclave economy study by Don Mar demonstrates not only the likelihood of low-wage employment in this situation, but also a lower wage level than in the secondary labor market with a non-Chinese employer.[9] In other words, employment within the ethnic economy places the worker within an even more exploited position in the subordinate segment of the working class. But it is important not to read this as the whole story of an employment structure for a community faced with many marginal economic opportunities. Students should be warned not to fall into an overly economistic (i.e., simplistic) view of the situation.

The result would be to obliterate mentally the existence of a way of life with its own ethnic-specific density of meaning and forms of social support for which society offers no substitute.

The garment industry in San Francisco provides a good illustration of the complexities associated with the contradictory interests generated by this example—not the only one—of increasing class differentiation within Asian American communities. Both small employers and workers are mainly immigrant Chinese. Recently, some larger-scale employers have located outside of Chinatown in the South of Market and Mission District areas. In the last two or three years, the local newspapers have frequently run front-page articles on the low pay and poor working conditions in the industry. While keeping in mind that these jobs also provide a flexibility of employment, social life, and convenience of location that satisfies important needs, it is also true that the irregularities in pay, long hours, unhealthy conditions, and wages below the legal minimum spell exploitation. The problem, however, goes beyond small employers taking advantage of immigrant workers. The political economic framework provides an analysis of the larger class context in which the subcontractor/worker relation is embedded, enabling the dominant capitalist class of (white) manufacturers and corporate retailers to draw the surplus value upwards to themselves. The key factor determining the level of exploitation of garment workers appears to be the unregulated, free market competition between the many small Chinese subcontractors, who underbid each other to gain contracts from the few large manufacturers. Aside from the mostly nonunionized state of Asian immigrant workers, one can see the political wisdom and ethnic sensitivity of the Asian Immigrant Women Advocates, AIWAs, current organizing strategy. It has avoided the traditional confrontational approach which would rend the community along the worker/small employer axis. Instead, they have identified a common Asian community interest in seeking a remedy through joint-liability legislation. This would force the manufacturers to accept a degree of corporate social responsibility by ensuring that their subcontractors are at least able to pay the legal minimum wage and meet other legal minimum labor conditions. At the same time, encouraging unionization should strengthen the voice of the garment workers in relation to the subcontractors so that the results will be delivered in the end. Meanwhile, however, the North American Free Trade Agreement and General Agreement on Tariffs and Trade represent a new threatening element on the horizon. Both trade agreements treat the low-wage job sector as expendable in a bid to improve national economic competitiveness and preserve higher-wage jobs. It is unclear how deep the impact will be, but there is potential in the situation for cutting very deeply into the welfare of the Asian American community, not only in the San Francisco and Oakland Chinatowns, but also in Silicon Valley. The silence on the issue among Bay Area economic commentators is, to my mind, part and parcel of the general political underrepresentation of immigrant worker and ethnic community interests.

From a theoretical viewpoint, there is nothing new here, I think, at least for old hands in Asian American studies. What is new, perhaps, is the growing class differentiation within Asian American communities, which has made the subject matter of Asian American studies more complex. I find the approach valuable pedagogically because it offers a way to conceptualize the relation between system and situation in Asian American studies. If the values underlying a critical social cognitive mapping are also conveyed, it should cause the student to pause to think more deeply about the implications of politically underrepresented interests within the Asian American community.

Notes

1. "An aesthetic of cognitive mapping—a pedagogical political culture which seeks to endow the individual subject with some new heightened sense of its place in the global system. . . ." Frederick Jameson, "Postmodernism, or the Cultural Logic of Late Capitalism," New Left Review 146 (July–August 1984): 92. Or also: ". . . the incapacity to map socially is as crippling to political experience as the analogous incapacity to map spatially is for urban experience." Frederick Jameson, "Cognitive Mapping," in Marxism and the Interpretation of Culture, Cary Nelson and Lawrence Grossberg, eds. (Urbana: University of Illinois Press, 1988), 353.

2. The AAS 680 course is entitled "Asian American Communities: Development and Change." It is intended to be a culminating course in a three-course Asian American cluster satisfying the universitywide Segment III (upper-division) general education requirement at San Francisco State University. The prerequisites listed in the bulletin include completion of one of the upper-division Asian American history courses (Japanese, Chinese, Filipino, Southeast Asian) and one of the upper-division Asian American humanities, culture, or psychology courses.

3. Dick Walker and Bay Area Study Group, "The Playground of U.S. Capitalism? The Political Economy of the San Francisco Bay Area in the 1980s," in Fire in the Hearth: The Radical Politics of Place in America: The Year Left, Mike Davis, et al., eds. (London: Verso, 1990).

4. Mario Barrera, Race and Class in the Southwest: A Theory of Racial Inequality (Notre Dame: University of Notre Dame Press, 1979).

5. It might be noted, in relation to old concerns about theoretical priority in race/class theory debates, that a "subordinate segment" within a class refers not to groups, but to inferior positions or locations within a class (e.g., secondary labor market jobs) where racial segmentation produces a concentration of racial minorities. While class relations appear more fundamental in the sense that racial

segmentation is represented as operated on a substratum of class positions, the question of which principle, class division or racism, is deeper or potentially more long lasting is left open here, in fact.

6. Wing-Cheung Ng, "An Evaluation of the Labor Market Status of Chinese Americans," *Amerasia Journal* 4, no. 2 (1977): 101–22.

7. Frederick M. Wirt, *Power in the City: Decision Making in San Francisco* (Berkeley: University of California Press, 1974).

8. Jonathan H. Turner and Edna Bonacich, "Toward a Composite Theory of Middleman Minorities," *Ethnicity* 7 (1980): 144–58. The point of difference in the American context is the weaker link between the "hostility" and the "economic concentration" conditions. For Asian Americans, the relatively open educational opportunities in the United States for the second generation provide a characteristic avenue out of the middle-man minority position.

9. Don Mar, "Another Look at the Enclave Economy Thesis: Chinese Immigrants in the Ethnic Labor Market," *Amerasia Journal* 17, no. 3 (1991): 5–21.

6

Critical Pedagogy in Asian American Studies: Reflections on an Experiment in Teaching

KEITH OSAJIMA

In 1969, when Third World students at San Francisco State College embarked on the longest student strike in U.S. history, they articulated an extraordinary vision that sought to change higher education on three levels. First, critical of elitist admissions practices, they demanded that greater access be granted to working-class students and students of color. Second, understanding that the Eurocentric organization of curriculum excluded and denigrated the experiences of Third World peoples, they insisted that a College of Ethnic Studies be established which would offer a "relevant" education, i.e., curriculum and materials which focused on the experiences of people of color in the context of a critical analysis of American capitalism, imperialism, and racism.

Third, implicit in their demands was a prescription for pedagogical change. The desire for a relevant education meant not only broadening the scope of educational inquiry and the curricula, but developing new teaching practices and educational objectives. Not content to have students merely absorb or consume new knowledge, Ethnic studies and Asian American studies proponents sought to develop teaching strategies which would instill a desire to transform that knowledge into political praxis to effect social change in their communities. Field work and community courses sent students into Chinatowns, Japantowns, and Manilatowns to work in the newly formed social service organizations, community groups, and public schools. Often staffed by community activists, these courses broadened traditional notions of who could teach in the university.[1]

For twenty-five years, people have been trying to turn the goals of the Third World Strike into reality. It has been a difficult challenge. In Asian American studies, the most significant impact on higher education lies in the area of institutional and curricular change. The continued existence of Asian American studies departments and programs at San Francisco State University, the University of California at Berkeley, UCLA, UC Davis, along with the substantial growth of courses and programs, particularly on campuses "east of California" speaks to a significant level of institutional success. This endurance and growth has been fueled by the growing body of groundbreaking scholarly literature and resources documenting and analyzing the Asian American experience.

But building that institutional presence of Asian American studies in academe has consumed a considerable amount of energy and has made it difficult to develop other initiatives, particularly with respect to formulating a systematic understanding of effective teaching practices. On large research-oriented campuses, personal and professional survival of Asian Americanists hinge on a narrow reward system that values scholarly research, often at the expense of teaching and community work.[2] At comprehensive state-supported institutions, the pressures to publish are less, but the heavy teaching demands and large class size leave little room for pedagogical innovation.[3]

In this context of constraint and disincentive, the challenge to develop innovative, alternative teaching strategies in Asian American studies has not been met.[4] All too often, large class size, or simply the familiarity and security of controlled lecture settings, has made it easier to fall into what Paulo Friere calls the "banking style" of teaching.[5] While cogent, well-delivered lectures, full of counterhegemonic and critical information can inspire and transform students, I worry that our teaching has become one-dimensional, at the expense of exploring and taking risks with alternative strategies.

It is critically important to turn our attention to issues of teaching in Asian American studies. Our long-term survival and growth depends on how well we can inspire new generations of students to take up the challenge raised by the Third World Strike. This is a formidable task. As Michael Omi observed, "it just ain't the sixties anymore."[6] In the 1990s, conservative perspectives, signified most dramatically in the passage of California's Proposition 187 and the rise of Newt Gingrich, dominate the popular discourse and common sense understandings of many students. The life experiences of our students are likely to be more influenced by the Reagan/Bush viewpoints than by the vision of the Third World Strike. A 1994 survey of college freshman reports that "this year's college freshmen are more disengaged from politics than any previous entering class."[7] The survey also revealed that for the second year in a row there were "substantial declines in the percentages of students who felt it is important to participate in programs to promote racial understanding."[8] Faced with students who may be apathetic or resistant to critical perspectives, we in Asian American studies must think more seriously about how well we are reaching students in our classrooms. We must augment the body of knowledge we have built about Asian Americans with a body of knowledge about how best to teach Asian American studies.

In the remainder of this article, I take some tentative steps toward developing that pedagogical knowledge. My approach is not to offer broad prescriptions for change, nor a neatly packaged formula for good teaching. Instead, I look specifically at one class where I experimented with alternative structures and teaching methods. The struggles, problems, and rewards of trying to do something different in that course provide a number of insights into teaching that might be useful in other contexts.

Initial Course Organization and Objectives

In fall 1994, I was scheduled to teach a course entitled, "Language and Educational Issues of Asian Immigrant Students," at the University of California, Davis. I had always seen this course as a potential arena for experimentation, but the pressures to publish and worries that too much innovation might risk negative student evaluations had steered me away from change. A decision to accept a job at another university effectively freed me from these concerns and I decided to experiment with the course. Here, my lame duck status unfortunately does not allow me to address the difficult issue of how to develop alternative teaching practices while keeping up with the many other institutional and faculty demands.

In planning the course, I wanted to meet three objectives. First, I wanted to reposition students in relation to knowledge, which meant challenging the common "consumer" or banking orientation in which teachers possess the knowledge and deposit it, mainly via lectures, into the students. The tendency in this model is for the student to passively sit and consume the information, rather than take an active role in their learning. I wanted students to see themselves as not only consumers of knowledge but also as transformers and creators of knowledge.

A second related objective was to reposition students in relation to the use of knowledge. Many students see education primarily as a vehicle for individual development, i.e., as a means for improving one's skills and knowledge for personal advancement. This runs counter to the community activist spirit of the Third World Strike and I wanted to redirect the purpose of students' work outward toward benefiting a particular community outside of campus. Third, I wanted to give students an opportunity to learn about substantive issues affecting the education of Asian immigrant students.

To meet these objectives, I decided to organize the course around two group projects. The first project was designed to respond to the rapid influx of Asian immigrant students in California public schools. The goal was to develop resource materials of high quality that could be distributed to teachers and administrators, educating them about the experiences of various Asian groups. The second project responded to the need for curriculum materials on Asian American topics. Students were to produce lesson plans and guides that could help teachers to teach about Asian American issues.

The projects were to be the main activity of the course and the class meetings were designed to facilitate the completion of those projects. Students were given the freedom and responsibility to determine what they did with that time. They could meet to plan their work, or go off to the library or computer center. I planned no formal lecture presentations in the course after the first week, and aside from some resource books I wanted to make available, there were no assigned readings. Students were expected to find necessary research information they would need to put together the project materials.

Focusing the entire class on group projects marked a significant departure from my previous experiences. I had often incorporated group projects into courses, but they were only small portions of the course work, never the whole focus. I wanted to see what gains could be made by making the projects the main emphasis of the course. In particular, I hoped that students would take the project and their own work more seriously, that they would have time to produce a higher level of work, and they would learn about how to work well with other students.

Throughout the planning of the course, I struggled with questions about what my role as instructor should be. My overall goal was to "empower" students, but how one does that in a ten-week quarter remained a mystery.[9] How much should I exercise my authority as instructor to shape the educational experiences of students when what I wanted was for them to take major responsibility for their work? Are students "empowered" when I am using my power to tell them how the course is going to be organized and run? Do I need to relinquish my power in order for students to be empowered?

In the end, I decided that it was important for me to take active responsibility for structuring the students' experience. In part this decision was made for practical and logistical reasons. The ten-week quarter goes by quickly and I wanted to move students into what I thought was the heart of the course, the projects. Also, since this would be my first time offering this version of the course, I knew that students would enter the class with expectations different from my own. They had no idea of the project-oriented plans I had in mind and did not know when they were signing up that this would be the structure of the class. In this context, I felt it was important to strongly define and delineate my expectations from day one, and to let them decide if they wanted to stay in the class. Were I to continue offering the course, thus building up a history and reputation for how it is structured, then perhaps my role would be less prominent.

Beyond these logistical reasons, the decision to take a strong role as instructor reflects my latest (not necessarily last) thinking with respect to critical pedagogy and the meaning of empowerment. I have come to believe that empowering students does not absolve the teacher from taking responsibility for a course. This position has emerged from my rethinking of Paulo Friere's work. Freire is well known for his efforts to empower peasants in Brazil to see themselves as active agents in history, capable of knowing, naming, and changing their worlds. While his writings suggest that the process of "conscientization" is principally in the hands of empowered peasants, a careful reading of his practice reveals that Friere did not simply turn peasants loose without guidance.[10] He always had a clear idea of the critical analysis of power and inequality that he wanted the peasants to arrive at and guided the learning process in that direction. Realizing that Freire does not relinquish responsibility for creating distinctive learning environments has helped me to resolve questions about my role as instructor.

The Class

On the first day, my main objective was to make clear the intents and structure of the class. I handed out a syllabus which described my pedagogical assumptions and how I wanted to organize the course. I wanted students to know right away what they were getting into and to give them the opportunity to decide whether to participate or not. A brief student survey was distributed to gather background information from the students and to generate a general discussion on education. I was fortunate that the class size was relatively small by UC Davis standards. A total of twenty-eight students came, and that number held steady for the remainder of the course. Had the course been much larger, group work might have been logistically impossible.

The next two days were spent laying a foundation for the projects. We spent time talking about group work—identifying what people needed to do to make groups work well and what problems needed to be avoided. We also talked about what information would be important to include in a packet for teachers. I brought in several examples of booklets and pamphlets on immigrant students as potential models for their work.

Next came the process of formulating groups, during which the question of how much control I should exert surfaced. Initially, I simply asked them to choose an Asian immigrant they would like to focus on, thinking that this would be the easiest way to form groups. But when they stated their choices, two potential problems appeared. First, it seemed that some students chose groups because they wanted to be with friends. Since I wanted students to learn how to work with people they did not already know, I worried about this tendency. Second, a group of students decided that they wanted to do a project on Japanese students. I thought this was problematic because the numbers of Japanese school-aged immigrants is negligible and there is a more pressing need to develop packets on other Asian groups that were arriving in greater numbers.

I decided to call for another round of thinking about group selection on the next day. I narrowed the field of choice to the largest Asian immigrant groups, thereby eliminating the Japanese as an option. I also encouraged them to select a group on the basis of what they were interested in, not on if their friends were in it. A total of five groups were formed, ranging in size from four to six persons, covering: Filipinos, Koreans, Vietnamese, Chinese (which would compare Taiwan, Hong Kong, and China), and Hmong. The groups met to begin plans for the project. Unfortunately, five students were absent on that day and did not join a group. Rather than give them a choice of groups the next day, which could potentially disrupt the ongoing groups, I decided to put these students together in their own group, and they chose to work on Asian Indians. As it turned out, this group experienced problems during the course, perhaps because they were not full participants in the group formation process.

With groups formed, class meetings were then devoted to planning the projects and gathering research materials. The original goal was to complete a pamphlet by the fifth week, but it soon became evident that this was unrealistic as the process of building an effective working group took longer than anticipated. Some groups coalesced quickly, figured out what information they needed, went off to the library together during class time, and effectively delegated responsibilities for work between meetings. Other groups started more slowly. Erratic attendance by some members hurt progress; overly busy schedules slowed others. One group consisted of three friends and one outsider, and it was difficult for them to work as one. My role consisted of going around the room, meeting with each group to see how their work was going and to offer suggestions about content, research strategies, and organization of the work.

By the fourth week, I wanted groups to start preliminary writing. We reserved a computer lab and met there so groups could work together on the initial write-up. At this point, I pushed back the deadline and told them that I wanted to give them time to produce a rough draft, and then to rewrite and revise toward higher quality. The decision not to "rush" the end product was made to break a student tendency to write course papers at the very last minute. I wanted them to see their work as more than a class exercise, but as a high quality product that could be distributed to a wider audience.

A fortuitous call from a teacher in the Davis school district helped to support this goal. The district was planning an in-service workshop on immigration in December, and the teacher wondered if I could help them out. Suddenly, I had a real audience for the student pamphlets. I went back to my class and told them of the in-service workshop and that I thought it would be great if we could produce pamphlets on Asian immigrant students that could be distributed to Davis teachers. They agreed, and from that moment I used the workshop to motivate them to work on the project. I could always ask, "Do you think this is clear enough, complete enough, coherent enough, etc., to give to teachers in Davis?" The in-service workshop played a pivotal role in helping to turn the orientation of our work outward, toward the community. Now there was more at stake for the students. I wasn't going to be the only one looking at the work. The prospect of wider distribution helped them to take the work more seriously and to sharpen their editorial eyes.

My "fortuitous" experience can, and should, be more deliberately structured into future courses. Prior discussions and arrangements with organizations or groups can identify a range of specific projects they need to have accomplished. These real community needs can then be the basis for defining student projects. This approach to community-service learning draws from the work of Brown University's Campus Compact and the Haas Center for Public Service at Stanford. They try to structure the community/student relationship in mutually beneficial ways so that community organizations get a substantive service they need (i.e., research or writing or materials they alone could not produce), and students do real work (not just filing or xeroxing). I believe the community-service learning model can help Asian American studies refine its long-standing commitment to community activism.

Weeks five through seven were difficult times for most groups. As they started to produce drafts, my main role was to read them and give critical feedback. My continual push for clearer, more organized, better-supported writing, combined with the lengthening time it was taking to do the projects proved wearing on the groups. Some got frustrated with my critiques; others wanted a firm deadline to really force them to finish; others began to panic that they were not progressing. As instructor, I had to figure out how to be supportive and understanding, yet firm and demanding. Having a real purpose for the work helped enormously as I could always justify my requests for more revisions by arguing that the writing must be strong enough to communicate the information to the teachers.

In addition to working on the content of the booklets. I encouraged them to pay attention to the form of presentation. This area produced a wonderful dynamic among the students. Being unfamiliar with desktop publishing programs, I could not take a lead role in this area. Fortunately one of the students had worked for the campus newspaper and was quite expert at desktop publishing. Early in the class, she produced some "dummy" pages demonstrating the graphics capabilities of various programs. Students could see that they could creatively format and present their materials in a professional manner, which contributed to them seeing their work as more than just a class paper. Later, when I had asked students to bring in a close-to-final draft, the Hmong group brought in a draft featuring scanned graphics, tables, side boxes with text, and variable fonts. Their work inspired others and became the standard for all to follow. As final production neared, students helped each other to design and format the booklets.

We decided to make the day before Thanksgiving, in week eight of the quarter, the final deadline for the booklets. On that day, each group brought in their work, and the class time was devoted to sharing the booklets with each other over coffee and donuts. The final projects were impressive. All the groups took advantage of desktop publishing capabilities to produce beautifully formatted booklets, full of creative and visually impressive features. It was rewarding to see groups excited about another group's work, and excited and proud of their own project. There was some unevenness in the quality of the final products, but overall I can say that each group made substantial progress during the course.

On December 4, I carried over copies of the booklets to the Davis in-service workshop and displayed them on a table. Teachers came over, thumbed through them, and were uniformly impressed when I told them that this was the work of my class. I left a set with the district for future reference and also left a set with the Asian American studies program. With only two weeks left in the quarter, ideas for a second project obviously were abandoned. Instead we spent the time discussing an Asian American studies major and assessing the course as a whole.

Assessing the Effort

As a final assignment, I asked each student to write up a short assessment of the course, organized around the following questions: What did you find valuable about how the course was organized and run? How beneficial were the group projects? What lessons did you learn? How could the course be improved? How would you assess your effort in the group? How did the group work together? Do you think a course of this type should be in the Asian American studies curriculum?

Overall, the responses indicate a positive view of the course and its organization. Students found the course to be a "refreshing change" from their other classes. They appreciated the flexibility and the relaxed learning environment. Some students noted that they felt comfortable speaking out in class because they did not feel intimidated and did not feel a "distance" between themselves and the instructor. Many said that the course organization made it possible to learn from other students, not just from the one instructor.

With respect to lessons learned, students mentioned a range of items. Several said that the group project allowed them to learn about one group in great depth. One wrote that he now feels like an "expert" on the Hmong and that he learned more about them than any instructor could have taught. In a related vein, two students noted that they appreciated learning about an ethnic group that they were not a member of. Students also noted that the "applied" nature of the projects enhanced their learning. One woman said she could better "see the value" of the work because it was going to benefit someone. Other students said that they learned research, editing, and computer desktop publishing skills through the project.

For virtually all students, the major educational impact of the course fell in the area of learning to work in groups. This was not one of my original objectives, but it emerged as a key aspect of the experience. Students said that the challenge of working together with other students to produce a joint project was the most difficult and educational aspect of the course. For some, the group work helped them to develop leadership and communication skills. Others said that the group work forced them to think about issues of compromise and criticism and how to build consensus out of difference. Some said they developed their problem-solving skills. For many, the unstructured nature of the group work challenged them to think for themselves and to take responsibility for their learning experience. One woman best described these benefits when she wrote:

> With the project, I was able to use more of my own head to think about what was right, what was wrong, what was relevant, and what was not. With a lot more freedom, I think I worked harder and felt as if I learned more practical things.

Though largely unintended, the educational value of group work is not surprising. In the past decade, educators across disciplines and grade levels have come to value cooperative or collaborative learning as a reform to improve academic performance and to develop positive interpersonal behavior.[11] Moreover, the movement toward collaborative work has been bolstered by a growing recognition that the real world often requires that people work together with others.[12] Developing good communication skills, problem-solving abilities, and a sense of community, which are central goals of cooperative learning, are precisely the outcomes students in my class identified as important.

Many of the lessons students learned were borne from emotional struggle. While ideally the learning experience would be enjoyable and positive, the reality of the course was that the frustration, anger, and difficulty of working in a group often served as the most effective teacher. All groups had challenges to overcome. In two groups, some students felt resentful that others were not working as hard. In another, tensions arose when two students' work was criticized and edited by others in a hurtful way. In another, one student's "perfectionism" had to be tempered so that the project could move on. For all, trouble finding time to get together outside of class heightened feelings of panic and anxiety. That all groups managed to pull together outstanding final products speaks to how they learned to work through differences and tensions. In the end, every student said the course should be part of the Asian American studies curriculum.

Learning from Experience

Overall, I think the basic approach and objectives of the course were sound. The final outcomes—the six pamphlets on Asian immigrant groups and the generally positive response of the students—affirm the decision to risk stepping out of my own comfort zone. Giving the projects a real purpose was a useful way to turn their efforts toward the community and to help them take their work more seriously. In the future, I think stronger connections between the student projects and the community can strengthen this aspect of the course. For example, one might have students give a presentation of their work to a community group or have them meet periodically with a community organization to talk about the progress and focus of the project.

This course, however, was far from perfect. The problems and mistakes were often glaring. The students offered insightful criticisms that help to define how the course structure and my role as instructor could be improved. In general, the experience and criticisms point to a need for better balance and time management in the course. In retrospect, the original idea of having students complete two projects in ten weeks was too ambitious and threw the whole course out of balance. It forced me to get students into groups and to start working on the first project too fast, without enough preparation. Then, when it became apparent that there would not be enough time for a second project and the deadline was extended for the first project, students were thrown off by the change of expectations and were not sure how to plan their time as the deadline kept shifting.

There was a need to lay a stronger and deeper foundation from which the student projects could be built. I spent a little bit of time talking about group work and about the goals of the project, but this was not enough to stave off problems. As one student noted, more structured reading at the beginning of the course could have provided a better base of knowledge from which to do the project. Another said that it would be good to read about group building, communication, and leadership skills as a foundation for later work. In the future, readings on cooperative learning and critical and feminist pedagogy should be assigned to help build that foundation.[13] A better balance between structured learning at the beginning and the independent, less-structured group project at the end would be a wiser way to organize the class next time.

In terms of working with groups, my role could benefit from a better balance between giving assistance on content and process. For the most part, I focused on the content aspect of the projects, advising them on what points should be included, where to find resources, and on how to organize the write-up. Less attention was paid to how the groups were actually working. I knew that some were experiencing internal difficulties, but I did not work much on group dynamics. In the future, I think time should be set aside to discuss how the groups are functioning. To prepare for this, I would need to figure out how to effectively mediate tensions and differences, and to help group members work through them. Again, the issue of balance is key. On the one hand, students should be given the main responsibility for building working relationships in the group and not rely on me to solve their problems. On the other, it is my responsibility to make sure that groups function well, and that might necessitate my active intervention to make sure that potentially destructive tensions do not run unchecked.

Another problem related to balance is easier to correct. Students noted that they learned a great deal about the ethnic group they worked on, but did not learn much about the work of other groups. In the future, more time should be allotted for sharing the group's work. This would be useful while the projects are developing so that students could learn from how others are approaching the project. It would also be useful for groups to formally present the projects to their peers.

Finally, as I near the end of this paper, it has dawned on me that I have made no mention of student assessment and grading. In part this reflects a conscious decision to place less emphasis on this area, as this is an institutional requirement that often runs counter to pedagogical goals. Less emphasis, however, did not absolve me from having to assign grades and I tried a number of alternative approaches. There were no midterms or quizzes, or other traditional assessment measures. I started with the idea of having students produce a portfolio of their quarter's work, but that didn't get fully implemented. Instead, I kept rather unsystematic track of how groups were doing and how individuals were contributing to the group work. I asked students to assess their own performance. This, combined with their final product, provided sufficient information upon which to assign letter grades. I was not entirely happy with the process of grading, but interestingly students did not focus a lot of attention on the issue. This may indicate that they did find more value in the educational experience than in the letter grade (that, however, may be wishful thinking on my part).

Developing Pedagogical Knowledge

Often, in our efforts to improve teaching, intuition tells us to seek out the exemplary teacher, the confident, experienced one with beautifully constructed courses and innovative ideas. While these exemplars can indeed be inspirational, sometimes their polish can intimidate, making those of us with less experience wonder if we can ever reach that level.

In this article, I present another approach to developing pedagogical knowledge. Here, the important focus is not to produce a neatly packaged prescription of readings, topics, and teaching strategies. Instead, I maintain that good teaching develops by looking more closely and candidly at the oftentimes messy process by which our courses and teaching develop. Better teaching usually emerges from our struggles, failures, and desperate attempts to recover from mistakes. Unfortunately, these don't always get into articles on teaching, or we're too embarrassed to bring them into print. Yet it is the process of making our goals and assumptions explicit, of reflecting on how well our practice reached those goals, and of figuring out how we might do them differently next time that holds the key to improved teaching.

Notes

1. Karen Umemoto, " 'On Strike!' S.F. State College Strike, 1968–69," *Amerasia Journal* 15, no. 1 (1989): 3–41.

2. Lane Ryo Hirabayashi and Marilyn Alquizola, "Asian American Studies:

Reevaluating for the 1990's," in *The State of Asian America: Activism and Resistance in the 1990s*, Karen Aguilar-San Juan, ed. (Boston: South End Press, 1994), 351–64.

3. Raymond Lou, " 'Unknown Jerome': Asian American Studies in the California State University System," in *Reflections on Shattered Windows: Promises and Prospects for Asian American Studies*, Gary Okihiro, Shirley Hune, Arthur Hansen, John Liu, eds. (Pullman: Washington State University Press, 1988), 24–30.

4. This is not to suggest that there are no innovative teaching initiatives. A recent *Los Angeles Times* story, 11 March 1995, entitled, "UCLA Class Puts Theory to Test in the Real World," by Connie Kang, reports on Glenn Omatsu's UCLA Asian American studies class on social movements. A key part of the course involved students going into the community to help Latino employees to organize a union at the Japanese-owned New Otani Hotel. In addition, the students reported on their work at a community forum.

5. Paulo Friere, *Pedagogy of the Oppressed (New* York: Seabury Press, 1973).

6. Michael Omi, "It Just Ain't the Sixties No More: The Contemporary Dilemmas of Asian American Studies," in Reflections *on Shattered Windows: Promises and Prospects for Asian American Studies, Gary* Okihiro, Shirley Hune, Arthur Hansen, and John Liu, eds. (Pullman: Washington State University Press, 1988), 31–36.

7. Amy Wallace, "Survey Finds Political Apathy among Freshmen," *Los Angeles Times*, 9 January 1995, A1, A14.

8. Wallace, Survey Finds Political Apathy . . ."

9. Both Elizabeth Ellsworth [Elizabeth Ellsworth, "Why Doesn't This Feel Empowering? Working Through the Repressive Myths of Critical Pedagogy," *Harvard Educational Review*, 59, no. 3: 237–324] and Jennifer Gore [Jennifer Gore, "What Can We *Do* For You! What *Can* We Do For You? Struggling Over Empowerment in Critical and Feminist Pedagogy," *Educational Foundations* 4, no. 3: 5–26] have raised important critical questions with respect to issues of "empowerment." They note that while "empowering students" has become a common goal in critical and feminist pedagogy, we know little about what that actually means and how one can realize such goals. From them I knew that simply claiming a desire to empower students meant nothing. I needed to pay greater attention to what we mean by empowerment and what role teachers play in bringing it about.

10. Paulo Friere, *Pedagogy of the Oppressed*, and *Education for Critical* Consciousness (New York: Seabury Press, 1978).

11. Mara Sapon-Shevin, "If Cooperative Learning's the Answer, What Are the Questions," *Journal of Education* 174, no. 2: 11–37.

12. U.S. Department of Labor, *What Work Requires of Schools—A SCANS Report for America 2000* (Washington, D.C.: U.S. Department of Labor, 1991).

13. For example, see Barbara G. Davis, *Tools for Teaching* (San Francisco: Josey-Bass, 1993); Friere, *Education for Critical Consciousness*; Henry Giroux, *Teachers as Intellectuals: Toward a Critical Pedagogy of Learning* (South Hadley,

Mass.: Bergin and Garvey, 1988); Susan Hill, *The Collaborative Classroom: A Guide to Cooperative Learning* (Portsmouth, N.H.: Heinemann, 1990); David Johnson and Roger Johnson, *Learning Together and Alone* (Englewood Cliffs, N.J.: Prentice-Hall, 1987); Carmen Luke and Jennifer Gore, eds., *Feminisms and Critical Pedagogy* (New York: Routledge, 1992); and Ira Shor, *Freire for the Classroom* (N.H: Boynton and Cook, 1987).

7

Unity of Theory and Practice: Integrating Feminist Pedagogy into Asian American Studies

DIANE C. FUJINO

Introduction

The first ethnic studies program in the nation was born at San Francisco State College in 1969. The labor was prolonged and the delivery pains sharp. It took a five-month strike by the student-led Third World Liberation Front, with the support of faculty and staff, to birth ethnic studies. So began the Asian American movement, which originated in the late-1960s out of the struggle centering on ethnic studies programs, opposition to the Vietnam War and U.S. imperialism, and the development of a pan-Asian identity.[1] Throughout the past three decades, women and some men have struggled against sexism and for the inclusion of feminist discourse in Asian American studies and in the larger social movement.[2] We have made some progress in this area, which can be seen in the proliferation of books and scholarly articles on Asian American women produced by Asian American scholars in the past decade. Various Asian American studies programs have placed increasing priority on women's issues.

In this chapter, I will examine Asian Americanist and feminist pedagogy through college courses I have taught on Asian American feminist issues, Asian American gender relations, and women of color experiences. As a beginning teacher, I certainly do not claim to have all the answers. But by examining pedagogical issues through my teaching and reteaching of gender courses, I recognize issues that are common to those teaching race and gender courses. I will discuss the content and process of teaching Asian American gender courses with an emphasis on the unity of theory and practice; gender, race, and power in the classroom; and the feminist challenge to the field of Asian American studies. It is my hope that this chapter's focus on curriculum materials and pedagogical issues will be of use to those teaching gender-specific courses and to those integrating gender themes into other courses.

Unity of Theory and Practice

The "unity of theory and practice" underlies my pedagogical approach to teaching Asian American gender courses. This is not surprising, given that early ethnic studies programs emphasized applying academic knowledge to serve the community and feminist scholarship promotes "the personal is political." The unity of theory and practice emphasizes the dialectical process of integrating academic knowledge and lived experiences. Personal experiences inform one's intellectual knowledge; in turn, theory can frame the interpretation of one's experiences. In the classroom, the unity of theory and practice contains at least three layers of meaning: (a) the continuity between the content and process of teaching; (b) the integration of intellectual and experiential or emotional knowledge; and (c) the application of academic learning to community service.

The Integration of Content and Process

There are two main approaches to structuring the content of Asian American gender courses. One approach organizes the material by ethnicity; one or two weeks are spent on each of the many Asian ethnic groups. The second approach organizes the material thematically around issues of importance to several or all Asian ethnic groups. The strength of the ethnicity approach lies in its the attempt to emphasize marginalized Asian groups by equally representing each Asian group.[3] In practice, however, the ethnicity approach tends to result in a superficial coverage of each group, continues to privilege certain groups, given the uneven availability of reading and video materials, and often fails to make useful comparative analyses. In contrast, the thematic approach provides an analytic framework for understanding Asian American women's issues by structuring the curriculum around important concepts and issues. Despite wide heterogeneity in Asian American women's experiences in terms of class, immigration status, language, sexual orientation, and so forth, these themes are relevant to most Asian groups and tend to bridge our experiences.

Ideally, the teacher would integrate both approaches by subsuming ethnicity within the thematic approach. Within each theme the teacher would make comparative analyses between ethnic groups and would highlight underrepresented Asian groups such as the Hmong, Cambodians, and Sri Lankans. I must admit that, in practice, I fall rather short of the ideal. The limitations of a ten-week quarter or even a fifteen-week semester, the disparate availability of curriculum materials, and the diverse backgrounds of students render this an arduous task. For example, some students are simply working to grasp elementary Asian American history and concepts, and find it overwhelming to differentiate among Asian groups. However, I do attempt to approach this ideal by contextualizing a group's experiences historically and culturally; by consciously including at least one article on underrepresented Asian groups, especially those groups represented at the university where I teach; and by making comparative analyses among Asian groups (e.g., comparing various Southeast Asian women's attitudes toward domestic violence).[4]

At UC Santa Barbara, I teach two gender-specific courses: Asian American gender relations and Asian American feminist issues. The size, level of the class, and the knowledge and motivation of students create differences in the content and process of teaching these two courses. Asian American gender relations is a two-hundred-student, lower-division course that fulfills the ethnicity requirement. Consequently, the students range from those with little knowledge about Asian America to Asian American studies majors who have already taken a dozen upper-division Asian American studies courses.[5] In addition, some students have little interest in the subject matter, enrolling solely to satisfy the ethnicity requirement. This creates a challenge in teaching students with diverse knowledge and motivations for Asian American gender issues. In contrast, Asian American feminism is a forty-five-student, upper-division course that does not fulfill the ethnicity requirement. Though the students represent diversity in terms of their ethnic and women's studies background, most are juniors and seniors who enroll because of a genuine interest in the subject matter.

I organize my gender relations and Asian feminist courses by the thematic approach, with an effort to represent ethnic diversity. First, I address gender and race as well as sexism and racism as social constructs. I begin the lower-division course by addressing the social construction of gender and race, gender and race discrimination, and gender role socialization. In the upper-division course, I spend little time on issues of social construction, assuming students should understand this. Instead I focus on how interlocking systems of racism, sexism, classism, and heterosexism operate. I find that students have a better understanding of sexism and racism, but have little knowledge about the economic system of capitalism. A cogent, readable, and interesting article by Edna Bonacich is useful for explaining economic inequalities,[6] which I augment with an overview of capitalism. I also use the U.S. overthrow of Hawaii to concretize the concepts of capitalism, imperialism, racism, and patriarchy.[7] Finally, I discuss the linkages between sexism and heterosexism; for example, both systems function to uphold the nuclear family which enables society to benefit from women's unpaid reproductive work. Second, I place Asian American gender experiences in a historical context. In addition to addressing the impact of U.S. legislation on sex ratio imbalances, gender roles, family, and work, I also explore the possible existence of matriarchal (i.e., egalitarian and communal) societies in Asia and influences such as imperialism and Confucianism that changed gender roles and fostered patriarchy.[8]

The third section focuses on the role of social institutions in shaping contemporary gender relations or Asian women's experiences in the areas of media representations, education, productive and reproductive work, violence (e.g., rape, domestic violence, hate crimes), and social relationships including gay/lesbian and interracial relationships. The lower-division course provides an overview of a wider number of topics. The upper-division course examines topics in more depth, from a structural analysis, and with an international focus, including the globalization of Asian women's labor and the sex industry around U.S. military bases in the Philippines, Korea, and Okinawa, and via tourism in Thailand, Cambodia, and India.[9] Finally, I end the courses with a focus on resistance and activism. I believe it is important to show Asian American women, stereotyped as the most passive of all women, as agents of change. Racism and sexism do not completely determine our lives; we also think, feel, and act upon our environment.[10]

The upper-division course differs from its lower-division counterpart by analyzing gender and race through interlocking systems of domination more than an individual-level approach, by presenting information in an international in addition to a domestic context, and of course, by focusing on women's experiences rather than relations between women and men. In sum, while the lower-division course emphasizes applying material to the students' personal lives at the individual level, the upper-division course focuses on how systems of domination operate at a structural level nationally and internationally.

A good teacher attends to the process of the classroom learning as much as to the content (i.e., the syllabus, readings, and lectures). In contrast to "traditional" teaching methods, feminist pedagogies strive to incorporate the concepts of participatory learning, cooperation, democracy, equality, and the unity of theory and practice into the classroom.[11] What many discussion-oriented teachers quickly learn is that most students have not had the opportunity to learn how to participate in their education. The influence of what Paulo Freire terms the "banking system" of education, based on the assumption that memorizing knowledge and regurgitating it on exams represents meaningful learning, has a powerful grip on students' minds. Part of our job involves teaching students how to think critically and participate in a discussion. While it is easier to generate discussion in smaller classes and teaching-assistant-led discussion sections, I have learned through experience that large classes do not preclude discussion.

One of the first steps in encouraging student participation is to facilitate speaking out. While I do promote students' articulating their ideas, it is important to acknowledge cultural differences in speaking out. On the first day of class, when discussing my pedagogical approach, I acknowledge that Asian and women's cultures tend to emphasize collectivism rather than individualism, making it more difficult to speak out.[12] Speaking out implies that my individual opinion matters. For Asian Americans, we often speak out only after carefully thinking over the content and delivery of our ideas. I recall that as an undergraduate student, even when I knew the answer to the professor's questions, I often thought it too obvious and simplistic to state publicly. I would then notice how the professor praised the comments of students who expressed the same ideas I had. I learned that people do not necessarily have profound thoughts, nor are they necessarily articulate when they speak out. And only through practice will we improve our speaking and critical thinking. For pragmatic reasons, speaking out is a good skill to develop in an individualistically oriented society. More importantly, speaking out is not necessarily an individualistic enterprise. It depends on one's goals. It is individualistic to speak out simply to draw attention to oneself or to help improve one's grade. However, speaking out is collective when one uses it to improve society by resisting stereotypes, racism, and sexism.

Promoting speaking out also requires creating space for those students who are hesitant to speak or those who miss openings in the discussion because their pacing or timing is slower. Women tend to wait until the speaker completes his/her thought, but then are unable to enter the conversation when a more aggressive student, often male and/or white as a result of unexamined privilege, jumps into the conversation or cuts off the speaker. I deal with this in a number of ways. First, I ask students to raise their hands to be called on, which facilitates speaking by all who want to speak. Second, I ask people who have not yet spoken to respond first. This creates a space for quieter students to speak. Moreover, this makes talkative students more aware of how their speaking affects other students. My students have reacted positively to creating opportunities for quieter students to participate. However, a couple students reacted strongly when a colleague of mine, Christine So, implemented a provocative classroom experiment. She gave varying numbers of tickets to students depending on the degree to which they spoke out; students who spoke rarely received four tickets, students who participated actively received two tickets. Students used one ticket each time they spoke. This exercise did promote speaking out by some quieter students. It also had an unanticipated effect on talkative students. After using their tickets, a couple of students expressed anger and frustration at being silenced: one put her head on her desk, another walked out of the room because she felt she could not learn without speaking. I interpret this to mean she cannot learn by listening to her classmates because most students acknowledge learning when the teacher lectures. Given that students have had few opportunities to appreciate learning from each other, I regularly emphasize the importance of listening to classmates who have valuable experiences and ideas to share.

Third, I allow silence, which requires the teacher to be comfortable with a period of nonspeaking, or rephrase the question in different ways to allow students time to think and to formulate their words. Fourth, I call on students whose nonverbal expressions imply they are responding to the discussion. Though other teachers call on students randomly to keep them sharp, I tend not to do this because I believe it can become a traumatizing experience that hinders further public speaking. I do believe, and state this to students, that I often learn by listening. It is not imperative to speak out, though I do encourage student participation. Fifth, I ask students to participate in some exercise, such as introducing themselves or their partners on the first day of class. I believe that students will have an easier time speaking out if they have done so at least once. Sixth, I've had students discuss in small groups, which encourages quieter students to express their ideas, and then reconvene as a large group. Finally, when students share a meaningful experience or idea with me, I encourage them to express the idea in class.

I believe in interspersing lecture material with structured discussions (i.e., dialogue with a focus and goals, rather than simply rapping about issues). Throughout my lectures and structured discussions, I do provide opportunities for students to ask questions and make comments. Students also raise different questions than those I had prepared as topics for discussion and we incorporate these ideas into our class discussions. In other words, while I have my own goals and topics in mind, there is flexibility in the classroom to incorporate what students want to learn. Clearly, discussion is important for students to learn to think critically, articulate their ideas, and engage in dialogue with their classmates. Without discussion, students rely too heavily on the "banking system" of teaching.

The Unity of Intellectual and Experiential Knowledge

Ethnic studies programs emerged in 1969 as a result of students protesting the exclusion of Third World people's experiences from the curriculum. The first Asian American women's course was taught at UC Berkeley in 1970 and at UCLA in 1972.[13] In the early Asian women's seminars, the lack of resources necessitated a reliance on experiential information. Students would interview their mothers or grandmothers about their experiences, and these oral histories became the basis of class discussion. Three decades later, academics and students have produced substantial materials on Asian American women's experiences. Still, oral histories and personal experiences remain a critical component of the curriculum.

Asking students to share their experiences brings alive academic concepts and material. I regularly ask students to share their experiences with, for example, race discrimination or sexual harassment. This information counters the myth that Asian Americans, as the model minority, experience no discrimination. It also counters a tendency I have observed in students to argue that discrimination exists largely among older people in politically conservative locations, or is a thing of the past. Having Asian American students tell their stories about how they were called a "gook, chink, or jap" on campus, how they received poor service at a store or restaurant, or how they were abused by police vividly illustrates that race discrimination affects Asian American youth today. Our class discussions on sexual harassment are usually quite lively, with several women sharing poignant stories about being sexually harassed and other students inquiring about boundaries for ethical behavior; for example, can a man ever ask a coworker out on a date? These discussions also legitimize the reality of sexual harassment, rape, domestic violence, and race discrimination experienced by Asian American women and men. One of my most dramatic experiences with a student testimony occurred in response to a white male student expressing disbelief about the prevalence of domestic violence. In the midst of tears and anger, a student shared how, two weeks earlier, her Asian American friend had been killed by the friend's boyfriend after years of abuse. Moreover, our classroom discussions send a message that it is appropriate to discuss these issues and break the code of silence that exists in Asian American communities. Giving voice to these problems is an initial step towards their resolution.

Journal entries are another tool that facilitates bridging students' intellectual and emotional lives. While women's studies faculty have long assigned journals, these assignments tend to veer towards what Berry and Black call "true confessions" or "cold knowledge."[14] Ideally, journals would be a dialectical forum for students to react emotionally to mental knowledge and to use the intellectual material to help them analyze their personal experiences. However, there are cognitive barriers that hinder students from integrating emotional and intellectual knowledge. One barrier arises from students' years of schooling based on logic that promotes binary thinking. Having compartmentalized intellectual from emotional spheres, it is difficult to integrate these experiences within a one-quarter or one-semester course. Another barrier arises when students struggle with emotional stress caused by academic material that challenges their fundamental worldview. At such a point, it is difficult for students to intellectually analyze dominant ideologies in a journal assignment. Conversely, framing the journal as a diary may help students to express their emotional turmoil, which may lift their emotional burden and enable them to be self-reflective or as is more likely the case, it may simply verify their confusion. In the latter case, the unstructured emotional diary does not facilitate analyzing and contextualizing personal experiences. Moreover, emotional assignments are hard to grade.

As a solution, Berry and Black present the integrative learning journal, which provides a sequential framework for increasing dialectical thinking. The first journal assignments involve diary entries requiring students to respond emotionally to academic material. The second type of journal assignments involve notebook entries which help students to engage intellectually through assignments such as summaries or critiques of lectures and readings or a response to a question posed by the teacher. At the next level of dialogue entries, students "talk" to the teacher in a written interaction by discussing issues she may have been uncomfortable raising in class. The next level, integrative entries, gives students practice at synthesizing emotional and intellectual knowledge by applying academic concepts to a personal struggle or by using personal experiences to support or contradict academic material. Finally, evaluative entries ask students to assess their progress in the class, and revision entries require students to modify previous entries based on new knowledge. Berry and Black require students to write one diary and one notebook entry each week, to attempt an integrative entry every two weeks, and three times a quarter, students write an evaluative entry before turning in journals to be graded.

Finally, videotapes offer a powerful medium to explore the experiences of Asian Americans and to elicit discussion among students. Videos such as *The Color of Fear, Mixed Blood, Picturing Oriental Girls*, and *Two Lies* can be used to explore how students feel, respectively, about discrimination, interracial relationships, media representations of Asian American women, and the use of eyelid surgery so Asian American women can approximate European standards of beauty.

The Application of Academic Knowledge to Changing Social Realities

In the spirit of the roots of Asian American studies, our courses can include projects that apply academic knowledge to community service and social change. Though I have not assigned such a project in my courses on gender relations and Asian women's issues, the experience in my Asian American social movements course can be easily applied to gender-specific courses. In addition to the academic goal of teaching Asian American movement history, the experiential goal of my Asian American social movement course is to help students understand they could help create social change. Based on the premise that to gain knowledge, one must participate in the practice of changing social realities, the course requires a hands-on, outside-the-classroom project, which focuses on Asians in the garment industry. The various small groups organized educational forums at a local high school and at the university, created an eye-catching visual display in a residence hall, produced a video, accessed the local media, and organized a picket in downtown Santa Barbara.

The class projects successfully met the goal of changing reality by increasing public awareness about labor exploitation. The students learned that they are teachers. Significantly, the students learned that changing reality also involves personal growth for participants. Most students in the class had no previous grass roots experience and were apprehensive about leaving the safe zone of the classroom. Several students admitted they started participating strictly for the grade. But as the class progressed, many of these same students began to get excited about their projects and to understand the academic material in a new light. As they began integrating personal and academic knowledge, most students struggled with their individual behaviors. How could they as consumers reduce their complicit role in exploiting garment workers? This is an especially difficult question for appearance-conscious youth. But, some decided to make sacrifices by boycotting their much-beloved Nike shoes. As one student said, "This class changed my life style."

Perhaps the most important lesson learned by students is that the power to create social change lies within each of us. As they touched people's lives and sparked an interest in others, many realized they could influence what happens in this world. They felt they had made a genuine difference in at least one other person's life. Through the frustrations and rewards of organizing their projects, the students came to understand the collective power of students to change social realities. Projects such as this that require hands-on participation advance the student's ability to integrate theory and practice as well as to integrate intellectual and experiential knowledge. These projects also have the potential to inspire a desire to apply academic knowledge to serving the community.

Gender, Race, and Power in the Classroom

Issues of gender and race present multiple pedagogical issues in teaching Asian American women and gender courses. The content of such courses

obviously necessitate a discussion of gender and race. If the course analyzes structural dimensions, one must address sexism and racism. This
often leads to emotionally charged discussions which are problematized
because students have been taught to understand the individual level—
and not to see the systemic level—at which race and gender operate. Individual-level thinking occurs, for example, when the student can offer an
anecdotal example that counters the systemic patterns presented by the
teacher and the readings. Individual-level thinking also occurs when the
student attributes behavior to personal choices and minimizes the influence of social institutions. When discussing the gendered division of reproductive work, an Asian male student of mine had difficulty
understanding that this gendered division is primarily socially constructed. He argued that women are "naturally" better at raising children
because of our biological ability to bear children. After some debate, we
moved onto discussing housework. Though the student had never considered housework to be socially constructed, a light bulb clicked on as
he had problems explaining why women are "naturally" better cooks
and cleaners. He then began to question his biological-deterministic view
of child rearing. I could see the beginnings of his ability to contextualize
reproductive work in patriarchal constructs, though no doubt he will slip
in and out of his individual-level thinking for quite some time.

In my teaching, I have noticed that race raises even more controversy
than gender. For example, when discussing affirmative action, some students, particularly whites and to a lesser extent Asians, have difficulty
seeing beyond the individual level. Their constant arguments are based
on "my friend didn't get into [UC] Berkeley because a less-qualified African [or Chicano] took her spot." No matter how much we discuss the
ways systemic racism and sexism function to limit opportunities, a position with which most of these students agree, their arguments spiral back
to a forced choice between two individuals (who they assume live equally
free from racism because they went to the same high school). Note too
that affirmative action has been framed as a race issue, though white
women are the major beneficiaries. Clearly, it is difficult for students,
especially younger students, to see beyond their personal experiences because they have been trained to see the world only on an individual level.
In addition, I believe some students' emotional investment in their worldview (e.g., that society is fair and offers opportunities equally to all)
blocks their ability to view the topic from a systemic perspective. This
rigid grasp on their worldview explains why they are unable to incorporate new, rational information on this particular topic, though their logic
operates well on other less emotionally charged topics.

For more privileged groups, it is difficult to acknowledge the ways that
race and gender hierarchies systemically advantage whites and men, re-

spectively. While students may recognize that some groups are discriminated against, it is very difficult for them to also understand that this same discrimination privileges their own group. I find an article by Peggy McIntosh useful for discussing white privilege and male privilege. McIntosh explains how, as a woman, she readily recognizes sexism and male privilege. But as a white person, her racial privilege blinded her from recognizing subtle forms of racism and the ways she benefits from white privilege. Moreover, she notes that, "Whites are carefully taught not to recognize White privilege. . . . Whites are taught to think of their lives as morally neutral, normative, and average, and also ideal, so that when we work to benefit others, this is seen as work that will allow 'them' to be more like 'us' ".[15] McIntosh identifies ways she benefits from white privilege such as, "I am never asked to speak for all the people of my racial group," "I can choose blemish cover or bandages in 'flesh' color and have them more or less match my skin," and "My culture gives me little fear about ignoring the perspectives and powers of people of other races." I extend this material to address forms of male privilege such as, "I can go talk to a professor, most of whom are male, without worrying that I may be sexually harassed" and "I can turn on the television or open a magazine without having to see countless pictures of my body being used as a commodity to sell beer and cars." I also apply this to discuss heterosexual privilege, including "I can talk about what I did over the weekend with my partner and not have to worry about which gender pronoun to use" and "I can marry legally and obtain the associated legal benefits such as tax breaks and spousal health care." These discussions have been eye-opening to many students. Significantly, they also help clarify how privileged groups benefit from racial, gender, and sexual hierarchies, though they are not slave owners, neo-Nazis, rapists, or gay bashers themselves.

As McIntosh illustrates, I have also found that men have difficulty understanding subtle sexism, whites understanding subtle racism, and straights understanding subtle heterosexism. A tool that I have found useful is to first discuss the student's personal experiences with discrimination and then make parallels to other forms of discrimination. For example, an Asian American male student of mine understood anti-Asian violence, but held beliefs that women who are raped somehow "asked for it." I asked the student, "Did Vincent Chin 'ask' to be beaten to death because he went to a bar filled with white men?"[16] This student's insight into how experiences are racialized facilitated his understanding of gendered experiences.

In my Asian women's courses, I also deal with stereotypes students have about Asian Americans or women, in general, and about Asian American women, in particular. Several non-Asian students have told me they prefer to fulfill the campus ethnicity requirement[17] by taking a course in Asian American studies rather than Black or Chicano studies, which they view as politically charged and radical. The stereotype of Asian Americans as the passive model minority[18] presupposes that our courses will not directly challenge the racial hierarchy and thus will be a safe space to discuss diversity without any discomfort or guilt. So when our classes do confront racism and sexism, those students holding the model minority stereotype become upset. In the lower-division gender relations course, I show the video *Stolen Ground* to illustrate how Asian American men experience race discrimination. A white female student, who made the effort to come to office hours because she cared enough to grapple with race issues, told me she thought the video showed militant reactions that are not representative of Asian America. She was particularly disturbed when one Asian American man in the video described how he wanted to, but never had, respond to race discrimination by screaming "fuck you" to the perpetrator. The student further explained that this behavior would only separate whites and Asians; in fact, she has noticed that Asian American student organizations segregate themselves from whites. I asked her, "Would you have reacted in the same way had the person been African American?"[19] She was surprised to discover that she would not have been disturbed. She explained that she often hears African Americans get angry about race discrimination, but she never knew Asians also felt discrimination. This conflicted with her image of Asian Americans as fitting into America as the model minority. (I also explained that historically race-conscious organizations developed because white Americans excluded people of color from their organizations, not vice versa as she characterized "the problem.")

The misimage of Asian America as the model minority also affects how students view our classes as well as ourselves as teachers. As a teacher, I visibly fit the "lotus blossom" image of a passive, subservient Asian woman. I am female, Asian, short, and youthful in appearance, the latter two being related to my race and gender. Some students have told me they were surprised that I was the professor, or that I was so articulate, or that I had strong and intelligent perspectives, or that I got angry about certain issues. Just as the white female student reacted to the video *Stolen Ground*, I believe some students react negatively to my discussions of racism and sexism because they expect me not to challenge dominant ideologies, their privileges, or their worldviews. Some of these students' worldviews attempt to be race and gender neutral, and they become disturbed when I reflect how society operates in race- and gender-conscious ways. In response, some white or male students react with feelings of guilt, denials that race or gender discrimination are barriers, and accusations of white and male bashing. I would also argue that these students are conflating systemic-level analyses that I present with their own individual-level perspectives. And no matter how often I explicitly differentiate between group and individual analyses and acknowledge the difficulty in seeing the structural level, some students do not understand the systemic analysis for reasons discussed earlier. Certainly, any teacher who addresses race and gender hierarchies will be met with strong reactions by some students, but I suspect that students react more strongly when an Asian woman discusses these same issues. I will add that for many students, their views of me as bashing men and whites changed as the course progressed (that is, as they were able to understand systemic perspectives) or when they came to talk to me in office hours.

It is important to acknowledge the difficulties an Asian male colleague of mine experienced when teaching Asian American men's studies from a pro-feminist perspective. Some male students were outraged at Professor Jachinson Chan, accusing him of "selling out" to feminism. Some of these same students had never directly challenged me because they (correctly) perceived me to be a feminist. Just as whites, and to a lesser extent "model minority" Asian Americans, are expected to uphold the racial hierarchy, men are expected to uphold male dominance. Dominant group members who oppose oppressive ideologies can be attacked as vehemently as minority group members.[20] On another level, however, whites who oppose racism and men who oppose sexism hold ascribed credibility. White and male privilege enhances their authority, and because their opposition to dominant ideologies is unexpected, students may listen more carefully to their reasoning.[21] I should note the location of Asian American female teachers in this dialectical process. On one hand, some students see us as the racial minority group who has not been adversely affected by discrimination and are disturbed when we raise strong voices challenging racism and sexism. On the other hand, some students dismiss our perspectives because, unlike white teachers, we lack proscribed racial authority and some students see us as selfishly promoting our own race issues. In a parallel fashion, as female teachers, we lack the male privilege to enhance our credibility and we may be dismissed as promoting our own self-interested gender issues. Conversely, some students react positively because they expect and want us to discuss feminist perspectives. To counter these often unconscious processes, I believe it is important to explicitly articulate how race and gender operate in the classroom and to discuss these issues when they arise.

I also want to address that the flip side of physical attributes; my size, gender, race, and youthful appearance also function to reduce the hierarchical distance between teacher and student. Some students tell me that they feel more comfortable speaking out in class, questioning what I'm teaching (which can be both positive and negative), and talking to me about school or more personal matters because I'm more "approach-able," that is, I look like many of my students. Moreover, many students are excited to find a course that addresses their own experiences (or the experiences of an underrepresented group) in an antiracist and antisexist context. Clearly, gender and race operate in multifaceted ways in the classroom. And the more we attend to the nuanced ways gender and race are manifested, the more we, as teachers, will be able to confront racism and sexism in the content as well as the process of our teaching.

The Feminist Challenge to Asian American Studies

From the beginnings of Asian American studies and the Asian American movement, there has been a lively and dynamic struggle to prioritize feminist works, to fight against sexism, and to integrate issues of race, class, and gender. In fact, it was through the Asian American movement that many women increased their consciousness of patriarchal structures.[22] In the early 1970s, women, especially college women, in the Asian American movement created their own courses[23] and publications focusing on Asian women, including UC Berkeley's *Asian Women* (1971) and two special issues of *Gidra* (January 1971, April 1972).

There is no doubt that the social movements for race, gender, class, and sexual equality have advanced our knowledge and analysis of Asian feminist issues. I have noticed that college students today integrate, rather than dichotomize, race and gender issues in their thinking much more readily than we did a decade ago. The field has advanced in terms of the number of gender courses taught on a regular basis as well as in the integration of gender issues into other courses. For example, at UC Santa Barbara where I teach, the Asian American studies department provides a focus on gender issues, offering numerous courses on Asian American gender relations, Asian feminism, women's history, women's literature, and perhaps the only such course in the nation, Asian American men's issues; many other courses contain at least some focus on gender.

Despite the increased gender focus in Asian American studies, binary thinking continues to border our field of inquiry. Issues of race and gender are too often pitted against one another rather than being integrated within a field. One obvious area in which women's experiences and feminist perspectives have been minimized is early Asian American history, a core area of Asian American studies. Though efforts have been made to integrate women's experiences and perspectives into our history courses, these courses continue to be primarily taught as a history of single Asian men, with references to women in terms of their relation and function to men.[24] Note that historical writings also assume a heterosexual norm:

that all Asian men were heterosexual and longing for a wife in America. It would be interesting to study the lives of gay men among our early Asian American ancestors.[25]

I believe a current challenge to our field is to prioritize the integration of Asian feminist perspectives into our curriculum materials, pedagogies, and standard course offerings. This would require hiring ladder-rank faculty to teach Asian American gender courses on a regular basis. It would also require providing resources to develop feminist curriculum and research material for use in both gender-specific and nongender-specific courses. The integration of gender issues into the nongender-specific courses is necessary to ensure a comprehensive study of gender rather than the ghettoization of women's issues within Asian American studies. Finally, this requires that we attend not only to the content, but also to the process of teaching. From a feminist perspective, this means incorporating the unity of theory and practice. It also means evaluating how we assess knowledge, using assignments that assess experience and personal application, such as journals and group projects, instead of or in addition to (masculine) material, such as multiple-choice tests.

Intensifying the inclusion of feminist issues into Asian American studies provides an exciting challenge and opportunity for the field to integrate issues of race and gender along with class and sexuality. This creates complexity and also more closely approximates the multilayered realities that exist in society. Moreover, the integration of feminist discourse also foregrounds gay and lesbian experiences given the connection between sexism and heterosexism. In a slightly different context, Franz Fanon said, "Each generation out of its relative obscurity must either fulfill their mission or betray it." Three decades after the birth of ethnic studies, it is up our generation of scholars and students to determine how well Asian American studies will fulfill this feminist challenge.

Notes

Author's note. I would like to thank Lane Hirabayashi for his editorial suggestions and advice, my colleagues for their pedagogical guidance and support, and my students for their enthusiasm, inspiration, and intellectual inquiry that keeps teaching a rewarding and challenging enterprise.

1. In contrast to ethnic-specific identities of previous generations, the development of a pan-Asian identity grew out of the Asian American movement in an effort to recognize common oppression, to forge new solidarities within Asian America and with other racial minority groups, and to consolidate political power. It was Asian American student activists who developed the now widely recognized term, "Asian American," as an act of self-determination in opposition to the pejorative term, "Oriental." See Yen Le Espiritu, *Asian American Paneth-*

nicity: Bridging Institutions and Identities (Philadelphia: Temple University Press, 1992); Yuri Kochiyama's talk on the Asian American movement at UC Santa Barbara, April 29, 1997; Karen Umemoto, " 'On Strike!' San Francisco State College Strike, 1968–69: The Role of Asian American Students," *Amerasia Journal* 15 (1989): 3–41; William Wei, *The Asian American Movement* (Philadelphia: Temple University Press, 1993).

2. Judy Chu, "Asian American Women's Studies Courses: A Look Back at Our Beginnings," *Frontiers* 8 (1986): 96–101; Lane Ryo Hirabayashi and Marilyn C. Alquizola, "Asian American Studies: Reevaluating for the 1990s," in *The State of Asian America: Activism and Resistance in the 1990s*, Karin Aguilar-San Juan, ed. (Boston: South End Press, 1994); Susie Ling, "The Mountain Movers: Asian American Women's Movement in Los Angeles," *Amerasia Journal* 15 (1989): 51–67; Wei, *The Asian American Movement*.

3. An ongoing debate in Asian American studies centers on who is represented by the term "Asian America." Certain groups, in particular the Chinese and Japanese, men, heterosexuals, and early immigrants, have been privileged in the research and curriculum materials, teaching positions, course offerings, etc. Some argue that the pan-Asian discourse is largely rhetorical and strategic, failing to include Southeast Asians and South Asians. Others argue that the field is genuinely striving for meaningful representation though the hurdles are significant. Another aspect of the debate questions which groups should be included under the socially constructed pan-Asian identity; e.g., "Are Asian Indians part of Asian America?" and "Given the geographic location of the Philippines, are Pilipinos Asian, Southeast Asian, or Pacific Islanders?" The debate gets murkier: Do Pilipinos constitute one cultural grouping given the diversity in language, religion, etc.? Also note that this large archipelago was not socially constructed as a single nation or known as the "Philippines" until Spain colonized the Philippines in the sixteenth century. The contours of this debate are dynamic and changing. Partly resulting from demographic changes, newer immigrant groups such as Koreans, Pilipinos, Vietnamese, and Asian Indians are increasing their role within the field and the prominent role of older immigrant groups, such as the Japanese, is being reduced.

4. Christine K. Ho, "An Analysis of Domestic Violence in Asian American Communities: A Multicultural Approach to Counseling," *Women & Therapy* 12 (1990): 129–50.

5. Because the Asian American studies major was implemented two years ago, many upper-division students have not yet fulfilled their lower-division course work.

6. Edna Bonacich, "Inequality in America: The Failure of the American System for People of Color," in *Race, Class & Gender: An Anthology,* Andersen and Collins, eds. (Belmont, Calif.: Wadsworth Publishing, 1992).

7. The video *Act of War* and the introduction from Haunani-kay Trask, *From a Native Daughter* (Monroe, Maine: Common Courage Press, 1992) are useful teaching material.

8. Yen Le Espiritu's book, *Asian American Women and Men* (Newbury Park, Calif.: Sage, 1996) provides an overview of gender relations in three time periods:

1840s–1930s, World War II and postwar years, and the post-1965 period. *Making Waves: An Anthology of Writings by and about Asian American Women,* Asian Women United of California, eds. (Boston: Beacon Press, 1989) contains several articles on Asian American women's herstory. Elizabeth Uy Eviota's book, *The Political Economy of Gender: Women and the Sexual Division of Labor in the Philippines* (London: Zed Books, 1992) describes the impact of imperialism on gender relations in Philippine society. Yunshik Chang's article, "Women in a Confucian Society: The Case of Chosun Dynasty Korea (1392–1910)," in *Traditional Thoughts and Practices in Korea,* Eiu Young Yu and Phillips, eds. (Los Angeles: Center for Korean-American and Korean Studies, California State University, Los Angeles, 1983) illustrates how the introduction of Confucian ideology into Korea changed women's roles and rights.

9. For information on gender and labor in an international context, see Cynthia Enloe, *Bananas, Beaches, and Bases: Making Feminist Sense of International Politics* (Berkeley: University of California Press, 1990). For information on the sex industry, see Saundra Pollock Sturdevant and Brenda Stoltzfus, *Let the Good Times Roll: Prostitution and the U.S. Military in Asia* (New York: The News Press, 1992); also Robert Friedman, "India's Shame: Sexual Slavery and Political Corruption are Leading to an AIDS Catastrophe," *The Nation,* 8 April 1996; Lillian Robinson, "Touring Thailand's Sex Industry," *The Nation,* 1 November 1993; and Thanh-Dam Truong, *Sex, Money and Morality: Prostitution and Tourism in Southeast Asia* (London: Zed Books, 1990). One poignant film on global labor is *The Global Assembly* Line and two excellent videos on the sex industry are *Sin City Diary* (on the Philippines) and *The Women Outside* (on South Korea).

10. I show the powerful video *Yuri Kochiyama: Passion for Justice* produced by Rea Tajiri and Patricia Saunders, 1994.

11. Nancy Schniedewind, "Teaching Feminist Process in the 1990s," *Women's Studies Quarterly* 21 (1993): 17–30; Carolyn M. Shrewbury, "What is Feminist Pedagogy?" *Women's Studies Quarterly* 21 (1993): 8–16.

12. As an example, I contrast the collective adage "the nail that sticks out gets pounded down" with the individualistic adage, "the squeaky wheel gets the grease." In making this general statement about cultural differences, I recognize the great heterogeneity that exists within any group. Certainly some Asian students are quite outspoken and verbally confident. Others are situationally outspoken, quiet in the classroom, yet downright aggressive in protesting grades.

13. Judy Chu, "Asian American Women's Studies Courses: A Look Back at Our Beginnings," *Frontiers* 8 (1986): 96–101.

14. Ellen Berry and Elizabeth Black, "The Integrative Learning Journal (or, Getting Beyond 'True Confessions' and 'Cold Knowledge')," *Women's Studies Quarterly* 21 (1993): 88–106.

15. Peggy McIntosh, "White Privilege and Male Privilege: A Personal Account of Coming to See Correspondences through Work in Women's Studies," in *Race, Class and Gender: An Anthology,* Andersen and Collins, eds. (Belmont, Calif.: Wadsworth Publishing, 1992), 71, 73.

16. The Vincent Chin case is the most widely known contemporary case of

anti-Asian violence. Chin, a 27-year-old Chinese American man, got into a bar-room brawl with two white male autoworkers, one of whom referred to Chin in racist terms. After the brawl ended, the two men, Ronald Ebens and Michael Nitz, found Chin and beat him to death with a baseball bat. This murder occurred in Detroit in 1982 at a time when anti-Japanese and anti-Asian sentiment ran high as a result of scapegoating Japan for the slump in the American auto industry. For more information, see Yen Le Espiritu, *Asian American Pan-Ethnicity* (Philadelphia: Temple University Press, 1992).

17. In an effort to reduce Eurocentrism, students at the University of California, Santa Barbara fought for and won the implementation of an ethnicity requirement in 1989. For more information on how the ethnicity requirement affects Asian American studies courses, see Sucheng Chan, "On the Ethnic Studies Requirement," *Amerasia Journal* 15 (1989): 267–80.

18. The "model minority" stereotype emerged in the 1960s to lift up Asian America as a group that has succeeded in America despite disadvantages. This contrasts sharply from earlier stereotypes of Asian Americans as sneaky, manipulative, untrustworthy, manual laborers. The model minority stereotype, developed at the same time African Americans, Chicanos, and Asian Americans were struggling against racism, functions to locate Asian America as the wedge group. As the wedge group, we are used to buffer rich whites against direct assaults by people of color as seen in the "Black-Korean conflict." As the wedge group, we are also used to show that America is an open society and with enough hard work, any one can make it in the United States. High levels of unemployment, incarceration, and poverty among African Americans, Chicanos, and indigenous peoples can then be explained by their own laziness and incompetence. This victim-blame explanation ignores the role systemic racism plays in creating marginalization within society as well as the hard work exerted by most working-class people.

19. My response to this student stemmed from an incident described by Mitsuye Yamada in which her students were offended by the radical voices of Asian Americans in the introduction to *Aiiieeeee!*. These students were not offended by the militancy of African Americans, Chicanos, or Native Americans, but reacted to Asian American militancy. One student said, "Their anger made me angry because I didn't even know the Asian Americans felt oppressed. I didn't expect their anger." See Cherrie Moraga and Gloria Anzaldua, eds., *This Bridge Called My Back: Writings by Radical Women of Color* (New York: Kitchen Table, 1983), 35.

20. Consider, for example, the murders of the three civil rights workers—two Whites, Michael Schwerner and Andrew Goodman, and an African American, James Chaney—in Mississippi in 1964. The three were missing after being released from jail, and months later, a group of whites, including police officers, were implicated in the murders; see Carson, Garrow, Gill, Harding & Hine, eds., *The Eyes on the Prize Civil Rights Reader* (New York: Penguin Books, 1991).

21. Sucheng Chan describes how having seen videos that contained scenes of white male scholars—"who look and talk like the white male authority figures with whom all students are familiar"—opposing racism, students were better able to accept her analysis; Chan, "On the Ethnic Studies Requirement," 279.

22. Susie Ling, "The Mountain Movers: Asian American Women's Movement in Los Angeles," *Amerasia Journal* 15 (1989): 51–67.

23. Judy Chu, "Asian American Women's Studies Courses," 96–101.

24. Gary Okihiro, *Margins and Mainstreams* (Seattle: University of Washington Press, 1994); Sylvia Yanagisako, "Transforming Orientalism: Gender, Nationality, and Class in Asian American Studies," in *Naturalizing Power,* Sylvia J. Yanagisako and Carol Delaney, eds. (New York: Routledge, 1995).

25. Some studies discuss notions of homosexuality or alternative forms of heterosexuality in Asian American history: *Amerasia Journal,* special issue on "Dimensions of Desire," 20, 1994; Jennifer Ting, "Bachelor Society: Deviant Heterosexuality and Asian American Historiography," in *Privileging Positions: The Sites of Asian American Studies,* Gary Y. Okihiro, Marilyn C. Alquizola, Dorothy Rony, and K. Scott Wong, eds. (Pullman: Washington State University Press, 1995), 271–79.

8

Contemporary Asian American Men's Issues

JACHINSON W. CHAN

To gain insight into how young Asian American men in the 1990s perceive themselves and gender-related issues, I taught one of the first Asian American men's studies course at the university level in the United States during the spring quarter of 1996.[1] This course was developed because I felt that Asian American men have not been given an opportunity to articulate their perspectives on gender issues on an institutional level. Furthermore, my research and analysis of Asian American masculinities made me realize the urgent need to familiarize students with current debates on gender and race relations and to encourage them to reject an oppressive masculinity and embrace a profeminist ideology of manhood. I anticipated, however, that my goal to transform lives in ten weeks was destined to fail. I admitted this on the first day of class. Redefining Asian American male identities is necessarily a lifelong project.

The process of redefining Asian American male identities begins with the evaluation of whether definitions are viable and effective tools toward understanding Asian American men or men in general. Will definitions reduce the complexity of Asian American male identities to simple discursive categories? Is it even possible to define Asian American masculinities when there are so many generational, ethnic, and class differences among Asian American men?

In the 1970s, the coeditors of *Aiiieeeee!* argued that "the deprivation of language in a verbal society like this country's has contributed to the lack of a recognized Asian-American cultural integrity . . . and the lack of a recognized style of Asian-American manhood."[2] After almost two decades, the same editors are still angry because stereotypes of Asian American men not only continue to be prevalent in American culture but they have been further perpetuated by Asian Americans themselves:

It is an article of white liberal American faith today that Chinese men, at their best, are effeminate closet queens like Charlie Chan and, at their worst,

93

are homosexual menaces like Fu Manchu. No wonder David Henry
Hwang's derivative *M. Butterfly* won the Tony for best new play of 1988.
The good Chinese man, at his best, is the fulfillment of white male homosexual fantasy, literally kissing white ass. Now Hwang and the stereotype are
inextricably one.[3]

The coeditors of *Aiiieeeee!* and *The Big Aiiieeeee!* have been fighting for
decades to regain, in part, a model of hetero-masculinity on behalf of
Asian American men. What such a recognizable heterosexual manhood
should be like for Asian Americans, however, is not clearly articulated by
the coeditors. One reason that an Asian American hetero-masculinity is
so vague is the problematic assumption that there are essential physical,
psychological, and behavioral qualities in heterosexual men: athletic, aggressive, virile, rational, and decisive. Given these pervasive social prescriptions of manhood, men in general strive to live up to the standards;
when they fail, they experience what Joseph Pleck calls "sex role strain."[4]
When white American men are used by popular culture as standard bear-
ers of hetero-masculinity, Asian Americans are forced to accept the racial
hierarchy embedded in the discourse of American manhood. In effect,
Asian American men are given a false choice: either we emulate white
American notions of masculinity or accept the fact that we are not men.
The discursive formation of Asian American masculinities is thus
burdened by the need to prove our "hetero-masculinity" while simultaneously finding alternative ways to redefine social definitions of "masculinity."

On a representational level, Asian American men need to resist the
cultural inheritance forced upon us by Sax Rohmer and Earl Derr Big-
gers, among others. There is an urgency to find alternative ways of defining Asian American male identities. I believe that on a political level, the
question of redefining Asian American masculinities ultimately rests on
how men respond to feminism and gender issues. Criticizing and putting
pressure on the media to be more responsible in how they represent Asian
Americans is an important step towards limiting the reproduction of stereotypes. However, the idea of understanding Asian American male identities must also begin with dialogue—a critical evaluation and discussion
of how Asian American men feel about their lives, environment, family,
relationships, beliefs, and particularly how they view themselves as Asian
men in America.

At the conceptual stage of the Asian American men's issues course, I
did not expect many male students to enroll in this course nor did I expect the ones who did to speak freely until they trusted me. According to
colleagues who have taught men's studies classes at other universities,
male students seldom enroll in such courses so I was pleasantly surprised

to find nineteen Asian American men among the thirty-four students.[5] During the first five weeks, we read critical essays on sports[6] and novels by Asian American male writers,[7] viewed videos,[8] and attended a performance by a group of Asian American male performance artists based in Los Angeles.[9] Throughout the first five weeks, it was obvious that most of the men were not actively engaged in the discussions about the social constructions of masculinities, so during the seventh week I decided to throw away the syllabus and address the men's silence.

I instructed all the men to sit in a circle and asked the women to sit in an outer circle, facing outwards. The female students would get their chance to speak among themselves the following week. I proceeded to explain to the men why I was not going to finish the next three weeks without addressing the apparent disinterest among them. I then asked a series of questions to engage them in a discussion. Although there was some reluctance at first, soon almost everyone joined in and our conversation continued well beyond the end of the class period. Unfortunately, I did not record the conversation but I asked students to write down what they thought about the "men's rap" session and there seems to be some consistency in how the men responded to the "men's only" discussion.

All of the male students who participated in the "men's rap" session felt that the male-only discussion was a positive experience. Some of the more typical responses were:

> It opened the first doors for me to express my views . . . This forum was needed to release some of the tensions that were building up among the males in this class . . . I think that this was definitely the climax of the class . . . I feel that the last three weeks of class were the most beneficial . . . I felt rejuvenated after the men's rap session . . . I found the format quite interesting and comfortable . . . For the first time in the class I heard something that I have also experienced and can really relate to.

The men's discussion group was so comfortable that a student felt that this should have been an all-male class. On the opposite end, another student felt that this class needs to include women because one's masculinity is usually defined in relation to women. Finally, there were four students who felt that the men spoke about the "truths" and "realities" of Asian American men's experiences. These students were, in part, responding to the women in the class since they felt that many of the women were being too politically correct in answering some of the questions posed to them.

Some of the topics that were addressed in the men's discussion session revolved around interracial dating, internalized self-hatred, the obstacles that some "vertically" challenged students face, and the subculture of car racing among Asian American men in Los Angeles. Some of the men felt misled because of the title of the course. They wanted to learn about Asian American "men's issues" but the issues seem to be dictated by the female students in the class. They revealed that they felt bashed by me. One student said that until the rap session, he thought that I was always

> trying to be impartial (which is good) but then again sometimes you side with the women. Come to think of it, I don't recall many instances when you sided with us men on any discussion that we have had in the past. [During the rap session] it seemed more empowering to us since you were sitting among us guys and somewhat seeing where we were coming from.

Ten out of sixteen students would have preferred a course that empowers Asian American men as opposed to a profeminist approach to masculinity. One student said specifically that he enrolled in this class because he wanted to feel good about being an Asian American man. Instead, he felt that this course was just another male-bashing course, like women's studies courses, and that he was disappointed when the first week focused on showing how "sports is bad."

In retrospect, I felt that I made a strategic pedagogical mistake by not confronting the issue of reaffirming Asian American hetero-masculinity. I wanted to skip the macho posturing, which is often interpreted as an important component of "regaining" one's masculinity, and move into a more critical and/or self-critical level of analysis, focusing on the ways in which patriarchal powers permeate the infrastructure of society, including sports, and how men become complicit in the way power is distributed along the contours of race, gender, sexuality, and class. Judging from the responses, I believe that it might have been wise to "empower" Asian American "manhood" first, then question why such affirmations are needed and critique the consequences of empowering Asian American men.

The issue of dating dominated a large part of the ensuing discussion. One student said that Asian American men are the "lowest of the low," in terms of the social hierarchy of men in America, which elicited comments from almost all of the men in the group. Some men explained that Asian American women have the option of dating white men because of the existing stereotypes of Asian and Asian American women, while stereotypes of Asian American men do not give them the same capital when it comes to dating white American women or women in general. Further, a few of the men were angered by the fact that some Asian women prefer to date white American men.

Unfortunately, in the course of these discussions, the word "some" was not used. In turn, the women who were listening to this conversation were upset that they were lumped together with those Asian American women who date only white men. When the women had a chance to do their rap session the following week, their disappointment was quite evident. As I sat inside their circle, I paid close attention to what they said. Consequently, I was not aware of how the men were reacting to the women's discussion. In the written responses by the female students I learned that some of the men were "listening to their Walkmans, playing cards, talking, and laughing." One female student observed that "they [the men] were busy playing cards, laughing, eating, sleeping, or doing homework. They didn't take us seriously." Another female student remarked that the men's behavior was "a slap in the face." Unfortunately, I was not aware of such behavior at the time and could not explain to the men that their actions were highly inappropriate and offensive.

Most of the women in the class were, understandably, disappointed with the men. Although they thought that it was a good thing that the men had a forum to speak their true feelings and vulnerabilities, the content of the men's discussion offended and upset some of the female students:

> But when they did start to speak up, I was so appalled. They were blaming all of their problems on Asian American women . . . What I heard from the guy's group discussion was very disappointing . . . I really felt that letting the men talk as a group was a great idea. I felt that they opened up to a certain degree. However, after listening to what they had to say, I was a bit upset . . . It hurts because it is usually a negative confirmation and completely opposite of what you thought or wanted to hear . . . It was interesting but disappointing to hear them talk.

For one student, she was so disappointed with the "superficiality" of the men that she declared "I can tell you now . . . I hate men. I REALLY hate men!! I have lost all sense of faith and compassion for men."

Many of the women complained that the men dealt with superficial things such as their inability to find dates, lack of sexual experiences, and not looking beyond stereotypes. More importantly, though, the women felt that the men were not fair in saying that the women in the class were oppressive towards them: "I don't understand why the men feel that we were oppressing them. I feel that the women in the class have always supported the men (till this Tuesday) . . . They were blaming all their problems on Asian American women."

It is unfortunate that the men felt "threatened" by some of the female students since most of the Asian American women were prepared to support Asian American men's issues. As one female student remarked, "when Asian American men rise, the status of Asian American women also rises, and when Asian men fall, we fall . . . and vice versa." I firmly believe that the women in the class were sincere in their support for Asian American men but, as the same student pointed out, she is "not here to empower Asian American men, just to support them." For some women, apparently, "empowering Asian American men" implies a reproduction of a patriarchal social order. This is perhaps one of the more crucial distinctions that underlies some of the animosity between the two groups: the men want to be "empowered" as Asian American men, so "support" seems insufficient. Further, the men did not feel that the women were in fact supportive since the more vocal women in the class were relentlessly critical of patriarchy and hegemonic masculinities.[10]

Asian American men, much like many of their white counterparts, do not feel "privileged" or empowered simply because they are men. Indeed, most Asian American men are very aware of the fact that there are racialized roadblocks toward accessing the dividends of a white patriarchal society. Lynne Segal argues that "men can and do change"[11] and some of my male students have changed, albeit slowly. Some of the female students spoke with individual male students after class and noticed that "after hearing the women's discussion, they seemed more aware and sensitive to what was said by the women. One of the males in our class even stated that he realized the men's session was just a "superficial-complaining-whining-bitching about everything" session. At the other end of the spectrum, a female student said that "I have lost all sense of faith in men because the men's circle just reaffirmed that there is no hope."

The question of how men can change is crucial to an understanding of Asian American men, or men in general. For some feminists, the struggles against sexism and the fight for equal rights have been a long and arduous process. The frustration felt by some of the feminists in my course is understandable since women have been challenging patriarchy and sexism for decades; yet, many men do not seem to be sympathetic to their cause. One student commented that men should take more women's studies courses for their own personal growth and understanding. Some men responded by saying that they do and they feel bashed over and over again. The underlying issue comes down to this: how can men embrace feminism without feeling threatened?

Segal observes that there is a clash between "thought and deed in men's apparently increasing commitment to a more participatory, egalitarian role in child care and housework." She wants to explore the underlying reasons for the discrepancy between theory and practice. As a self-identified profeminist scholar, I am constantly challenging my own behavior at home and it is frustrating to witness the ease in which I slip into traditional gender roles. Segal explains the dilemma:

> Some, like Tony Bradham, blame society—the inflexible and relentless pressures of men's working lives: "Men have changed . . . but society itself hasn't changed sufficiently to make life easier for fathers (and for families)—and so we have this dilemma." Others would argue that men have no real wish to change, that they are happy, as a sex, to exploit women by leaving the labour of loving and caring to them. Such critics could point, for example, to the evidence that unemployed men often do less domestic work than men in jobs, even when the mothers in their household have full-time jobs.[12]

Critiquing society for perpetuating fundamental differences between men and women is not sufficient to help resolve the conflict among men who intellectually and politically want to change but find, in practice, that change is indeed hard work. Role models can provide motivation to relearn one's domestic responsibilities. For instance, my uncle in San Leandro, California, enjoys cooking, cleaning, taking care of grandchildren and the elderly. Every time I catch myself lounging in front of the television, I think of him and immediately get up to do something around the house. My spouse thinks that I should think of my uncle more often.

Redefining gender roles with a strategically indeterminate sexual identity is one way to embrace both "masculine" and "feminine" traits on a conceptual and literal level.[13] The fusion of masculinity and femininity elides psychological and biological differences and, admittedly, oversimplifies the complexities of sexual politics. Nonetheless, for Asian American men, thinking about masculinities as heterogeneous and conflictual enhances our ability to navigate the spectrum of competing masculine identities and gestures toward a nonessentialist identity formation. A strategically indeterminate gendered identity also resists the overidentification with a hegemonic masculinity that defines itself in terms of oppositions and negatives: not homosexual, not woman, not inferior, not weak (mentally and/or physically).

The playfulness of an indeterminate sexual identity should not mask the urgency of a more serious agenda of dismantling gender hierarchies. Neither macho posturing nor wallowing in self-pity will create a space where men and women can dialogue. Segal's anticynicism towards gender and sexual politics provides a positive starting point for a socialist feminist agenda. As she suggests, we cannot jump to a utopic vision of egalitarianism without understanding the roots of racial, cultural, class, and sexual differences and committing oneself to social change.

In the 1990s, the subject of Asian American "masculinity" is still underresearched and undertheorized. As we begin to trace the different ways in which Asian American masculinities have been constructed historically, I believe we must also work towards the future. The empowerment of Asian American men must begin with the premise of not subordinating women or gay men. It must also begin with a critique of what masculinity means and what it represents on an individual as well as a social level. This process must involve dialogue with other men as well as with women, since women play an influential part in shaping a man's sense of manhood. One of the consequences of not having critical tools, research data, and creative writings on the topic of Asian American masculinity is the slow development of a theoretical discourse on Asian American men. Finding the language to express one's ideologies, cultural upbringing, and emotional experiences is one step towards a nonoppressive form of empowerment.

At the beginning of this course, I argued that Asian American masculinity should not be determined by a hegemonic masculinity and that the construct of "masculinity" needs to be critiqued, redefined, and constantly challenged. After teaching this course, it is apparent that "Asian American men's studies" need to develop critical tools to navigate competing masculinities. My Asian American male students may have been resistant to a critique of patriarchy because some of the men have not yet had access or can even look forward to enjoying the dividends of patriarchy. How can they critique patriarchy when they do not feel that American culture and society have provided them with a sense of power as men?[14] For others, this was the first time that they had to confront their own sense of masculinity and it was difficult for them to articulate what masculinity means. The frustration of not having neatly packaged answers to the questions of "masculinity" was felt by many of the students, but at least some of the students have started the process of broadening their definitions of masculinity and de-reifying conventional social expectations of men and women.[15]

Asian American masculinity, as a social construct, has been defined largely by the reproduction of stereotypes in American popular culture. Stuart Hall's analysis of the ideological effects perpetuated by the media helps to explain how the representational relationship between Asian Americans and the mainstream media in America have been "naturalized" in such an effective way that Asian American men have been rendered, for the most part, invisible. As such, Asian American men have the responsibility to reclaim the discourse on masculinity on our own terms. The rigid social and cultural definitions of masculinity and femininity have been contested by feminists and profeminist men on a conceptual level for decades but the actual practice of reconceptualizing "masculine" and "feminine" behavioral traits continues to be resisted in a patriarchal society. We need to explore strategies to confront such a project. Discarding the rigid binarism of femininity and masculinity and the consequent reinvention of sexual identities is only one among many ways to subvert the boundaries of gender. Michael Kimmel argues that "we need a democratic manhood" which he defines as "a gender politics of inclusion, of standing up against injustice based on difference. Some men have embraced feminism, gay liberation, and multiculturalism as a blueprint for the reconstruction of masculinity."[16] For Asian Americans, the importance of a politics of alliance with gays/lesbians of color and straight women/men of color may provide men of color opportunities to dismantle gender hierarchies and find ways to overcome homophobia and sexism. Conceptually, it is easy to specify the goals to be attained but on a practical level, there is much work to be done. While we contest the misrepresentations of Asian American men in the media, Asian American men need to find alternative models of masculinity and not be complicit in a patriarchal social order. More importantly, we need to look beyond the compulsory heterosexual model of masculinity that has been scripted and rescripted by the editors of *Aiiieeeee!* since the 1970s.[17] Writings and performances by Asian American men and discussions within Asian American men's groups offer ways to contribute to an Asian American "masculinist" discourse that is less concerned with accessing patriarchy and more invested in articulating a fluid and self-critical sense of masculinity. Asian American men need to move beyond the stereotypes and to develop strategies to empower ourselves in opposition to patriarchal traditions and sexist ideologies.

Notes

1. I want to take this opportunity to thank all the students who took my first *Contemporary Asian American Men's Issues* course. It was a tremendous learning experience for me and thanks for the wonderful conversations on masculinities and related issues.

2. Frank Chin, Jeffery Paul Chan, Lawson Fusao Inada, Shawn Hsu Wong, eds., *Aiiieeeee!* (Washington, D.C.: Howard University Press, 1974), xxxviii.

3. Jeffery Paul Chan, Frank Chin, Lawson Fusao Inada, and Shawn Wong, eds., *The Big Aiiieeeee!* (New York: Meridian, 1991), xiii.

4. Joseph H. Pleck, *The Myth of Masculinity* (Cambridge: MIT Press, 1981), 160.

5. Two of these male students eventually withdrew from the class due to nonacademic related reasons. All of my students were, incidentally, Asian American students.

6. Michael Messner, *Power at Play* (Boston: Beacon Press, 1992), 1–23; and selected articles from Michael Messner and Donald F. Sabo, eds., *Sport, Men,*

and the Gender Order: Critical Feminist Perspectives (Champaign: Human Ki-netics Books, 1990).

7. Gus Lee, *China Boy* (New York: Signet, 1992); Shawn Wong, *Homebase* (New York: Plume, 1991).

8. Valerie Soe, *Picturing Oriental Girls* (1992); Jachinson Chan, *American Inheritance* (1995); Lee Mun Wah, *Color of Fear* (1995).

9. Dan Kwong's Asian Men's Writing/Performing Workshop has been per-forming "EVERYTHING YOU EVER WANTED TO KNOW ABOUT ASIAN MEN**but didn't give enough of a shit to ask" since 1994.

10. Many of the responses that are not produced here are personal critiques of individual students. Since many of the students know each other, they told me, in confidence, personal information about each other. Therefore, when I refer to the ways in which students "felt," I am using confidential conversations and writings to support my claims.

11. Lynne Segal, *Slow Motion: Changing Masculinities, Changing Men* (Lon-don: Virago Press, 1990), xiii.

12. Segal, *Slow Motion*, 35.

13. I agree with Michael Kimmel that androgyny, a simple blurring of mascu-linity and femininity into "a melange of some vaguely defined 'human' qualities," is not helpful because it reduces difference into sameness. My notion of a strategi-cally indeterminant gendered identity refers to a more targeted approach towards appropriating normative gender traits. For instance, redefining domestic work as a shared responsibility, not a gendered one; but more importantly, one needs to be able to reject the social stigma of redefining a space and not be affected by emasculatory comments.

14. A colleague of mine suggested using Peggy McIntosh's "White Privilege: Unpacking the Invisible Knapsack," in *Experiencing Race, Class, and Gender in the United States*, Virginia Cyrus, ed. (Mountain View, Calif.: Mayfield Publish-ing, 1993), as a model to investigate Asian American male privilege.

15. Students were divided into groups and were responsible for different proj-ects. The last group decided to write a performance piece that reflected some of the concerns raised in class and it was clear that these students creatively ex-pressed some of the problems in which gender roles are constructed.

16. Michael Kimmel, *Manhood in America* (New York: The Free Press, 1996), p. 333.

17. It was not surprising to me that many of my students reproduced, in differ-ent forms, the single trajectory of frustrated heterosexual desire articulated by the editors of *Aiiieeeee!* It seems that the politics of inclusion overrides the politics of alliance as these male students were more interested in changing the ways in which Asian American men are represented in popular culture than revisioning or redefining the ways in which masculinities are constructed by alternative mod-els of masculinity, such as learning from Asian American gay men. With the advent of Hong Kong movie stars, I believe that some Asian American men would rather appropriate "imported" models of masculinity than challenge pre-vailing notions of heteromasculinity. Some students, at the end of the quarter, did raise the issue of homophobia among Asian American men and I believe that there is an urgent need to unlearn homophobia before we can redefine heteromas-culinity.

9

Teaching Against the Grain: Thoughts on Asian American Studies and "Nontraditional" Students

ROBERT JI-SONG KU

The Metamorphosis

A few years ago, on route from New York City to Los Angeles, I sat in a plane flying somewhere over middle America and thought of the film, *The Fly*—not the old Vincent Price affair but the recent one by David Cronenberg. *The Fly* did not buzz into my mind at that moment simply because I happened to be in flight. No, that would have been too silly. Rather, I thought of *The Fly* because I recalled something the main character, Seth Brundle, uttered in midst of his rather absurd metamorphosis from average human to giant insect. The gist of it was: "I once was a man who dreamt he was a fly. Now, I am a fly who once dreamt he was a man."

That was quite a meaningful moment for me—no, not the moment in the film, but the moment in the plane as I flew over Iowa. You see, I was flying to Los Angeles from New York because I was changing graduate schools and also homes. I loved being a New Yorker, but, due to powers and circumstances I did not quite understand or could control, I was quickly—actually, at about five hundred miles per hour at thirty thousand feet—metamorphosing into a Los Angeleno, something that was to me at the time perhaps worse than becoming a giant, furry insect.

Fortunately, today I am back in New York City. (Yes, I am a New Yorker who just once dreamt he was a Los Angeleno.) Although I am still a graduate student, for the past three years I have spent most of my time and energy not being a graduate student, but being a teacher, and, in effect, abandoning my own studies in the process. And so, when I sat in my office at Hunter College preparing to teach a class recently, it was not unusual that I once again thought of the film, *The Fly,* and uttered to myself: "I once was a student who dreamt he was a teacher. Now, I am a teacher who once dreamt he was a student." But, unlike the moment in the plane over Iowa, and certainly unlike Seth "The Fly" Brundle I was not afraid of my liminality, my metamorphosis. When the time came, I calmly gathered my things and went to teach, and forgot all about my life as an insect. At least for awhile.

Six Questions, or Maybe Seven

Before I subject you to my questions, I want to ask you to play a game with me. Close your eyes and ask yourself what comes to mind when someone says "nontraditional student." (Yes, I know, this is a bit contrived, but bear with me.)

Question A: Who or what is a nontraditional student? Is he or she the same as what some in the field of education refer to as an "at-risk" or a problem student? I ask this because I hear this term, "nontraditional," used quite often as I teach and talk about teaching, and I think I know to whom this term is referring, but I want to be as precise as I can about it. Perhaps instead of defining it, I should describe it, try to make a list of traits that a nontraditional student might have.

1. The "nontraditional" student is the first in his or her family to attend college.
2. She is often older than 18 years of age when she starts college.
3. She is usually of color.
4. She is of working class.
5. She commutes to school.
6. She lives in the inner city.
7. She is herself a parent.
8. She has a full-time job or a demanding part-time job.
9. She has a poor background in the basic skills—reading, writing, and math.
10. She attends a community college or night classes.

Of course, I should not stop here; surely there are many more traits that can be recorded. Or maybe some of what I already listed should be amended or even omitted. At any rate, I want to stop here because I am feeling unsatisfied with this approach, dreadfully unsatisfied. How many of these traits must a student have before she can be considered a nontraditional student?

Question B: Can an entire college campus be considered a nontraditional campus if most of the students attending it are considered nontraditional? For instance, is Bard College or Columbia University *less* nontraditional than, say, the Borough of Manhattan Community College or Hunter College?

Question C: Can a teacher be considered a nontraditional teacher if most of her students are nontraditional, or if she teaches at a campus where most of the students attending it are considered nontraditional, or if she herself was once considered a nontraditional student?

Question D: Can a field of study, i.e., Asian American studies, be considered a nontraditional discipline if it is taught to students who are considered nontraditional by a nontraditional teacher teaching at a nontraditional campus? Simply put, are there two kinds of Asian American studies—one for traditional students and one for nontraditional students? Or does it all depend on things too complicated to articulate in a form of a simple question such as this?

Question E: Is nontraditional a value-free term? In other words, should a student not take offense when she is called a nontraditional student?

Question F: Are some students called nontraditional because they are the sum of the kind of traits I listed in Question A or, rather, are they called nontraditional because they force teachers and educational institutions to be challenged in ways that they are not accustomed or trained or simply do not care to?

Question G: Am I dated? Has someone already asked these questions, did a lot better job at it, and thought of answers to go with them?

You Must Pay Your Dues to the Emperor of Ice Cream

It is no secret that graduate English programs do not train their students to do the single most important thing they will end up doing once they obtain their Ph.D.'s. Graduate English programs do not teach their students how to teach, let alone let them know *why* they will eventually teach. But, perhaps this is just as well. With a few notable exceptions, I do not think I would like to learn how to teach from the professors who teach in my department.

I recently ran into a colleague of mine, a fellow graduate student in my department, in the hallway. We taught for a semester at the same community college. He seemed noticeably upset so I inquired as to why? "I just had a horrible class," he said. I knew he was referring to his freshman composition class, the same course I was teaching at the time. "The class was so dead. It's like they just don't care. No one said a word. It's getting worse every day." "What did you do in class?" I asked. "Wallace Stevens's 'The Emperor of Ice Cream,' " he answered. "That's not a difficult poem. I feel like I'm teaching in high school." Before I could speak to him any further, he walked away.

I felt bad for him. Over the past two years, he and I had been in the same courses together at the graduate school since we both identified ourselves as Americanists. I recall him quite vividly in those classes because he was always one of the most outspoken and animated. I *envied* him in those classes because I could sense that he found pleasure, much more so than I did, in talking about "literature," about, for instance, the different Calvinisms in Hawthorn and Melville, and the complimentary use of *tableux vivants* in Henry James's and Edith Wharton's realist fiction.

Yes, I felt bad for him, but soon decided I felt worse for his students, much, much worse.

Most of us graduate students in English, even before we earn our Ph.D.'s, will have to teach remedial writing, basic or freshman composition, or introduction to literature to students who might be labeled "nontraditional." Only a select few of us will avoid what most people in our discipline consider to be menial or blue-collar work. In my profession, teaching basic composition to nontraditional students is likened to working in the mailroom of a corporate office. And, of course, everyone in the mailroom, if he or she knows any better, aspires to be up on the fortieth floor in a board meeting, doing the things that *really* matter. Graduate English programs feed their graduate students a fantasy: Yes, you will someday be in the boardroom; you just have to pay your dues in the mailroom, in the basic composition classroom.

My colleague in the hallway feels he is paying his dues. "Someday," he is thinking, "I will be teaching graduate seminars on the poetics of Wallace Stevens." In order to prepare himself, my colleague in the hallway has brought to his nontraditional students Wallace Stevens and his "Emperor of Ice Cream." But, instead of the intellectual fulfillment he has fantasized about, has been promised, he finds resentment. On the one hand, he resents his students because they are not graduate students in English like himself, because they cannot read or write well enough in his mind to be "real" college students, because they do not pay attention in class, because they regularly come to class late, because they never read the assigned texts, because they interrupt the class with silly questions, and because they are too difficult. "What is this," my colleague asks, "high school?" On the other hand, his students resent him because they know how he feels. They are not stupid.

My colleague will not so much end up hating his students than hating the position he is in because of his students. He, along with many others like him, cannot wait until the class is over, until the day is over, until the semester is over, until this phase of his career is over, until he can finally do what he was trained to do, to teach students who love literature as he loves it, to teach students who will willingly talk about "The Emperor of Ice Cream" without giggling, students who know already how to read and write basic English, students who will challenge him with their young, enthusiastic minds. He cannot wait until he can finally teach "real" students, as Socrates taught Plato, as Plato taught Aristotle. The sadness my colleague felt in the hallway is the sadness Seth Brundle feels in midst of his transformation into the fly. My colleague was once a bright-eyed graduate student who dreamt he was a university professor. Now, he is a social worker. And he is wide awake. And so, he cannot wait for the day he can finally teach his own graduate students in graduate seminars. And, when the time comes, he will tell them the truth. He will tell them how things *really* are in this profession of teaching English. He will teach them how to pay their dues, how to work in mailrooms. He will teach them to persevere as he has—survive teaching in nontraditional schools—because they, too, like himself, will eventually reap the benefits. After five minutes of teaching them to pay their dues, he will officially start class and ask everyone to turn to Wallace Stevens's "The Emperor of Ice Cream." He will enjoy the fruits of his labor. After all, he deserves it. He has paid his dues.

The Seduction, or They're "Different"

Clearly, I was being wooed, not with flowers and compliments about the smell of honey in my hair, but with a newly built library, an intellectually stimulating environment, 10 to 1 student to faculty ratio, and students who are sure to be "different" than those students I was used to teaching at the city university.

"Tell me, how will you teach this course?" asked the dean during my interview. "How will you teach this Asian American literature course? Do you have any ideas?" "Oh, yes. As you know, I've been teaching this course at the city university for two years, and . . ." "Well, that's wonderful, I'm sure. But, you *do* know that the students here are, ahhh . . . different. You'll probably find them much more demanding and they'll challenge you in ways you are not accustomed. Our students are special, exceptional. They're different."

Although he did not say it, his message was clear: "We are doing *you* a favor. We are taking you away from the unpleasantness. We are accepting you as one of our own. You are one of the fortunate ones. You do not have to pay your dues."

A few hours later, I was back home in Brooklyn. I got out of my suit and tie and sat on the couch thinking what a peaceful campus I had just visited. I thought about calling my parents to tell them about the interview. Surely, they will be happy for me, proud of my achievement. After all, they still see in me the face of Horatio Alger. I wanted to be happy for myself, but, instead, I felt sad, not the sadness of Seth Brundle or my colleague in the hallway, but their sadness turned inside out, the negative impression of their sadness. However, despite my sadness, or rather because of it, I took the job.

The Will to Remember

I realize now that I went into Asian American studies, both studying and teaching it, because I wanted to engage in "nontraditional" pedagogy, although I have not yet figured out what that is. What I do know is that I want to believe in Asian American studies, to believe that it is somehow different than "traditional" studies. I want to believe that studying and teaching American literature "traditionally," for example, is different from studying and teaching *Asian* American literature.

I want to believe that Asian American studies started as a "nontraditional" field of study concerned directly with "nontraditional" issues, issues that "traditional" studies ignored, denied, or erased. I want to believe in radical pedagogy, whether one teaches at Bard College, Hunter College, the Borough of Manhattan Community College, or Columbia University.

But, sadly, I sense that Asian American studies is being seduced, not with flowers and compliments about the smell of honey in its hair, but with the possibility that it no longer has to pay its dues, that it has already paid its dues, that it no longer should be situated within the mailroom.

Asian American studies was once an illegitimate discipline which dreamt it was legitimate. Now, it is in danger of fast becoming a discipline that has forgotten how to dream.

Question H: Should Asian American studies by its very nature confront issues that confront nontraditional students or should it just replicate the attitudes of the larger academy, hoping to become invited into the boardrooms?

Questions I, J, and K: Will Asian American studies, like so many other fields of study, end up believing that cream rises to the top? Will it embrace the trickle-down theory of pedagogy? Will it kowtow to the emperor of its own ice cream?

Sadly, I have given up hope on the larger academy, but, happily, I have not given up hope on Asian American studies—not yet, at least, because I have not given up hope on my colleagues within the field. Furthermore, I have not given up hope on myself, and, more importantly, I have not given up hope for my students. I want to remember to remember.

It's the Shoes

I had a homeless student in class last year at the community college where I periodically teach. I knew he was homeless because he one day came up to me after class and asked if I could hold onto his portable stereo. "This is the only valuable thing I own," he said. The student, in his mid-forties, had once been an active jazz musician, a drummer, and had regularly played at the Blue Note in Greenwich Village. He told me this with more sadness than pride. He asked me to hang on to his portable stereo because he was being moved to a different homeless shelter. He was very upset about this. He briefly talked about how awful these shelters were and how dangerous they could be. He was unsure about this next shelter, so, just to be safe, he wanted me to hang on to his portable stereo, at least until he got himself settled.

A few days later, it snowed all day and rained all night. An army of trucks had dumped salt over most of the city streets, followed later by giant snowplows. The streets were a mess. It was one of those dreaded New York winter mornings when I left home for school.

Although it was already 8:15 A.M., I had not yet started class. The class officially started at 8:00, but only half the class was present. I decided to wait a bit longer, to give more time to those fighting the icy, slushy terrain of the city. As I sat in my chair reviewing my notes, I overheard a conversation between the jazz musician and a young woman who always sat behind him. I did not recall ever seeing those two speak to each other before.

"Why do you have those plastic bags over your shoes?" she asked. He turned around to face her, and with some hesitancy, said: "These are the only pair of shoes I have and it's very wet outside." "Oh," she said, and went back to *The Daily News* she had been reading.

The next morning, the young woman calmly sat behind the jazz musician and handed him a bulky plastic bag. "Here," she said to him, "these are my father's. He doesn't wear them anymore." In the bag were two pairs of worn shoes. I heard the musician say, "Thank you." Then, somewhat in a daze, I announced: "Okay, let's get started. Please take out yesterday's essay and start proofreading out loud."

I still had the musician's portable stereo back in my Brooklyn apartment. He had not yet asked for it back. Three weeks had passed since he had brought it to me.

A Correction

I was wrong. I have not metamorphosed into a teacher after all. Neither have I abandoned my studies, and I am still very much a student learning from the best teachers I can ever hope to come across—my students, "nontraditional" or otherwise.

Yes, for a change, Spike Lee and Nike might be right. It's the shoes. That's what matters, no matter what the emperor, the Emperor of Ice Cream, says.

10

Reflections on Diversity and Inclusion: South Asians and Asian American Studies

MADHULIKA S. KHANDELWAL

In the Q-and-A part of a pedagogy session at a recent Asian American studies conference, a question was asked, "What should I do when I walk into a classroom to teach an Asian American studies course and am not considered an Asian American by the students?" The question—posed by a scholar of South Asian descent—drew a silence. With nobody in the well-attended room willing to respond or pursue the subject of the inquiry, the session moved onto other important but less awkward pedagogical issues of the Asian American classroom.[1]

The above experience of a South Asian teacher is not an isolated incidence: it is an issue that is omnipresent in all conversations of South Asians that have any relation with Asian American studies, and often initiates intense arguments over concepts of diversity and inclusion. Few South Asian students enroll in Asian American courses, and there are but a handful of South Asians in teaching and curricula designing of Asian American courses. The numerical representation is tied to inclusion in the curriculum: few Asian American programs deal with South Asians as an integral part of the communities they intend to respond to. At best, nominal representation is attempted by including basic statistics, mention of a literary work, or making a reference to them. In general, attitudes towards South Asians range from sheer ignorance about their characteristics to their dismissal as a "non-Asian" or a "very different group."[2]

As Asian American demographics change rapidly, a range of ethnic, language, and cultural groups emerge within the expanded population. This requires analytical discussion of approaches towards diversity among Asian Americans and diversity's impact on the study of Asian Americans. The discussion over South Asians and Asian American studies has been presented by South Asian scholars in various forums, but has been confined to a primarily South Asian audience and has failed to generate discussion over diversity in the field at large.[3]

111

The objective of this paper is not to make an appeal for including South Asians in Asian American studies, but to explore the foundations for a meaningful integration of diverse groups into the field. I initiate this effort with an examination of existing approaches of inclusion of groups such as South Asians, followed by a brief overview of South Asian presence in the United States. Subsequently, I discuss three selected themes— "difference," race, and diaspora—to delineate dynamics of South Asians as well as the role of such concepts in charting the direction of Asian American studies.

Approaches to Diversity

The purpose of studying existing approaches is to think about strategies to deal with the growing diversity among Asian Americans in a meaningful way. In this effort, examples of similar processes in other groups and fields may be helpful. I found strong parallels in reflections offered by Patricia Zavella regarding diversity among Chicanas and particularly its impact on women studies. She writes:

> simply recognizing the richness of diversity can lead to an atheoretical pluralism where diversity seems overwhelming, and it is difficult to discern the basis of commonality and difference among women. Moreover, expanding the feminist canon to include other women can sometimes replicate stereotypes about internal similarities among the category of women being integrated.[4]

I divide the existing approaches into three categories.

The first approach supports inclusion of South Asians but is ineffective. The teachers and curriculum designers in this category would like to include South Asians in Asian American studies, but would treat them as any other ethnic group, without analyzing their distinct dynamics. The present approach, in striking similarity to some patched-up diversity panels and programs, establishes power of the supervisor over diverse groups, providing a small spot or a piece of pie to each one of them. It wants a neatly packaged homogenized version of the culture with no emphasis on evaluating its internal dynamics. Such an approach to inclusion is a crude additive strategy that results only in tokenism without including more than a handful of a group's representatives. It also manages to keep the different groups separate from each other, working *in the confines* of the space provided to them.

A second approach offers an explanation of noninclusion of South

Asians. They are treated as a "new" Asian group whose small numbers in the field are explained by their short history in this country. The assumption is, therefore, that inclusion will take place automatically once the group is old enough. This approach not only establishes hegemonic relationship between "old" and "new" groups (reminiscent of nativism?), but also renders any analysis of the inclusion unnecessary.[5] It denies the history of South Asians in this country which is characterized by their arrival, albeit in small numbers, since the eighteenth century, and their first sizable populations that settled on the West Coast in the early years of the twentieth century. Ample work is available on the largely Sikh communities of northern California who experienced explicit discrimination and exclusion with their other Asian contemporaries.[6] That the history of South Asians can be ignored more easily and that the same measure of "late coming" is not applied to other Asian groups indicates that distinction between old and new groups is an inadequate and inaccurate response to the call for inclusion.[7]

The third approach is of plain acceptance of noninclusion of South Asians by establishing them as a "different" group that has little in common with other Asian groups. These scholars who believe that South Asians will not and cannot be part of Asian American studies because of their inherent "difference" are engaged in freezing the definition of Asian Americans by ahistorically locking it in a certain period. I address this approach by examining these so-called differences between South Asians and other Asian groups. Through this approach I highlight not only distinct South Asian characteristics but also what many may have accepted as "standard" constitutive characteristics of Asian American populations.

In this discussion, I ask if our struggles of inclusion, diversity, and equity for Asian Americans in American society and its polity diminish the issue of diversity within ourselves? In other words, are we creating homogenized and standardized notions of who Asian Americans are, according to which groups are included or excluded, treated as normal or different, or even old and new to Asian American studies? Moreover, if we confine ourselves to the established notions of "normal" and "different" groups along national/ethnic lines, are we running into the trap of fragmenting and balkanizing Asian American populations and taking away emphases from their overlapping political struggles and social movements? Inadequate responses to issues of diversity and inclusion also support the assumption that groups *always* remain in watertight compartments, never crossing defined ethnic boundaries, and denies agency to historical cross-cultural changes.

South Asians in the United States

South Asians today are one of the largest groups among the Asian and Pacific Islander population category of the U.S. Census. In 1990, Asian Indians, the largest among them, were enumerated by the census as 815,447, Pakistanis as 81,371, Bangladeshis 11,838, and Srilankans 10,970.[8] In some regions such as the tristate area, they are particularly prominent and rapidly growing. In New York City, Asian Indians alone are the second largest Asian group after the Chinese. In New Jersey, they are the largest Asian ethnic group: their numbers jumping from 30,684 in 1980 to 79,440 in the 1990 census. These numbers obviously are much less than the actual populations, with substantial numbers of those who remain uncounted, particularly among immigrants who are undocumented or in the process of legalization, and/or who are not familiar with English language or U.S. racial categorization.

I mention three points in this brief profile of South Asians. First, considerable campaigning by certain Indian organizations convinced the U.S. census to allot them a separate ethnic category under the name "Asian Indians" in the Asian and Pacific Islander section of the 1980 U.S. Census.[9] This underscores the point that the government's racial and ethnic categories in the United States are not unchanging and should not be treated as natural and absolute.

Second, the South Asian population in the United States, like many other Asian groups, is predominantly though not exclusively, foreign-born, making ongoing immigration an important determinant in its demographics and dynamics. While a large number of these foreign-born South Asians come from the region of South Asia itself, reflecting its contemporary society, there are sizable numbers of others who are migrating from the worldwide South Asian diaspora. Large numbers of Guyanese and Trinidadians of Indian origin immigrate to the United States every year, and it is not at all uncommon to find twice or thrice migrants who have the multilayered diasporic experience of living in two or three continents before coming to the United States.

The South Asian population in the United States comprises of people from a range of nationalities, religions, subcultures, languages, and other social groups. Besides the amazing sociocultural diversity that is integral to their identity, South Asian populations in the United States have developed hierarchies and stratification that need to be looked at beyond ethnic homogeneity, stereotypes, and myths.[10]

Encountering Diversity: Within and Outside

Last year, I got a telephone call from another Asian American scholar friend. She was writing an article that covered different Asian groups and wanted some help from me on South Asians. As the conversation proceeded, I found her repeatedly asking me simple questions to which she expected simple and tailormade replies so that South Asians could be included in her pan-Asian work. In one of such attempts, she asked, "What is *the* philosophical/cultural system that you follow?" I tried to tell her that there was no *one* system that was followed all over South Asia by all groups, and that inclusion of South Asians into her format would require more research and understanding. She grew impatient. "We have a Confucian system. Don't you have *anything* like that?"

On various occasions, when I have presented glimpses of South Asian diversity in Asian American forums, the response has been either of non-interest or a feeling of threat. On one such panel that was addressing organizing strategies in different Asian communities, the chair exclaimed, "Oh, you will have to solve this problem (of internal diversity) first and then participate with other Asian American groups." Such calls for homogenization are alarming. It's almost as if diversity scares people, that it is a problem to be solved. Such reactions to internal diversity in a so-called ethnic group are caused when the cultural/ethnic boundaries are seen as absolute and overlook the potential common grounds for action and solidarity.

Indeed, diversity is not new to any nation, group, or culture. All Asian groups studied in Asian American studies can have their own patterns of diversity. Comparative studies on handling diversity within groups show that South Asians have a distinct (but not unique) heightened consciousness of it. Based on her 1970s research, Maxine Fisher concluded that

in 1975, New York Indians were an ethnic group composed of ethnic groups; and the latter were in turn, in many cases, still in some sense ethnically heterogeneous, incredible as that seems. This situation, though dizzying to contemplate, and the bane of government agencies concerned with ethnic groups derives quite naturally from the possibility of multiple identities."[11]

Fisher goes on to describe these multiple identities—based on language, religion, region, and place of origin within or outside of India—and compares them with such multilayered experiences among other groups such as Italians and Filipinos.

The contemporary South Asia comprises of many independent nations such as Bangladesh, India, Nepal, Pakistan, and Sri Lanka, with their own set of domestic and international issues, of shared cultural patterns as well as political contestations. Each nation has its own internal diversity and dynamics: a multitude of ethnic, language/dialect groupings, and different economic strata. The largest South Asian nation, India, has over twenty officially recognized language systems (and hundreds of dialects), virtually all major religions of the world are practiced there, as are multiple cultural systems of dress and food ways. This cultural diversity provides a glimpse of its complex social system—intricate networks of communities, urban and rural life patterns, lower and higher castes, affluence and poverty, different religions and regions. It also shows the postcolonial directions where South Asia sought to free itself from the colonial vestiges of British rule while moving toward economic development and at the same time keeping traditions alive. My intention is not to either defend this diversity or condemn it. I want to highlight, nevertheless, that through interplay of historical forces, amidst shaping of multiple identities, South Asia has developed its own power struggles and social movements, forces of change and preservation, and hierarchies and hegemonies that interact through its immigrants with American situations.

South Asians realize that their intense cultural diversity creates difficulties, particularly in organizing their ethnic community. However, there is no inclination to demolish these cultural traits; indeed most would nourish pride in the distinctness of their respective subcultures. The diversity has not fragmented the population into exclusive compartments but into multiple identities constantly in formation by interacting with each other. In many instances, people from different cultural backgrounds have crossed boundaries in favor of common interests of class, ideas, or social and political movements.

In one of the political attempts to deal with diversity of newly independent India, the slogan of "Unity in Diversity" was raised during the Nehruvian times. The term "South Asian" itself illustrates the reconstruction of new identities and alliances and is used by progressive elements of the population to connote a collective identity that crosses over political boundaries. There are no demarcated geographical boundaries of South Asia; the region could be defined as comprising of a few countries of that region to a list that may include Afghanistan and Myanmar as well.[12] The conception and implementation of diversity in a democratic way within the South Asians are as contentious issues as they are within Asian Americans or the larger American population. Naheed Islam voices her concerns about use of South Asian concept and its implications for the politics of its constituents in an essay "In the Belly of the Multicultural Beast I am Named South Asian."[13] The vigilance she calls for should not stop at the boundaries of any group, South Asian or Asian American.

In attempts to integrate South Asians as Asian Americans, it is imperative that we interrogate the representations from within the group. Currently, South Asians have been understood (whatever little of that exists) from self-definitions of a class-based dominant group of professionals and affluent immigrants. They represent not only their own economic interests but also their political and philosophical worldview. Such a viewpoint allies with the dominant forces in the American system, excludes issues of economically disadvantaged South Asians, and blocks out voices of women and "less-sophisticated" (read less-westernized) and younger South Asian American experiences.

Integration of South Asians seems particularly problematic if their postcolonial identities are made to fit in the bipolar model determined by stereotypes of East and West. I have often been told how South Asians are more western than eastern, and that all of them know English. Firstly, the definitions and constructions of East and West should be analyzed. Genealogy and many faces of orientalism may be one place to begin. Secondly, the view that all South Asians are westernized and therefore more western than eastern betrays lack of knowledge about the origins of the post-1965 immigrants from selected strata of urban societies most exposed to British rule.

Such stance towards South Asians is not only based on uninformed and stereotypical notions of the "other," but also betray disengagement with the critique of global colonialism and imperialism, including that in Asia.[14] This could be a serious limitation in conceptual development of Asian American studies since western perceptions and treatment of Asians in the United States have historical connections with their colonial presence in Asia. Can we afford to separate stereotypes of docile, passive, and "heathen" Asians in the United States from (post fifteenth century) western portrayals of Asia as a continent of ancient but stagnant people and cultures who waited for Europeans to be "opened up" and "be civilized?"[15] In its struggle against Eurocentrism in the United States—in fighting for ethnic studies courses and multicultural curriculum—Asian American studies should recognize and ally with hybrid identities that stem from oppressed and colonized societies and represent historical cross-cultural forces. In active challenge to ethnic Balkanization and notions of racial purity, it should encourage research and teaching of people of multiracial, multiethnic, and multicultural identities.

On the Anvil of Race

Confusion about "exact" race of South Asians have characterized the entire course of their history in the United States. In 1929, a few South Asians, in order to claim their right to naturalize, presented themselves as anthropologically Caucasian, citing their descent from the Aryan race. In 1965, President Lyndon Johnson canceled the visits of heads of state from India and Pakistan with the statement, "After all, what would Jim

Eastlan [the conservative senator from Mississippi] say if I brought those two niggers over here."[16]

These racial fluctuations in self-identification as well as perception of Americans can be explained by recognizing that South Asians (as many other groups in most of the world) do not subscribe to the U.S. racial classification system. Once again, centuries-old intercultural forces in South Asia have produced a population that is intensely multiracial and multicultural and at the same time has its own hierarchies and oppressive systems, such as the caste system, religious communalism, patriarchal structures, etc. Even though skin color is seen as a form of discrimination in South Asia—fair being good and beautiful as opposed to dark signifying bad and ugliness—it is not done so as a race indicator. The "confusion" and "ambivalence" of South Asians about race arises out of different conceptions of "difference" and "the other."

To a large extent, the difficulties in inclusion of South Asians as Asian Americans rests on the issue of race and the United States racial classifications. In the United States, where people are categorized on the basis of exclusive and pure racial groups, South Asians are ambivalent about their race. Not only do they cause unease and discomfort to the social norm, but also become invisible due to their inability to fit into established racial schema.[17] In Asian American studies, many have accepted the racialized categories without analyzing the political origins and implications of such definitions of their identities. (Asian and Pacific Islanders, as well as all other groups with the exception of Hispanics, are categorized as belonging to *one* race.) So, South Asians, who appear to be racially different from East Asians, the established and defining groups for Asian American studies, can be dismissed as a non-Asian group.

Thus, in dealing with inclusion of different groups in Asian American studies, we may have to remind ourselves that racial groupings are not exclusively determined by skin color, facial features, and blood types, but by historicizing race and racism and understanding its social and political construction.[18] Sucheta Mazumdar, in an article that interrogates the issue of race for South Asians and racism within the group, writes that the "essay seeks to understand the origins of racialism among a people who are black, but have sought to prove over and over again that they are white."[19] To substantiate her definition of South Asians as nonwhite and black people, Mazumdar gives examples of interplay of class, caste, and color through the history of South Asian diaspora and political struggles in South Asia. On one hand, some South Asian Americans have forged alliances with other oppressed and marginalized groups—Asian and other minorities. On the other, given the postcoloniality and upperclass profile of first waves of people in the post-1965 immigration, many have voiced an opposition to their minority status in the United States that brings them identification with other people of color.[20]

Diaspora: Testing the Boundaries

Another aspect of integration of South Asians into Asian Americans and their studies demands careful consideration of the Asian diasporic experience. Case studies from Asians in the Americas remind us that simplistic notions of immigration from *an* Asian place to *an* American one (usually United States, and usually West Coast) do not capture the multidimensional experience of Asian Americans. Through its several programs and publications, the Asian American Center at Queens College (City University of New York) has brought forth pioneering work in this area.[21]

As in other Asian groups, such as Filipinos, Chinese, Japanese, and Koreans, considerable numbers of South Asians migrated to Latin America and the Caribbean during the nineteenth and early twentieth century. These populations, generally known as East Indians, represent one of the largest indentured labor migrations in the world.[22] Besides influencing Asians in the United States from their sizable bases in their Latin American and Caribbean countries (East Indians are over 50 percent of the Guyanese population) and their constitutive roles in shaping political forces, they migrate to the United States in large numbers. In addition, there are other people of South Asian origin who come from Africa, Britain, the Middle East, Fiji, and Mauritius, to mention a few prominent concentrations from their global diaspora. Inclusion of these communities as Asian Americans requires models that take a second look at migrations from "Asia to America," as well as the construction of diverse trends in Asian communities in the United States.

I am not proposing an Asian American studies that is rendered borderless with incorporation of the entire Asian diaspora into its fold, but arguing to create spaces in our field so that it can be informed by dynamics of Asians that are not explained by simple formulas. South Asian diaspora—and Asian diaspora in general—opens avenues for comparative studies to discern cross-cultural and global forces from which neither the United States nor Asians living here have been immune.

The diaspora dimension of South Asian Americans is neither too global nor too abstract for their experiences in the United States. My research on a few blocks in Jackson Heights, in the New York City borough of Queens, which has one of the largest concentrations of South Asian businesses in the entire country, displays interaction of local neighborhood politics with the South Asian diasporic worldview.[23] In the ongoing process of cultural production, music and dance forms of *bhangra*

and *Raas-garba*, essentially originating in the Punjabi and Gujarati overseas communities of South Asians, are crossing national boundaries to
create new cultures. Concerts of popular musicians and film stars from
Bombay's movie industry attract tens of thousands of South Asian fans—
cutting across regional, religious, language, age, and other identities—at
different stops on their worldwide tours.[24] These cross-national South
Asian identities and their engagement with local and global issues is vividly portrayed in literature by South Asian writers such as Meena Alexander, Amitav Ghosh, and Salman Rushdie. One of the most recent
examples of interaction of different spaces can be seen in the memoirs of
Abraham Verghese, a South Asian medical doctor born in Ethiopia, who
wrote about his encounter with AIDS as it arrived in a small town in
Tennessee.[25]

In conclusion, in thinking about inclusion of South Asians in a way
that respects diversity and deals with it adequately, it is not sufficient to
add a South Asian reference in a literature course or to mention early
South Asians as another group that was discriminated against and excluded in Asian American history. We may have to look at some of the
patterns more closely to decipher how interethnic differences and commonalities have played out, how the early South Asian farm laborers
were different from their contemporary South Asians of educated and
upper classes, of the role that class plays in building of new Asian communities, and what may be shared grounds beyond and despite cultural
differences. Though separate courses on South Asian communities are
advised, their objective should be clearly defined in order to stimulate
interest in studies of particular communities that would lead to participation in interethnic and pan-Asian issues. They should be a step in strateg-
izing Asian American studies' future course rather than becoming the
goal that generates further segregation.

In short, the issue of diversity and inclusion (for South Asians and
other groups) should be dealt with in a way that it does not become a
liability but enriches our field with their distinct patterns and historical
lessons. We should be more cognizant of the impregnability of our ethnic
and racial boundaries than vigilant about preserving an unchanging core.

Notes

Author's note. I would like to express my gratitude to Sucheta Mazumdar,
Mustafa Aozami, Margery Wolf, and participants of the South Asian Caucus of
the annual conference of the Association for Asian American Studies at Ann
Arbor, Michigan, in 1994 for extensive discussions on the subject.

1. The reference is to the session "Teaching What Students 'Don't Want to

Know': Resistance to Asian American Studies" at the Annual Conference of the Association of Asian American Studies titled "Border/Crossings" at Ann Arbor, Michigan, in April 1994. The relatively minor interaction initiated by Naheed Islam's question reverberated in South Asian circles for the rest of the conference.

2. Often South Asians are not even mentioned while enumerating the different ethnic groups of Asian Americans or they are confused with Southeast Asians, an example of all "others" being lumped together in an undifferentiated mass.

3. As examples, I cite presentations by Nazli Kibria at the Association of Asian American Studies Conference at San Jose, California, in 1992, Sucheta Mazumdar at the East of California Asian American Studies Conference at Brown University, Rhode Island, in 1992, and Madhulika S. Khandelwal at the Association of Asian American Studies Conference at Honolulu, Hawaii, in 1991.

4. Patricia Zavella, "Reflections on Diversity among Chicanas," in *Race*, Steven Gregory and Roger Sanjek, eds. (New Brunswick, New Jersey: Rutgers University Press, 1994), 199–212.

5. See Sucheta Mazumdar, "What To Do With All These New Immigrants, or Refiguring Asian American History," in *Building Blocks for Asian American Studies*, 1992 East of California Asian American Studies Conference Proceedings, Robert Lee and Lihbin Shiao, eds. (Providence, Rhode Island: Brown University, 1992), 63–75.

6. Joan M. Jensen, *Passage From India* (New Haven, Conn.: Yale University Press, 1989); Karen Leonard, *Making Ethnic Choices: California's Punjabi Mexican Americans* (Philadelphia: Temple University Press, 1992).

7. Some Asian groups, for example, Koreans, are not seen as such a "different" group, though the issues of equal representation remain relevant for them as well.

8. *General Characteristics*, 1990 Census, U.S. Bureau of the Census.

9. Maxine Fisher, *Indians of New York City* (New Delhi: Heritage Publishers, 1980), chapter VIII.

10. Madhulika S. Khandelwal, *Patterns of Growth and Diversification: Indians in New York City, 1965–1990*, Ph.D. dissertation, Department of History, Carnegie Mellon University, 1992.

11. Fisher, *Indians of New York City*, 4.

12. As an example, see *Our Feet Walk the Sky: Women of the South Asian Diaspora*, South Asian Women Collective, eds. (San Francisco: Aunt Lute Books, 1993), xvi.

13. Naheed Islam, "In the Belly of the Multicultural Beast, I am Named South Asian" in *Our Feet Walk the Sky*, 242–45.

14. For a fuller discussion, see Sucheta Mazumdar, "Asian American and Asian Studies: Rethinking Roots" in *Asian Americans: Comparative and Global Perspectives* Shirley Hune, Hyung-chan Kim, Stephen S. Fugita, and Amy Ling, eds. (Pullman: Washington State University Press, 1991), 29–44.

15. K. N. Chaudhuri, *Asia Before Europe: Economy and Civilisation of the Indian Ocean from the Rise of Islam to 1750* (Cambridge: Cambridge University Press, 1990); Philip D. Curtin, *Cross-cultural Trade in World History* (Cambridge: Cambridge University Press, 1984).

16. Cited in Sucheta Mazumdar, "Race and Racism among South Asians" in *Frontiers of Asian American Studies: Writing, Research, and Community*, Gail M. Nomura, et al., eds. (Pullman: Washington State University Press, 1989), 25–38.

17. Michael Omi and Howard Winant, *Racial Formation in the United States From the 1960s to the 1990s* (New York: Routledge, 1994).

18. Roger Sanjek, "Introduction," in Sanjek and Gregory, *Race*, 1–17.

19. Sucheta Mazumdar, "Race and Racism Among South Asians," 25.

20. Fisher, *Indians of New York City*, chapter VIII.

21. For example, see Asian American Center publications *Asians in Latin America and the Caribbean: A Bibliography*, Lamgen Leon, ed.; *Caribbean Asians: Chinese, Indian, and Japanese Experiences in Trinidad and Dominican Republic*, Roger Sanjek, ed.; and *East Indian Diaspora: 150 Years of Survival, Contributions, and Achievements*, Tilokie Depoo, ed. (Flushing, N.Y.: Asian/American Center, Queens College).

22. Among others, see Basdeo Mangro, *Benevolent Neutrality: Indian Government Policy and Labour Migration to British Guiana, 1854–1884* (England: Hansib Publications, 1987), and Basdeo Mangru, *Indenture and Abolition: Sacrifice and Survival on the Guyanese Sugar Plantations* (Toronto: TSAR Publications, 1993).

23. Madhulika S. Khandelwal, "Patterns of Spatial Concentration and Distribution, 1965–1990" in *Nation and Migration: The Politics of Space in the South Asian Diaspora*, Peter van der Veer, ed. (Philadelphia: University of Pennsylvania Press, 1995), 178–96.

24. Somini Sengupta, "Out of India," *New York Newsday*, 19 September 1994.

25. Abraham Verghese, *My Own Country* (New York: Simon & Schuster, 1994).

Part II:

Reconsidering Communities

11

A Contending Pedagogy: Asian American Studies as Extracurricular Praxis

LAURA HYUN YI KANG

I am an indelible product of Asian American studies.[1] Before becoming myself a scholar and teacher, I was an undergraduate ethnic studies major at the University of California, Berkeley. Significantly, it was through taking Asian American studies classes that I found a habitable space within the university and wanted to become a teacher. Writing from this pivoting position of student/teacher, I submit that, as much as we provide information and perspectives unavailable through other courses, the Asian American studies classroom encourages students to critically engage the multiple and complex methods of knowledge production in the field. Beyond the dichotomy of filling absence with substance or replacing false stereotypes with authentic truths, a trenchant interdisciplinarity enables both teachers and students of Asian American studies to actively engage a broader politics of knowledge.[2] Calling into question the shifting and often arbitrary workings of knowledge in specific discursive contexts could resist the academic ghettoization of Asian American studies as an elective subdiscipline committed to the preservation of a marginalized collective *identity* rather than the praxis of intellectual rigor. Such persistent questioning of disciplinary demarcations can productively accompany a necessary reconceptualization of other important "borders/crossings" at this historical juncture in Asian American studies.

My self-critical ruminations upon the role of Asian American studies began as a "crisis of belief" while working as a teaching assistant (TA) in an introductory, lower-division course on the "Asian American Experience" in the winter of 1993. Until then I sought to impress upon students the long history of institutionally sanctioned abuse against Asians in the United States and the rich sociocultural vitality that is manifest in Asians' perseverance in the face of oppression. I stressed how this information was especially deserving of attention given the ways in which it has been omitted from or marginalized in educational curricula as well as the broader socio-cultural terrain of the United States. Primarily focused on matters of content—geopolitical exclusions, U.S. imperialisms in Asia, labor exploitation of Asian immigrants, cultural misrepresentations and stereotypes of Asian/American men and women, anti-Asian violence, etc.—I believed that this new knowledge would incite students into a more informed position which could critique and resist the operations of power, both on an institutional and interpersonal level. In short, I consciously and yet rather unproblematically sought to transform students into good antiracist, feminist, antihomophobic subjects.

Most challenging during these earlier teaching assignments were the students who offered up strident resistance to the materials and to my own explicitly politicized stance on issues. Very roughly, they fell into three allied positions: 1) individualism: "I am different from other Asian/ Americans"; or "We can't talk about a group because every person is unique"; 2) a self-conscious antiessentialism espoused by those students with some prior exposure to poststructuralism and/or feminist theory, and 3) pluralist optimism: "That was then, but this is now, and it is much better. Isn't the existence of this class or even your placement as my TA proof of these liberalizing changes?" While these students exacted a considerable amount of time and energy from me, I came to be less and less bothered by their querulous classroom presence.

I found myself increasingly troubled, instead, by those students who developed and/or demonstrated an utter conviction about and commitment to the course materials. Many of these students, both Asian and non-Asian, expressed outrage and sympathy for the Japanese American internees or the Southeast Asian refugees, often followed by indignance about never having heard or learned about such historical episodes in their prior education. Although there were no clear lines of separation along race/ethnicity, I would venture that such receptiveness had different resonances for non-Asian students than for the Asian American students.[3] It was alarming how several of the non-Asian students, even while earnestly voicing "appreciation" for the readings, spoke from a disturbingly anthropological position.[4] Granted they had certainly learned much through the course lectures and assigned texts, it seemed premature and even arrogant for anyone to think that they can come to "know" or "understand" Asian Americans through a ten-week course. According to this perspective, everything becomes sheer content or data to be absorbed and recorded rather than actively negotiated. Consequently, Asian Americans are figured less as historical actors, researchers, writers, and creative artists but more as (native *and* naive) informants who merely transmit information yet are unaware of what or *how* he or she is saying such and such. By taking for granted the "authenticity" and "representativeness" of a heterogeneous range of texts and authors, such reading practices minimize or ignore the complexities and internal differences of any singular "community" and the willful, peculiar manipulations of language and meaning exercised by different authors and researchers. This assumption of (auto)biographical and sociological mirroring in and through texts seemed especially misguided in relation to fictional literary works by Asian American writers. Such dynamics point to the dangers of presuming any pure correspondence between a discursive representation and the reality it purports to describe and analyze.[5]

This problem of unmediated acceptance had different implications for the Asian American students. I became more and more self-conscious about the awkward, forced, and often forceful pedagogical practice of directing them suddenly to imagine and to embrace an "Asian American" history and identity as their own. As the students seemed to do precisely this, I noticed the odd paradox of emphasizing the suffering of a diverse array of people with whom most students do not have any "natural," familial or communal relationship. This was done, presumably, with the ultimate goal of imbuing these same students with a sense of "pride in who they are." More than any single text or poststructuralist theories of the subject, such student reactions have convinced me of how "identity" is not given, but discursively constituted and pedagogically (en)forced.

Until then, I had believed that the promising part of a focus on "oppression" or "marginality" lay in provoking all students, but especially the Asian American ones, to develop what Gayatri Spivak has written as "a certain rage against the history that has written such an abject script for you."[6] Such a politicized anger could then ameliorate the self-abnegation and self-hatred that are the detrimental effects of being marked as racialized and gendered bodies in the United States. Beyond that, I hoped that it would lead students to a more active, ethically committed stance in a world so marked by power inequalities. While the class materials and my own teaching seemed to produce this effect on certain students, I learned that there could be perilous consequences as well. This recently found awareness of "who they are" also heightened and at times even generated a debilitating nihilism and a different sense of disempowerment in many other students. Rather than productively demystifying the conservative myths of "American" freedom and equality which suppress unequal hierarchies of race, class, gender, sexuality, the course materials merely exacerbated an already fraught negotiation of experience, memory, and desire. Having proceeded from the unquestioned belief that "knowledge is power," I was not prepared to address such viscerally painful consequences of my own pedagogical practices.

The students' "belief" in so readily accepting the assigned texts also tended to delimit the topical and conceptual range of classroom exchanges. Many student comments often could not and did not go beyond initial, emotional reactions: "That made me sad"; or "I was angry that this happened to them/us." Some added (auto)biographical anecdotes pertaining to themselves, their family, or their Asian American friends and acquaintances. Although some of these remarks illustrated how the "personal" can be "political" and vice versa, I began to grow wary of having discussion sections frequently devolve into free-for-all confessionals. When I would attempt to direct the group discussions into ones that more substantively addressed the assigned texts or the designated "theme" of the week, many seemed perplexed and disinterested. Furthermore, it was difficult to get students to articulate any critical interpretations or analyses beyond the superficial, i.e., "It was boring." I suspect that there was a conscious restraint at work in these silences: non-Asian students probably did not want to appear racist or even unappreciative and Asian American students did not want to appear ignorant (of their own "heritage") and "white-washed." Several students responded to my call for a critical response with the question: "How can you critique what happened in someone's life, especially when it is so sad?" Such attitudes clarify the pitfalls and limitations in labeling something as "*beyond* criticism;" even though students may have thought that they were pleasing me or being "culturally sensitive," their critical resistance also implies a patronizing attitude which presumes that Asian American texts do not merit a serious and creative intellectual interrogation. In order to move the discussion along, I found myself having to repeatedly take on an adversarial—at times sincere and at other times performative—position to the texts in the hopes that it would provoke or inspire students to refine and voice their own interpretations and critiques. However, this tactic frequently backfired with some students accusing me—both in person and in anonymous written evaluations—of being "too critical." Although my efforts did produce some exciting and insightful exchanges, I was still left with the question of what I was doing or, more to the point, *not* doing in terms of teaching them to be more confident and nuanced *thinkers*.

I realized increasingly that in order to shift the discussion beyond the reactionary and anecdotal, I had to direct them to pay critical attention to the form, structure, and rhetorical style of specific books and articles. In other words, they had to address the text as a mediated and strategic production, not a transparent window onto some individual or collective truth. This turn to a critique of representation was informed by a growing conviction that without encouraging and inciting students to attend to the specific constructedness and limitation of a text, I would be contributing to the intellectual ghettoizing of Asian American studies that

persists in the U.S. academy. As much as I have professional and economic stakes in combatting such hegemonic impulses, I feel that it is the
greater disservice to our students to perpetuate such dynamics. Beyond
asserting and buttressing a questionable and contested Asian American
identity, teachers in Asian American studies can explicate and demonstrate different *ways* of reading, thinking, and writing. It is through dis-
cerning and deconstructing the methodological assumptions and the
epistemological limitations of specific texts that students can also realize
how they could interface with and contribute to the growing vitality of
Asian American studies as a field of knowledge production and critical
inquiry. The discussions that emerged were productive and heterogeneous, raising important and at times innovative theoretical questions
about language, knowledge, and representation.

Along with these promises and possibilities, I should add that the shift
to a critique of representation can risk unsettling the legitimacy, credibility, and authenticity of the contents, which can inadvertently and indirectly challenge the political goals and scholarly richness of Asian
American studies itself. I want to refer to Le Ly Hayslip's *When Heaven
and Earth Changed Places* as a concrete example of these complicated
dynamics. Once the idea was introduced that Hayslip may have strategically constructed the book to produce certain effects on its readers, it
raised all sorts of questions about the possibilities of dramatization, exag-
geration, and invention by Hayslip herself as well as editors and the
oddly disembodied coauthor Jay Wurts. Even as the students were developing a critical awareness of the ways in which the text was mediated,
this aperture for criticism dismayingly provoked certain students to take
on a morally judgmental tone to Hayslip, both as author and as a figure
in the text. Some drew analogies between the instances in which she had
to be resourceful to survive to her embellished manipulations as a writer;
this was exactly the (auto)biographical fixation/determinism I wanted to
avoid. Such criticism does not sufficiently account for the complex meanings of what it meant to endure as a Vietnamese women in the midst of
immense sociopolitical turmoil and economic deprivation.

It is in response to such complicated and convoluted dynamics that I
want to qualify the ubiquitous exhortation to "think critically"—a slogan I myself have often extolled—with what Gayatri Spivak has called
"earning the right to criticize."[7] Insisting that the practice of criticism
begin with "a historical critique of your position as the investigating person," I find Spivak's comments helpful in the way that it points to the
ways in which any would-be critic is implicated in a broader terrain of
knowledge production and distribution which is linked to certain historically specific socioeconomic conditions; here, no innocent position of
judgment or detachment is tenable. With this in mind, I asked students

to consider whether their morally righteous assessments of Hayslip reflected the privilege of being upwardly mobile students sitting in a clean,
well-lighted classroom at a prestigious university, and would they, could
they have made decisions differently under similar circumstances. It was
only through such serious attention to their own specific embodiedness
that students could reevaluate their facile personalizing and moralizing
about Hayslip's sexual relations with American GIs. Instead, they began
to interrogate the broader historical forces that would have enforced such
limited choices for a Vietnamese peasant woman. Furthermore, I asked
them to shift their thinking about the book from being a "true life story"
to a strategically constituted text, which offers a contending version to
other accounts of the Vietnam war and Vietnamese women found in
dominant U.S. historiography or mass media. It was then that they
seemed to locate other meanings and the usefulness of the book beyond
its apparent content. I believe strongly that the promise of Asian American studies as a site of critical pedagogy lies in alerting students to the
shifting contours and dynamics of such an intertextual terrain.

On this point, I would recommend a very useful pedagogical exercise
I learned in a graduate seminar[8] in which groups of students were as-
signed to investigate how a specific text was produced and circulated
within a broader intellectual and political conversation. When I taught
my own seminar on "Asian Women in America," I decided to employ
this method on six books by and about Asian American women: Evelyn
Nakano Glenn's *Issei, Nisei, Warbride;* Mary Paik Lee's *Quiet Odyssey;*
Miné Okubo's *Citizen 10660;* Judy Yung's *Chinese Women in America:
A Pictorial History;* Le Ly Hayslip's *When Heaven and Earth Changed
Places;* the Women of South Asian Descent's Collective *Our Feet Walk
the Sky.*

The first six weeks of the semester sought to establish the rudimentary
contours of "Asian American women," looking at a range of articles
about immigration and settlement histories, socioeconomic positionings
both in the United States and in Asia, resistance and activism, sexualities
and subjectivities. Then, for the following six weeks, the six books were
scheduled to be read and discussed on their own as well as in comparison.
By focusing on a book a week, I wanted students to begin analyzing
texts beyond matters of content and instead look upon them as specific
productions of knowledge and discourse by specific Asian American
women (as) authors, artists, researchers, and scholars.

Along with the first assigned text, students read a very insightful article, "Bibliography and a Feminist Apparatus of Literary Production,"[9]
by Katie King. Calling for shifting "the frame of analysis from the world
in the text to the text in the world," King urges attention to what she
terms "writing technologies" alongside and against close readings of a

text which is often the privileged mode of teaching literature in the university classroom:

> The apparatus of literary production, simultaneously object for analysis and tool of analysis, intersects in art, business and technology, . . . From this perspective we begin to see that interpretation itself is an element within the apparatus of literary production requiring analysis. A study of the apparatus of literary production potentially exposes how our cultural expressions engage a global economy of language, technology, and multinational capital.

Such attention to the broader context of a text's production and exchange denaturalizes it as some pure, truthful communication between a singular author and an individual reader/student, revealing instead a host of actively mediating parties in the form of editors, publishers, reviewers, bookstore workers, and instructors. While the authenticity and autonomy of the text are problematized, such an approach also offers epistemological and political possibilities. In rejecting the absolute distancing between the producer and receiver of text, which accords the power of knowledge only to the author, the reader/student can seize upon their own agency in the production of meaning. Katie King holds that "writing technologies" can be especially instructive and useful for feminism and, I would add, for Asian American studies:

> Finally *stories about the production of stories* require feminists to engage in this story-making [about origins, crisis and identity], not merely to analyze it: there are no innocent positions from which one can only look on. The systems of publication and other forms of production, the valuations of the academy and the market, the explicit and implicit "political" uses of literacies (in the plural) both within the U.S. and internationally, must all be taken into account in an examination of the apparatus of literary production.

Keeping in mind the above insights of King's essay, I asked students to approach the assignment as an exercise in doing collective work and a collaborative critical investigation of how texts are constructed and transported from an author to the university classroom. Each group was directed to research the literal production or manufacture of the books and their distribution. Therefore, they had to look up any published book reviews and critical essays, arrange personal interviews with author(s), and talk with the publishers about marketing and sales. They would then present their findings and comments in an oral presentation.[10] Both the oral presentation and the written report were to present the main themes raised by the work as well as the students' specific interpretations of the book's content and form. Finally, I asked them to address *how* this specific text is significant for the field of Asian American women's studies. I hoped that the search would reveal the books to be less sites of information but as calculated productions and transmissions of knowledge.

What the six groups did with their presentations far exceeded my expectations. For example, the group assigned to investigate *Quiet Odyssey* produced a video which examined the dynamics of race, gender, culture, and class within the narrative as told by Mary Paik Lee, but also raised probing questions around the editorial role of Sucheng Chan. It critiqued the "Preface," the "Appendix" and even the title of the book for the ways in which they resituated and recontextualized the book, making it much more complex and complicated than a simple, transparent (auto)-biographical document. They further questioned the authorial choices and manipulations that could have been exercised by Mary Paik Lee, treating this Korean American woman as the *subject* of her story in both senses of that word. Finally, the concluding part provided a metacritique of their own knowledge–production in and through the video as well as their specific impositions of meaning on the text under the banner of interpretation and analysis. Each group spurred the next to equally thorough and nuanced examinations, using a variety of media: dramatizations of an intellectual conversation between scholars, a slide show, another video incorporating computer-generated images, a multivoiced audio presentation that echoed and engaged the construction of an anthology. The performative and written presentations further juxtaposed or supplemented the text by situating it alongside and against other representations on the same subject matter: dominant historiographies, contemporary popular culture, Asian American pop media, interviews with Asian American women students. These intertextual comparisons revealed the specific articulations by certain Asian/American women as one of many partial, competing claims to truth about Asian/American women. Needless to say, I learned a great deal from each of the group presentations.

I believe that a large part of why students were able to fashion such critically astute yet creative approaches to the text lay in the interdisciplinary structure of that particular class.[11] Since the articles and books we studied engaged the disciplines of literature, history, sociology, anthropology, visual culture, area studies, ethnic studies, and women's studies, examining them alongside and against each other clarified their different methods of constructing and conveying knowledge about Asian American women. That has reinforced for me how much the strength of Asian American studies lies in its interdisciplinarity.[12] The methodological and rhetorical diversity of the materials we choose to teach can allow for more nuanced explorations of the specific language and the ideological underpinnings of each text. These differences can in turn shed insight upon how cultural productions and scholarly studies emerge out of specific historical circumstances; discursive representations are enabled and constrained by a broader political economy that influence *which* Asian Americans become writers, artists, and filmmakers as well as the more specific one of funding and commerce. A purely or primarily thematic or issue-oriented approach can be limited and limiting if it fails to address this larger informing context.

Taking the ways in which interdisciplinarity troubles and renegotiates the demarcations of specific arenas of research and discourse, I would like to move onto a more thematic discussion of how other "borders/crossings" can be conceptualized for Asian American studies as we head into the twenty-first century. Given the parameters of this paper, I would like to briefly mention three arenas that seem the most crucial and promising to me: 1) the process of economic and cultural globalization and the paradoxically attendant questions around national identities; 2) the relationship between Asian Americans and other communities of color, of the working poor, and of lesbians and gay men; and, 3) the increasing internal cultural differences and socioeconomic inequalities amongst Asian Americans.

The first border I will address is that of the nation-state in this age of both economic and cultural globalization. The late scholarly attention to the process of globalization at the close of the twentieth century has certainly opened up and complicated ways of looking at certain international and intercultural encounters. Capitalist elites are joining together as transnational corporate bodies, spreading both their domains of production and consumption across the world. The diaspora of peoples and identities has enabled increased mobility as well as increasing exploitative possibilities. The travel of capital and of human bodies across and sometimes in spite of assumed or imposed geopolitical borders have challenged many a dream of homogeneity, stability, fixity, and knowability about individual subjects and nation-states. Given these global movements, the question that emerges forcefully is what does it mean for Asian Americans to continue to claim an American identity? The binary between the myth of assimilation and the defensive assertions of a "real" Asian identity is becoming less salient to a meaningful consideration of subject formation let alone radical politics. Furthermore, even a less conflictual conception of Asian American identity as a harmonious blend fails to adequately challenge the East–West dichotomy. Rather, I insist on a dialectical interaction marked by bumpiness, unevenness, and overlap.

What about Asia and the various nation-states that mark the first half of our many hyphenated identities? The insistence on a right American identity has been necessary to repudiate the hegemonic stereotyping of

Asians in the United States as "perpetual foreigners." In the process, however, I believe that the connection to the Asian countries of origin has been compromised and devalued. When Asia is invoked, it is too often in terms of a mythical past with a fixed culture. Conceptualizing Asia only in terms of culture and roots precludes a politicized consciousness about present-day Asia and its imbrication in global political economy. Commonalities and possible affinities as well as differences need to be discerned. More than ever, it is imperative for Asian American studies to be attentive to social, economic, and cultural conditions in the diverse Asian nations. After a week of studying the many ways in which Asian/American women are situated in the political economy of the United States, I devoted a week to studying the ways in which Asian women are disciplined and displaced in the global political economy. This latter group of readings was prefaced by the question of whether "Asian American" women faced different, and more precisely "better"—in terms of less exploitative and more liberatory—economic circumstances than Asian women in Asia. Against the developmental paradigm which posits that everything is better over here, I wanted students to discern the similar fates of a certain socioeconomic class of Asian women who are employed to do similar work in similar conditions both "over there" and "back here," and indeed throughout the world. Such a perspective forces the question of whether a Vietnamese immigrant woman working in the Silicon Valley would have more basis for identification and political alliance with a young Korean female factory worker employed by a multinational electronics firm in South Korea rather than a professional Sansei woman. Such barriers and possibilities break up the internal coherence of an "American" identity.

Complementing this examination of internal heterogeneity, we need to produce nuanced and complicitous understandings of the positioning of variously specific Asian American communities with other communities of color, working peoples, and lesbians/gays. Using the demarcations of "race" as an example, I would suggest that while we continue to monitor the shifting and problematic relationship between Asian Americans and the "dominant community," it is equally urgent to address the intercultural interactions and confrontations of both bodies and texts with the African-American, Latina/o, Caribbean, and Native communities. While we attend to the commonalities amongst people of color, we need to think through differences and acknowledge real tensions. Only through a judicious awareness of specific, localized circumstances in which Asian Americans must interact daily with members from these communities of color can political solidarity become more than a rhetorical slogan.[13]

On the practical level, I reserved a week of readings at the end of the semester about the possibilities for identifications and alliances between

Asian American women and other possible groupings: Third World women, postcolonial women, and women of color. Here too, I posed the question of how select writings by Chicanas, African American, and Native American women could be useful for Asian American women in negotiating the perils of race, class, gender, and sexuality. While pointing to some shared circumstances amongst women of color, I also asked my students to think about the implicit and explicit hierarchies that fracture that identity category along the lines of racism, ethnocentrism, nativism, or "degrees of oppression/authenticity/entitlement."

Finally, we need to direct students in analyzing the "borders" that mark Asian Americans from each other along the lines of class, gender, ethnicity, immigration, sexuality, and gender. I would like to make some cursory comments on some of these axes of internal difference. Asian Americans, like other groups, are represented at all levels of the socioeconomic hierarchy from the most powerfully wealthy to the underclass. However, in the attempts to debunk the model minority stereotype—which I readily admit is insidious and misleading—these internal class inequalities are often displaced or underemphasized by both instructors and students. Not thinking *through* class difference and privilege in a serious, consistent manner leads to a false sense that such issues are insignificant just at the historical moment when more than ever Asian Americans students from immigrant, working-class families are gaining access to the university. On this issue of class, we also have to be willing to address the ways in which certain Asian Americans benefit both directly and indirectly from the labor exploitation of other Asian Americans and other working peoples. For example, the class read and discussed several articles on the domestic garment industry with its infrastucture of subcontracting, through which middle-level Asian American factory owners accumulate capital by employing mostly Asian immigrant women for subminimum wages.

Similarly, we need to be attentive to the different dynamics of gender in Asian American communities. On this point, I would like to emphasize that though it is imperative to point out the inequalities and conflicts between Asian American women and men, we should be careful not to inscribe a too rigid picture of Asian patriarchy—which often inadvertently echoes the worst Orientalism about an unchanging culture of male tyranny—or of subscribing to some unique sphere of Asian American women's identity and experience. The class read about the "debate" surrounding Maxine Hong Kingston's *The Woman Warrior*, and attempted to deconstruct this "gendered" conflict within Asian American literary studies.

Relating to the problem of gender, we need to ask students to examine the *politics* of desires and sexualities. One hotly debated topic is the phenomena of interracial, sexual relations between Asian American women and European American men. The discussions of this issue often uncritically assume that the Asian American woman "must choose" between the Asian American man and the white man. Against this false choice—often cast in terms of ethnic loyalty and betrayal—I attempted to stress that while Asian American women should not be expected to adhere to such dubious prescriptions, we/they—like anyone else—could gain from thinking through how "desire" is not natural and apolitical, but rather informed and mediated by culture, social norms, and education. Additionally, just as they can discern that this society produces and reinforces desire for the white male, they should also be mindful of accepting the desirability of the Asian American male as necessarily more authentic or politically empowering.

A consideration of the politics of bi- or lesbian sexualities offers one alternative beyond the binary confines of such racialized heterosexuality. This involves more than devoting one class meeting or even a week to reading about and discussing Asian American lesbians; such compartmentalizing implicitly echoes the most simplistic forms of multiculturalism with its inconsequential containment policy of "Asian American week." Such strategies could end up merely reinforcing the solidity of subidentities which are only further fragmented and demarcated rather than deconstructed. What could be more productive is a persistent critique of how a patriarchal heterosexuality is assumed as an implicit normality and further buttressed in representations of Asian American women. Using the notion of "compulsory heterosexuality" as a starting point, I instructed students to look for and interrogate the nontreatment of sexualities not only in writings by Asian American lesbians, but also in the texts on immigration, work, activism, etc. For this same reason, I also chose not to reserve a separate space to talk about the significance of "family" for Asian American women because of the ways in which this organizing "thematic" can naturalize heterosexuality as an implicit norm.

In terms of the question of ethnicity, we need to attend to how cultural, linguistic, and national differences can be real barriers to any facile or organic Asian American "pan-ethnicity." There are visceral and long-standing prejudices which specific ethnonationalities harbor against others borne of a complicated history of intra-Asian relations as well as the geographical concentration and social segregation of specific ethnic communities. All of these social and historical conditions call into question the meaningfulness or desirability of an Asian American identification for Koreans, Vietnamese, Indians, and Filipinos as well as for Chinese and Japanese. Recent technological innovations in transportation and communications have enabled the "newer" immigrant communities such as Korean Americans to sustain an active involvement with (South) Korean politics and culture rather than the dominant American culture. Even the emergent body of Asian American literary and cultural productions is less compelling under such conditions of transnational and cultural affiliation. The different trajectories of various Asian immigration also call for different periodizations of Asian American history; rather than a linear narrative with successive appearances of different Asian nationalities, there may be multiple and divergent trajectories of immigration and settlement, and this applies to differences within each ethnonational grouping as well.

Related to this question of the many lines of social identification and political alliance amongst Asians in the United States, I submit that paying attention to such differences will force the question of how the materials of Asian American studies are in themselves "situated knowledges." Increasingly, we would need to ask who are the prominent figures of authority within Asian American studies. Why and how it is that a great many of its scholars and instructors continue to be U.S.-born, middle-class, Chinese or Japanese Americans? I raise this issue not to be factious or to subscribe to a kind of epistemological determinism in which identity corresponds to knowledge, but rather to suggest that rather than an organic community and field of study, Asian American studies is invariably shaped by certain historical and economic forces.

Asian American studies holds a necessarily critical/corrective relationship to both past scholarship on or about Asian Americans, largely by non-Asian Americans, and contemporary marginalizations of Asian American subjects within specific, more entrenched disciplines such as history, sociology, literature, etc. Partially due to this contentious relationship, there is a lack of critical attention to the methodological assumptions and discursive strategies that undergird works within Asian American studies. In an essay titled, "The Politics of Knowledge," Edward Said has warned about "an impoverishing politics of knowledge based only upon the assertion and reassertion of identity, an ultimately uninteresting alternation of presence and absence."[14] Because there is so much focus upon and indeed urgency around the need to fill an absence or lack, the presences we construct seem to escape the critical, vigilant gaze with which we attend to other works.

One of the most important things that Asian American studies as a site of pedagogical practices can do is to call attention to the specificities without forgetting and forgiving our own knowledge-making tactics. This has been a perilous terrain to negotiate, and it is not unique to Asian American studies. I have had numerous conversations about how to time the imparting of information versus demonstrating the methods of how to critique such data while teaching in women's studies and other disciplines. While simultaneity may be difficult if not impossible, but instead of teaching historical data in the first weeks and then moving onto critical interpretations of film/literature in the final weeks, I would encourage a critical discussion of how history, political economy, and sociology, anthropology, and literary criticism express specific modes of thought and representation. Rather than proceeding as if we "offer students 'good realism' as a remedy to the 'bad fictions' of stereotypes,"[15] we can encourage students to approach texts as what Donna Haraway has called "situated knowledges"[16] in their own right. At the same time, we need to be mindful of stressing how to critique something that is nevertheless valuable. In restrospect, I could have emphasized more strongly that although some of the scholarship seemed limited or dated, each work was a significant scholarly effort often undertaken in much more difficult times. Although this deconstruction produces a somewhat contentious approach to the authors and texts, I much prefer this to producing "belief."

Finally, all of this is borne out by a certain respect that I have for my students. I do not and indeed I cannot speak with them convincingly about something which is both an epistemological problem and an ongoing negotiation for myself. At the risk of some confusion as well as a loss of authority, I have attempted to approach my pedagogy not as someone who knows and must lecture to those who don't, but rather as a way to think out loud with them about the questions and issues that are most important and intriguing to me at that moment. I want to help students live their lives with a certain rage, yes, but more a certain confidence about their rights and responsibilities as thoughtful inhabitants in an increasingly complicated world. The complexities and contradictions need to be *taken on*—in a most contentious and resistant sense—rather than ignored and reduced through stereotypical slogans. In his illuminating essay, "Old and New Identities, Old and New Ethnicities," Stuart Hall quotes Hanif Kureishi on the issue of "the difficult moral position of the writer from an oppressed or persecuted group and the relation of that writing to the rest of society":

> A jejune protest or parochial literature, be it black, gay, or feminist, is in the long run no more politically effective than works which are merely public relations. What we need now, in this position, at this time, is imaginative writing that gives us a sense of the shifts and difficulties within our society as a whole.
>
>   If contemporary writing that emerges from oppressed groups ignores the central concerns and major conflicts of the larger society, and if these are willing simply to accept themselves as marginal, or enclave literatures, they will automatically consign themselves as permanently minor, as sub-genre. They must not allow themselves now to be rendered invisible and marginal-

ized in this way by stepping outside of the maelstrom of contemporary history.[17]

If by thus widening our field of critical vision, we displace the primacy of identity and take the pedagogical and political risk that students may conclude that there is nothing connecting some authentic, collective Asian American identity, I feel that this is nevertheless a necessary risk worth taking. Gayatri Spivak offers these sober thoughts:

> For the long haul emancipatory social intervention is not primarily a question of redressing victimage by the assertion of (class- or gender- or ethno-cultural) identity. It is a question of developing a vigilance for systematic appropriations of the underacknowledged social production of a differential that is one basis of exchange into the networks of the cultural politics of class- or gender-identification . . . In the field of ethnocultural politics, the postcolonial teacher can help to develop the vigilance rather than continue pathetically to dramatize victimage or assert a spurious identity.[18]

An intelligent and informed rejection of older, reliable forms of identification must necessarily respond to the still open question of what then is the most effective political strategy for a less polarized and more inhabitable world. The best we can do as teachers is to encourage students to take on this responsibility in a courageous, persistent, and creative manner.

This is where I think that Asian American studies can be an epistemologically and politically productive force in the university as well as the larger society as we head into the twenty-first century. Rather than acceding to the status of an established discipline, our pedagogy can emphasize and expand the *extracurricular praxis*[19] of being an (institutionally marginalized) interdisciplinary arena of study and teaching. The lack or loss of academic prestige can also mean resisting the accommodationist pressures to uphold older, dominant truth claims and forms of knowledge production. Appropriating this uncertain and fluid status, Asian American studies can be a truly contending and contentious pedagogical space which graduates students who have the intellectual confidence, political investment, and the critical tools to effectively engage and interrogate the "departmental homes" to which many must return.

Notes

1. I would like to thank the professors at the University of California, Santa Cruz whom I assisted and learned from as a graduate student instructor. Judy Yung has been a singularly inspiring model of pedagogical wisdom and commit-

ment. This piece is indebted and therefore dedicated to the students I have had the pleasure to share a classroom space with at both Santa Cruz and the University of California, Berkeley. The members of the "Asian Women in America" seminar in the spring of 1994 were especially important in reminding me that teaching is the best part and the last destination.

2. Edward Said, "The Politics of Knowledge," in *Race, Identity and Representation in Education*, Cameron McCarthy and Warren Crichlow, eds. (New York: Routledge, 1993), 306–14.

3. I readily admit that such divisions are artificial and arbitrary, bordering on essentialism. It is further complicated by the presence of other students of color in these classes whose responses were often to compare the course materials to their specific group histories.

4. I am reminded of a disturbing story told by a colleague teaching Asian American studies at a University of California campus with an "ethnic studies" requirement. He related to me how oversubscribed his courses were due to the many Euro-American students who preferred to fulfill their requirements in Asian American studies because they perceive these classroom spaces to be less "hostile" than African American or Chicano studies. Yet, since they are taking the course only to meet the requirement, they have little or no desire to seriously engage the course materials as evidenced in their absenteeism and careless written submissions. I responded to him about how dismayed I was to hear that since my commitment to teaching in Asian American studies, rather than a more established and institutionally privileged discipline such as English, is informed precisely by the fact that in return for loss of academic prestige, I am assured of at least getting students who are invested—personally and politically—in the course materials. I think these eventualities need to be taken into account in the serious reconsideration/restructuring of such requirements.

5. The authors of a recent article on multicultural pedagogy present an effective account of this danger of "supplying students with 'accurate' or 'authentic' representations of particular cultures in the hopes that such corrective gestures will automize tolerant attitudes":

> These newly represented cultures appear on the stage of curriculum either as a seamless parade of stable and unitary customs and traditions or in the individuated form of particular heroes modeling roles. The knowledge that scaffolds this view shuts out the controversies of how any knowledge— including multicultural—is constructed, mediated, governed, and implicated in forms of social regulation and normalization. The problem is that knowledge of a culture is presented as if unencumbered by the politics and poetics of representation. (188–89)

Deborah P. Britzman, Kelvin Santiago-Valles, Gladys Jiménez-Múnoz, and Laura Lamash, "Slips that Show and Tell: Fashioning Multiculture as a Problem of Representation," in *Race, Identity and Representation in Education*, Cameron McCarthy and Warren Crichlow, eds. (New York: Routledge, 1993), 188–200.

6. Gayatri Chakravorty Spivak, "Questions of Multi-culturalism," in *The Post Colonial Critic: Interviews, Strategies, Dialogues*, Sarah Haraysm, ed. (New York: Routledge, 1990). Although my bracketing is appropriate to the discus-

sion, the specific situation to which these words refer is quite different. The original context (page 62), reads:

> I will have an undergraduate class, let's say, a young, white male student, politically-correct, who will say: "I am only a bourgeois white male, I can't speak." In that situation . . . I say to them: "Why not develop a certain degree of rage against the history that has written such an abject script for you that you are silenced?" Then you begin to investigate what it is that silences you, rather than take this very deterministic position— . . .

7. Spivak, "Questions of Multi-culturalism."

8. In the winter of 1993, Donna Haraway deployed this method in a Feminist Theory seminar on "The Traffic in Feminism: Anthropology, Ethnography, and Politics from 1975 to 1992." In another, earlier seminar, she introduced me to the exciting work of Katie King. I thank her for these and other pedagogical tools she has taught me.

9. Katie King, "Bibliography and A Feminist Apparatus of Literary Production," *TEXT* 5 (1990): 91–103.

10. I strongly advocate having students lead and facilitate discussions. I have found that more often than not, this exercise helps them to demystify the position of the instructor as well as to gain a new sense of "sympathetic understanding" and respect about the challenges of engaging a group of people in a lively discussion. To make sure that they are prepared to do so, I met with each group in the week preceding their presentation, at which time they were expected to have some preliminary findings, a set of discussion questions and a rough sketch of their presentation.

11. Other contributing factors could have been the small seminar size of twenty-six students and that over half of them had had some prior course work in ethnic studies, Asian American studies and women's studies. I am aware that such preconditions are not possible in many pedagogical contexts.

12. In contrast, I felt that the course I taught in the following summer on "Asian Americans in Film and Video" was less interesting and productive. The following are some brief notes on my pedagogical strategies for this course. I thought of organizing the course in several ways: 1) by theme, 2) by individual film or video makers, or 3) through a linear history beginning with the earliest examples and finishing with the most recent. I ultimately decided to arrange the short course along genre, with some resonances of the other organizing logics. Beginning the first week with a section on "(Self)Representations," I showed Wayne Wang's "The Joy Luck Club" along with an article in the *Los Angeles Times* which heralded the film as a historic achievement of Asian American culture. If as the author contended, this narrative feature marked an apex, I wanted students to keep the film in mind as we would go on to survey earlier and/or less well-financed films and videos. The second half of that first week was devoted to viewing, *Slaying the Dragon*, and reading various articles on the legacy of Asian American misrepresentation in American popular culture and dominant cinema. Therefore, while one film supposedly marked a point of successful arrival, the other film was an exhaustive catalog of what we were supposed to have left behind in terms of Asian American image making. I asked my students to pay critical attention not only to their divergences but also to the possibilities of simi-

larity in both content and form that would complicate any simple teleology of progress.

The following weeks were organized under the rubric of "Documentaries," "Narrative Shorts," "Narrative Features" and "Experimental Film and Video." This ordering of genres roughly fits the temporal pattern of the emergence of Asian American film and video as it works under shifting political, economic, and aesthetic exigencies.

I also wanted to introduce students to some basic concepts and questions within film theory and criticism, and the specific "schools" that could be enlightening for thinking about the possibility for an Asian American film criticism. Here, it was difficult to fit the theoretical readings with the ways in which I had arranged the screenings of specific films and videos. However, I did want to introduce them to feminist, ethnicity and Third Cinema criticism, as possible places from which to glean useful theoretical and critical insights.

13. An example of how complicated this question of solidarity can be was forcefully posed by the Los Angeles Rebellion in April and May 1992, specifically in the ways in which this event was figured as a conflict between African Americans and Korean Americans. The ambiguous and ambivalent stance by other Asian Americans raised questions about both identificatory categories of "pan-Asian American" and "people of color."

14. Edward Said, "The Politics of Knowledge," in *Race, Identity and Representation in Education,* Cameron McCarthy and Warren Crichlow, eds. (New York: Routledge, 1993), 306–14.

15. Deborah P. Britzman, Kelvin Santiago-Valles, Gladys Jiménez-Múnoz, and Laura Lamash, "Slips that Show and Tell: Fashioning Multiculture as a Problem of Representation," in *Race, Identity and Representation in Education,* Cameron McCarthy and Warren Crichlow, eds. (Routledge: New York, 1993), 188–200.

16. Donna Haraway, "Situated Knowledges: The Science Question in Feminism and the Privilege of Partial Perspective," in *Simians, Cyborgs, and Women: The Reinvention of Nature* (New York: Routledge, 1991). Calling for a "feminist objectivity [as] *situated knowledges*" that do not fall into, but rather negotiate the poles of "radical constructivism versus feminist critical empiricism,"(188) Haraway writes:

> So, I think my problem and "our" problem is how to have *simultaneously* an account of radical historical contingency for all knowledge claims and knowing subjects, a critical practice for recognizing our own "semiotic technologies" for making meanings, *and* a no-nonsense commitment to faithful accounts of the "real" world, one that can be partially shared and friendly to earth-wide projects of finite freedom, adequate material abundance, modest meaning in suffering, and limited happiness. (187)

17. Stuart Hall, "Old and New Identities, Old and New Ethnicities," in *Culture, Globalization and the World-System*, Anthony D. King, ed. (Binghampton: State University of New York Press, 1991).

18. Gayatri Chakravorty Spivak, *Outside in the Teaching Machine* (New York: Routledge, 1993), 63.

19. I find intriguing one specific definition of "extracurricular" as "outside and in direct opposition to or violation of the conventionally established limits or rights of one's position;" *Webster's Third New International Dictionary* (Chicago: G. & C. Merriam Co., 1981), 538.

Of the many definitions of "praxis," I want to retain the implication of "teaching" not as a mere transfer of data but as a "coaching": "to train intensively by detailed instruction, frequent demonstration and repeated practice;" *Webster's Third New International Dictionary* (Chicago: G. & C. Merriam Co., 1981), 431.

12

Reflections on Teaching about Asian American Communities

TIMOTHY P. FONG

The challenge put forth by Chalsa Loo and Don Mar in their provocative essay, "Research and Asian Americans: Social Change or Empty Prize?,"[1] was without doubt a major influence on my decision to enter into an academic career and to focus my attention on community research. Loo and Mar succinctly described the need to develop a conceptual framework for community research, the importance of confronting academic barriers that work to create an artificial separation between researchers and the community, and encourage the emergence of "new breed" researchers who are equally well versed in rigorous data gathering and academic analysis, information dissemination, and political organizing.

The Loo and Mar essay was extremely important in establishing a solid foundation for my research on Asian American communities, and I continue to refer to it for guidance. As vital as their work has been to my *doing* community research, however, it has been both an inspiration and a frustration for the very different responsibility of *teaching* a course in Asian American community studies. Of all the courses I have taught, I found my course on Asian American communities to be the most difficult. I have often wondered—indeed struggled—with the reasons why this is so. In this essay I want to discuss some of my thoughts on the ideals and the realities of teaching a course on Asian American communities, as well as what I've found works in teaching a communities course and what still needs to be done.

The Community Ideal

Asian American studies and the emphasis on research on Asian American communities evolved around the dramatic Third World Strike at San Francisco State College (now University) in the fall of 1968. Several years prior to the student strike of 1968 was a period of student-initiated pro-grams that provided education and social services to the communities where the students themselves lived and worked. During this era of civil rights and social change it was believed that urban Asian American students should have an education that is both relevant and would serve the needs of their communities. In this case, "the community" for Asian Americans in San Francisco was easily defined as Chinatown, Japan-town, and Manilatown. The establishment of the first School of Ethnic Studies in the nation, which included Asian American studies, was clearly the most tangible accomplishment following the Third World Strike. Within a few years several more programs and courses in Asian American studies were created at colleges and universities throughout California, as well as in larger urban campuses across the country. The convergence of the activist and the academic came out of this growth of the Asian American studies movement.[2]

In the early days of this movement there was a great deal of literature and rich debate on how to do research in Asian American communities. For example, the book, *Issues in Community Research: Asian American Perspectives* (1980), includes several papers presented by Asian American scholars centering on such issues as traditional objectivity versus "action" research, the role of the researcher as community advocate, and new methodologies for ethnic communities.[3] In short, the emerging field of Asian American studies struggled to create and institutionalize a new form of social science research where the primary focus was to "serve the community." Underlying this community ideal was the notion that there was a cadre of dedicated indigenous community activists who were *coming to* the university who could be trained to effectively challenge the establishment and work for social change. Asian American studies programs would, therefore, be the groomers and the mentors for a new generation of leaders who would then return to empower the community.

The New Realities

As we all know, much has changed in over two-and-a-half decades since the Third World Strike at San Francisco State, and the assumptions held then no longer apply today. First of all there has been a tremendous political shift in the United States with an overall swing away from the progressive social gains of the 1960s towards a more individualistic and laissez-faire sensibility in the 1980s and 1990s.[4] In addition, increased social and spatial mobility of well-educated, professional, American-born Asians, coupled with large numbers of extremely diverse Asian immigrants, have served to make the traditionally defined urban community an obsolete ideal.

The second reality is that the vast majority of today's Asian American college students bear little resemblance to the students who were the very heart and foundation of the Asian American studies movement. Today relatively few students come from the easily definable Asian American "communities" of twenty-five years ago. On one hand, Asian American students are much more middle class and above, come from suburban areas, and are more used to white, rather than Asian American communities. This is especially true in the elite research-oriented universities in California and in the growing number of Asian American studies programs in colleges and universities outside of the West Coast. These Asian American students are much more interested in middle class issues that relate to their career and social lives. Such issues include alleged quotas in elite universities, professional glass-ceilings, interracial marriage, and Asian American images in the media. On the other hand, there is a great deal more diversity among Asian American students as the numbers of Chinese, Korean, Asian Indian, and Southeast Asian Americans have immigrated to the United States. Many Southeast Asian immigrant and refugee students are often the first generation in college, and their lack of fluency in English affects their reading comprehension, writing skills, and public-speaking abilities. Of primary concern for them is their own survival in college and the survival of their families in a new and sometimes hostile environment.

The third reality is quite simply a generational problem. In Michael Omi's article, "It Just Ain't the Sixties No More: The Contemporary Dilemmas of Asian American Studies," he recalls a conversation with a colleague, one of the founders of the field, who acknowledges that the people who lived during the turbulent 1960s were undeniably affected. Yet the colleague notes that the urgency of that period cannot be replicated in the classroom when the audience has lived a very different experience and has a very different base of knowledge.[5] During one lecture on the Civil Rights movement and its influence on the Asian Americans, one student abruptly stopped me because she didn't know who the Black Panthers were—she thought they were a rock 'n' roll band! The generation gap cannot be overestimated.[6]

The fourth reality is the increased separation between Asian American studies programs and the various communities. In the article, "On the Development of Asian American Studies Programs," Russell Endo and William Wei outline several reasons for this departure from the community ideal including: realistic limitations on Asian American studies programs, faculty members being too busy and overworked to participate in community affairs, and, in some circumstances, community groups have progressed beyond the need to rely on Asian American programs for support.[7] Equally important have been the efforts of programs to institutionalize and legitimize Asian American studies as an academic discipline, which has led many on the road towards more traditional research where the emphasis is on mainstream scholarship. This is something that greatly concerned Loo and Mar when they warned, what "is rewarded in academia is often not what is useful to communities."[8] While there is an increase in community studies by Asian American scholars, they are often narrowly written for other academics and the presentation is not accessible to the community, and above the comprehension of most students.

What Should be Taught and How

Overemphasis on the community ideal without acknowledgment and understanding of these new realities will inevitably lead to disappointment, especially in teaching a course on Asian American communities. As stated above, the Loo and Mar article was instrumental in my researching of Asian American communities, and served as an inspiration of what I wanted to pass along to students taking an Asian American communities course. In many ways, however, I relied on it too literally. As a result, the Loo and Mar article proved to be a source of frustration primarily because of my own inability to distinguish between the ideals that were the context for the sentiments expressed in the article and the realities of teaching.

At this point it might be useful to briefly describe my first experience teaching an Asian American communities course at the University of California at Davis during the winter 1993 quarter. I was a part-time lecturer freshly out of graduate school and this experience was most humbling because I placed too much emphasis on my own narrow assumptions and values, which were not necessarily compatible with the expectations and experiences of the students. The major miscalculation I had was an expectation that students were, as I was, ready, eager, and willing to leave the university campus to work in the field.

With this expectation in mind I spent the first half of the quarter reading the Loo and Mar article to set the conceptual framework for Asian American community research and then focused on research methodologies, strategies, and ethics. The second half of the class concentrated on a brief, comparative overview of various contemporary Asian American communities and their issues. The midterm paper was a three-to-five page human subjects protocol that was intended to get students to think about their community/problem analysis term paper, their methods for research, and an awareness of the rights of the individuals they wanted to study. The students were required to hand in a ten-to-fifteen page analysis paper at the end of the course. To my dismay, there was a great deal of student resistance to entering the field; they didn't know where to go or what to do, or how to engage others outside of the narrow confines of the university campus.

I quickly realized that I was teaching the course completely backwards: the students were *not* indigenous community activists who were coming to the university to be trained as effective change agents, but were curious individuals who wanted to learn about new and changing Asian American communities, and wanted to know where they fit in. My pedagogy was more intimidating and abstract than informative and inspirational. The second half of the course was clearly much more effective than the first, but since the emphasis was placed on immediately *doing* community research, the final papers were overwhelmingly disappointing. One of the most trying aspects of teaching in a quarter system is when you start off stumbling on the wrong foot, it is extremely difficult to recover and regain balance. Student reviews of the course were equally disappointing. The most common complaint was that the course felt like two separate courses crushed into one. Given the broad and grandiose assumptions I was working with, this criticism was quite valid.

The following year I taught the Asian American communities course again, and this time I used Peter Nien-chu Kiang's article, "Bringing It All Back Home: New Views of Asian American Studies and Community," as my pedagogical guide.[9] While Kiang's article focused on the influx of Southeast Asian refugees into Boston University, his student-centered teaching approach and reconfiguration of the curriculum to meet the changing needs of the new students and communities was quite applicable to my own situation. The new course still began with the Loo and Mar article as its foundation, but I expanded on what was done during the second half of the initial course. I focused mainly on taking a historical and comparative examination of various dynamic contemporary Asian American ethnic communities, and also featured examples of pan-Asian American activities, with emphasis on the creation and re-creation of a sense of community.[10] This time around the course was much more successful because it was more descriptive, keyed into the interests of the students, and engaged their own experiences directly. The diversity of the students in class and their experiences worked extremely well with the new format. Classroom discussions were easily generated, as students were able to teach each other and share their own community issues, along with what they read and heard in lectures.

While this second opportunity to teach the class was indeed a catharsis for me, two new challenges emerged. First, there was some of my own initial resistance because I thought I might somehow be compromising the progressive ideals of the past by not making students immediately

run out to the field to do "action research" and analysis. However, I have
always been a firm believer in experiential learning rather than didactic
education, and this first concern naturally resolved itself. I was very
pleased to find the most positive spin-off of this new format was that
several students genuinely *became* interested in going out to do community research and analysis and volunteering in Asian American community-based organizations. Certainly most all of the students who took the
course are now able to appreciate new Asian American communities in a
way they never would have before. In this second attempt I allowed the
students to think critically for themselves rather than force-feed their education.

The second challenge is much tougher, has no immediate solution or
spin-off, and is probably common in Asian American studies programs
across the country. UC Davis offers only one Asian American communities course, and there are only a few opportunities to channel students'
new-found interest in "the community." Some internships are available,
but they are neither well organized nor closely monitored. To capture
and maintain student interest, I favor the development of a "cluster" or
"sequence" approach to teaching about Asian American communities.
This approach acknowledges the changes in the societal context, changes
in today's students, and that a critical thinking approach to education is
an engaging *process*, not a singular *event* (or course).

Obviously a one-quarter course can only whet the appetites of interested students and does not come near to achieving the goals for community research articulated twenty-five years ago. At least one follow-up
Asian American communities course, much like the course I originally
taught, should be offered. This follow-up course would focus primarily
on how to do community research and analysis, what methods and strategies to use, and the individual and interpersonal ethics of community
studies. Only, this time, the students will be much more prepared and
motivated. Ideally, a third course should be added with the emphasis
being on a *student-initiated* individual or group community-research or -
organizing project. The requirements for this third course could also be
fulfilled through an internship with a community-based organization or
government agency. This approach can be effective because it encourages
students to make an active choice in their research and may also be used
towards a career path. For example, a student who is interested in dental
school may wish to do research on Asian American community health
issues or intern in a community health clinic. This expansive and self-
directed approach to community studies at an undergraduate level is appropriate even in areas where large Asian American communities do not
exist. In addition, this approach can easily be made into a two-course

sequence that fits within the semester system, which is found at most colleges and universities.

Conclusion: "New-Breed" Researchers

Asian America is rapidly growing and changing. As an academic discipline, Asian American studies must keep up with these changes and be an integral part of them. The time has come again to take community studies seriously and to integrate it fully into an Asian American studies curriculum. To this day I am still inspired by the words of Loo and Mar and it is my hope their work will continue to motivate a new generation of "new breed" researchers for the 1990s and beyond.

In order to meet this challenge, however, we must step back and continuously reevaluate our pedagogical process. In my eagerness and excitement to re-create the community "ideal" sentiment, I lost touch with the reality of teaching. Ironically, while I remembered the words of Loo and Mar about how to be a researcher, I forgot how to be an educator. In *Education for a Critical Consciousness* (1981), Paulo Freire wrote that true education can only be done "with the people and never for them or imposed upon them" and the "prerequisite for this task was a form of education enabling the people to reflect on themselves, their responsibilities, and their role in the new cultural climate . . ."[11]

I believe teaching about Asian American communities is clearly much more complex than teaching other Asian American studies courses. The integration of, and the conflicts between, theory and practice, idealism and reality, quality research and social advocacy, expediency and ethics all come into play and need to be addressed. My experiences teaching about Asian American communities has made me appreciate these factors, and has made conceptualizing such courses in an effective fashion, a real challenge. My experiences teaching about Asian American communities made me appreciate these factors even more. In the process I have evolved into both a better researcher and a more competent educator.

Notes

1. Chalsa Loo and Don Mar, "Research and Asian Americans: Social Change or Empty Prize?" *Amerasia Journal* 12, no. 2 (1985–1986): 85–93.

2. See Mike Murase, "Ethnic Studies and Higher Education for Asian Americans," in *Counterpoint: Perspectives on Asian America*, Emma Gee, ed. (Los Angeles: Asian American Studies Center, University of California, 1976), 223; Karen Umemoto, " 'On Strike!' San Francisco State College Strike, 1968–69:

The Role of Asian American Studies," *Amerasia* 15, no. 1 (1989): 3–41; William Wei, *The Asian American Movement* (Philadelphia: Temple University Press, 1993).

3. Alice K. Murata and Juanita Salvador-Burris, eds., *Issues in Community Research: Asian American Perspectives* (Chicago: Pacific/Asian American Mental Health Research Center, 1980).

4. See Michael Omi and Howard Winant, *Racial Formation: From the 1960s to the 1980s* (New York: Routledge & Kegan Paul, second edition, 1994).

5. Michael Omi, "It Just Ain't the Sixties No More: The Contemporary Dilemmas of Asian American Studies," in *Reflections on Shattered Windows: Promises and Prospects for Asian American Studies*, Gary Y. Okihiro, Shirley Hune, Arthur A. Hansen, and John M. Liu, eds. (Pullman: Washington State University Press, 1988), 31–36.

6. For an excellent analysis of the importance of generations see Jere Takahashi, "Japanese American Responses to Race Relations: The Formation of Nisei Perspectives," *Amerasia* 9, no. 1 (1982): 39–57.

7. Russell Endo and William Wei, "On the Development of Asian American Studies Programs," in *Reflections on Shattered Windows*, Gary Y. Okihiro, et al., eds. (Pullman: Washington State University Press, 1988), 5–15.

8. Loo and Mar, "Research and Asian Americans: Social Change or Empty Prize?" 88.

9. Peter Nien-chu Kiang, "Bringing It All Back Home: New Views of Asian American Studies and the Community," in *Frontiers of Asian American Studies*, Gail Nomura, Russell Endo, Stephen Sumida, and Russell Leong, eds. (Pullman: Washington State University Press, 1989), 305–314.

10. See Yen Le Espiritu, *Asian American Panethnicity: Bridging Institutions and Identities* (Philadelphia: Temple University Press, 1993).

11. Paulo Freire, *Education for Critical Consciousness* (New York: Continuum, 1981), 16.

13

Psychology and the Teaching of Asian American Studies

RAMSAY LIEM

Because of the politics involved in creating Asian American studies programs, a certain amount of anarchy has characterized their appearance on many campuses. Rarely are these programs primarily the result of faculty or administration initiatives to reform established disciplines or intellectual traditions. On the contrary, Asian American studies were historically and, to a large extent still are, the product of support and demand from below—from disaffected students, individual faculty or administrators, and community activists. Consequently, what is taught in these programs, with what methodologies, and by whom, is often an accident of the particular players who happen to initiate such a project at a given university. This is particularly the case during the formative years of an Asian American curriculum. While these conditions both reflect and enforce the marginalization of ethnic studies by the academic canon, they have contributed to a degree of openness and creativity in Asian American studies absent in the established disciplines.

This ad hoc path to Asian American studies describes our experience at Boston College and explains how the first, and now introductory course in the field, came to be offered by me, a psychologist.[1] Five years ago a small number of Asian American students on our campus began to voice their frustration with the usual menu of social activities offered by student clubs at that time. I happened to be the only faculty member available to support their concerns. Together, we worked to strengthen the organizational presence of Asian American students on campus and to create a critical mass of interest in Asian American studies, first among other students and then faculty and administrators.

Three years ago I began offering a course, "Self, Ethnic Identity, and Asian American History," through the Psychology department. This peculiar blend of psychological perspectives on the self and ethnic identity, history, Asian American literature, and contemporary issues was dictated

151

by the accident of my own departmental affiliation and the urgency students felt to "cover everything" in the single course available to them. In spite of the practical necessities that shaped this venture, there are a number of pedagogical and epistemological lessons that can be drawn from the disciplinary border crossings that occur in this course.

A note about audience. Many of the students who elect this course are second- or third-generation Asian Americans who share the experience of having been "invisible minorities" for much of their lives. The majority are also middle-class suburbanites and have grown up in predominantly white communities. They are initially attracted to Asian American studies because of "Who Am I?" questions rather than more abstract intellectual concerns or political sensibilities. Less-egocentric interests evolve in time, but the initial hook is clearly identity politics. The generational and class makeup of these students no doubt helps to account for the appeal of a psychological entre into the collective experience of Asians in America at Boston College.

Course Plan

In rough sequence, our course includes personal autobiographies and life stories of other cohorts of Asian Americans, psychological theory and research on the self and racial/ethnic identity, the early and more recent history of immigration to America from Asia, a brief foray into Asian American literature, and a discussion of selected contemporary issues. In addition to a variety of short writing assignments and exams, students conduct a term project that requires face-to-face interviewing and/or participant observation, preferably off-campus.[2]

While the course is continually being reshaped by our experiences with it, one theme seems to persist, which involves a core dialectic of the individual vs. collective played out on a variety of levels. This tension can be illustrated in several ways.

When students share their personal biographies at the beginning of the semester, they wrestle with experiences and memories which often feel highly idiosyncratic. One student wrote that shortly after she came to the United States, she took the name "Judy" from the television cartoon series, "The Jetsons." To a five year old, Judy Jetson was the essence of Americana. Judy herself, however, had never before disclosed her act of self definition. Another woman pondered why her family relocated so many times during her elementary and high school years. She thought they were "weird."

Following an assignment to "code" each others' autobiographies for similarities and differences, however, they and others were struck by the similarities in their experiences, much more so than by the differences. "Judy Jetson" came to be seen as one instance of dressing in the clothes of the "other" to resist marginalization. Residential instability provoked curiosity about why so many parents could not find an appropriate niche in the labor market. This discovery of common ground is quite spontaneous yet tempered by the desire to protect one's individuality.

This initial glimpse of collective identity is reinforced when students read personal narratives selected from the published writing of earlier cohorts of young Asian Americans.[3] Discovering themes of invisibility, isolation, exclusion, and embarrassment in preceding generations of Asian Americans sometimes then creates the desire to find explanations for these shared experiences and why students have been previously unaware of them.

We then explore the topic of self and identity formation as addressed in the psychological literature. We do this in two ways. The first introduces students to prominent models of ethnic, racial, and cultural identity development.[4] I ask students to examine the hidden assumptions behind these approaches as well as their content. Most are variations on a core developmental process envisioning the movement from unreflected immersion in the racial and cultural mainstream to a period of contested identity to resolution, whether partial or complete.

We consider the validity of the stages in the different models and the experiences that provoke change (using personal autobiographies and the research literature). However, we focus on the paradox between the individualistic nature of the resolution phase—identity formation as personal choice—and the fact that cultural, racial, and ethnic identities have their roots in common experiences, especially those of racial discrimination and exclusion. Some of our liveliest discussions, therefore, involve the question of whether or not there are contradictions inherent in reducing ethnic or racial identity to personal preference or personal definition.

The second phase of this exploration involves new contributions from cultural psychology and psychological anthropology regarding the fundamental nature of the self. The focus is less on answering the questions Who am I?, What is the substance of my identity?, and more on What is encompassed by the self or ego? Drawing on the work of various contributors,[5] we examine the distinction between self as autonomous and "self-contained" vs. "relational" or interdependent. One expression of this distinction that resonates with the experiences of Asian American students is the contrast between the person who feels very close to his/her family and the person whose sense of self incorporates the ascribed status of son or daughter. Students often share anecdotes about their frustration with European American friends who fail to comprehend their feelings of family attachment and recognize that their differing constructions of the self may diminish the basis for empathy. In addition, when they recognize that the individualistic self is not necessarily the Darwinian evolutionary ideal, they are able to dispel feelings of immaturity and selflessness cultivated by misrepresentations of their social attachments as overdependence.

An essay by Lowell Chun-Hoon[6] reflecting on the early years in the life of Jade Snow Wong complements this examination of the cultural construction of the self. His inquiry centers on Wong's struggle to define herself apart from her tradition-bound, ascribed statuses, e.g., fifth Chinese daughter, taken for granted by her new immigrant reality. What Chun-Hoon describes, however, is not the liberation of Wong's incipient, individualized, "true" self, but the discovery of a third way; one in which tradition accommodates Jade Snow's desire for educational and professional success not only in service of self but the family and community as well. He portrays the mature Jade Snow Wong as *both* "bounded up" with and differentiated from her family.

This examination of the self departs radically from mainstream psychological theory because it proposes that the fundamental structure of the ego or self is particular to one's cultural and social practices, and that privileging the individualistic self is a product of cultural imperialism and racial exclusion. It problematizes the very notion of the autonomous, self-contained ego that is deeply embedded in the American psychological tradition. At the same time it challenges students to envision how institutional practices need to be transformed to accommodate other ways of "being-in-the-world" better suited to the inclinations of Asian Americans and other ethnic and racial minorities.

The remainder of my comments address the integration of identity politics with students' exposure to Asian American history and contemporary issues. What I have learned from my students is that, when elaborated through a critical psychological perspective, their more egocentric concerns about self and identity lead to many questions that are fundamentally historical in nature.

While many students enter the course expecting to study the history of East, South, and Southeast Asia, by this point in the semester they have begun to imagine a history of Asian America, many for the first time. They have also become aware of being "strangers within their own shores" and needing to claim a denied history to help resolve the dilemmas of ethnic and racial identity they have just encountered.

In the best-case scenario, students enter history as active questioners with some realization that their curiosities can only be allayed by knowledge of what preceded their own experiences in the United States. Many look for answers to personal questions: Why are there so many Filipino medical practitioners in the United States?; why are arranged marriages still common among Asian Indians?; why are there no Japantowns? Given the tension between the complexity and diversity of Asian American history and the practical constraints of time (usually about a half semester), I encourage students to explore several general themes: 1) the dialectic of subject/object, actor/victim operative throughout Asian American history; 2) exclusion and resistance to being shut out as a common expression of this dialectic across different Asian American communities; 3) continuity and discontinuity between past and contemporary barriers to equality for Asian Americans; and 4) the leading role that ordinary people like ourselves play in making Asian American history. The nineteenth-century and early twentieth-century recruitment of plantation labor to Hawaii, for example, provides an opportunity to examine community formation as the product of the competing interests of labor and capital, resistance through the building of worker solidarity, and similarities between this earlier manipulation of ethnic chauvinism and the provocation of contemporary interethnic, interracial conflict.

When this reading of history is successful, students are able not only to relate to the concerns of their historical predecessors, but also to begin to conceive of roles for themselves as makers of history. This awareness is based on several discoveries: that struggles against racism, the manipulation of interethnic and racial competition, cultural invisibility and the like are unfinished legacies of early Asian American history; that these struggles continually reshape the social, economic, and political life of Asian American communities; and that as an ascribed member of these communities, one's action or inaction is consequential. I do not mean to suggest that all students arrive at this kind of appreciation of Asian American history, but for those who do, history serves not only to clarify their identities but also to motivate and guide their future actions.

This approach to Asian American history is then reinforced through an examination of selected issues relevant to contemporary Asian American communities. The topics change from year to year, e.g., anti-Asian violence, the glass ceiling and model minority myth, labor market segregation, Japan bashing, anti-immigration sentiment, interracial conflict, educational and curriculum reform; but their contribution to the course is similar. They anchor history in the present as well as the past through their resemblance to earlier struggles with which they share common, if not identical, social, economic, and political origins. They also require students to consider a central lesson of history, that the totality of individual responses to these challenges—including apathy and denial—defines the Asian American experience and will determine the legacy passed on to future generations. In this sense there is no escape from one's status as an Asian American and a historical actor. One has only the choice to enact these roles more or less self-consciously.

Several years ago this process of discovery came to fruition toward the end of the semester when a local radio station advertised a "Bash Japanese Products" campaign. Listeners were invited to bring appliances manufactured in Japan to the station to be steamrolled. Several students in the class heard the broadcast and quickly set in motion a call for action on our campus and from surrounding colleges. They organized a counter-demonstration and telephone campaign which, in less than forty-eight hours, succeeded in blocking the event and wresting an apology. One new activist reached the governor of Massachusetts, who in turn made a direct appeal to the radio station.

The discussions sparked by this incident revealed not only the euphoria of "victory" among the students but an emerging recognition that their actions connected them in a small way to the legacy of struggle they had begun to discover in their foray into Asian American history. Acting in the present they also reflected on their place in the history of future Asian Americans who might, like they, come to appreciate events of the past as the foundation for their own identities and choices as Asian Americans. They recalled an excerpt from a poem assigned earlier in the semester:

b
haiku
        for sisters who have given, still give
you have shared vision
as I will ever try to
share my own with you
c
the work yet to be done[7]

Students in my classes leave with a variety of new ambitions—a change of major from accounting to education and sociology, a psychology honors thesis on engendered sibling relations in Asian Indian families, a senior thesis in sociology on stereotypes of Asian American women in the cinema, graduate school in clinical psychology and minority mental health, Peace Corps volunteering in Nepal, a first trip to China, Indonesia, or Japan. They also assume leadership roles in Asian American and multiracial student organizations and work to mobilize support for an expanded curriculum in Asian American studies. Others, I have come to learn, reconfigure their identities and lives months and years following their discovery of Asian American history.

The Contributions of Psychology

In retrospect, the ability to foster an appreciation of one's self as a historical actor strikes me as a special contribution of the integration of psychology into the teaching of Asian American studies. Psychology affirms the quest for identity and validates students' personal needs to know more about themselves. It can also cultivate interest in Asian American history and contemporary issues, ironically, because of its limited conceptualization of the meaning of ethnic and racial identity. History, on the other hand, reveals that Asian American identity is not a fixed composite of abstract attributes or values but an affinity for the varieties of resistance and exclusion, ambition and resignation enacted and experienced by preceding generations of Asian immigrants and their descendants. The concept of identity as common ways of being or acting under conditions of shared marginalization is then reinforced when history is brought into the present and related to the struggles of contemporary Asian Americans.

Students who acquire this understanding of Asian American identity become actors in the history of future generations of Asian Americans. For them, "Asian American studies has reached beyond the level of introspection and identity, the asking of 'Who Am I?' questions, to serious inquiries about the political, economic, and historical forces affecting Asian Americans."[8] Action can then take many forms from participation in campus and community struggles to the pursuit of more intensive historical, literary, or social science inquiry. Even the occasional student who discovers such projects through an introduction to Asian American studies confirms the value of this marginalized discipline.

The Impact of Asian American Studies on Psychology

Although psychology can animate students' introduction to Asian American studies, integrating it with the history and contemporary struggles of Asian Americans also exposes its own limitations, most notably its unbridled reductionism. Identity construed in psychological terms is fundamentally an attribute of the individual, comprised of temperament, constitutional dispositions, and unique interpersonal and social experiences. It signifies individuality and is generally experienced as what is most personal. This construction of personhood is also deeply embedded in the U.S. cultural ethos with which second- and third-generation Asian Americans are often closely and unself-consciously identified. The wholesale adoption of this approach to identity could reduce Asian American studies to a survey of historical and cultural artifacts with which to adorn one's primary sense of self.

There are, however, alternatives to this peculiarly individualistic discourse on personhood that dominates American psychology. For example, feminist psychology has identified this cultural ideal as masculine and contrasted it with women's sense of self as "in relation";[9] the psychological study of ethnicity and race has revived interest in social identity;[10] and cultural psychology has exposed the cultural particularity of "self-contained" individualism.[11] These challenges to the dominant psychological conception of the person have also been joined by critical theorists in sociology and anthropology. Together, they represent an effort to wrest identity, motivation, action, and morality from the fiction of a universal, autonomous individuality.

Still, what is absent in these efforts to "resocialize" personhood and identity is the extension of the self through time beyond personal autobiography to the history of those groups with whom one is associated. Psychology, in other words, is essentially ahistorical if not asocial. Human consciousness as rendered in American psychology lacks historical imagination. This striking omission has been the most important revelation for me as I have worked with students to incorporate a psychological perspective in the teaching of Asian American studies. Without an organic attachment to the collective experiences of Asian immigrants in America, students are prone to adopt ethnic or racial identity as one might put on a new dress or coat. It adds color and variety but little moral imperative.

What I have learned from crossing disciplinary boundaries in Asian American studies, therefore, is not only that history and psychology are complementary but that a historical sensibility is integral to human psychology. It is the psychological mechanism that enables us to experience ethnic and racial identity not only as belonging to a social group but as sharing in its current fate and participating in constructing its future.

Notes

1. The writer was trained in clinical/community psychology and has a background of Asian American and Korean American community activism.

2. Highlights of these projects are presented in class and have addressed such topics as Asian American gangs, interracial marriage and dating, interethnic relations in Boston's Chinatown, the plight of restaurant workers, Asian American mental health, African American/Korean American community relations, and campus relations between first- and second-generation Asian Americans.

3. Joann Lee, *Asian American Experiences in the United States* (Jefferson, N.C.: McFarland Press, 1991).

4. Jean Phinney, "Ethnic Identity in Adolescents and Adults: Review of Research," *Psychological Bulletin* 108 (1990): 499–514. Derald Sue and David Sue, "Racial/cultural identity development," in *Counseling the Culturally Different*, D. Sue and D. Sue, eds. (New York: John Wiley, 1990).

5. Clifford Geertz, *The Interpretation of Cultures: Selected Essays* (New

York: Basic Books, 1973); Takie Lebra, "Shame and guilt: A Psychocultural View of the Japanese Self," *Ethos* 11 (1983): 192–209; Helen Markus and Shinobu Kitayama, "Culture and the Self: Implications for Cognition, Emotion, and Motivation," *Psychological Review* 98 (1991): 224–53.

6. Lowell Chun-Hoon, "Jade Snow Wong and the Fate of Asian American Identity" in *Asian Americans: Psychological Perspectives*, S. Sue and N. Wagner, eds. (Ben Lomond, California: Science and Behavior Books, 1973).

7. Joannie Chang, "Three parts," *Asian American Spirit 5* (Boston, Mass.: East Coast Asian Student Union, 1990).

8. Don T. Nakanishi and Russell Leong, "Toward the Second Decade: A National Survey of Asian American Studies Programs in 1978." *Amerasia Journal 5*, no. 3 (1978): 1–19.

9. Carol Gilligan, *In a Different Voice: Psychological Theory and Women's Development* (Cambridge: Harvard University Press, 1982).

10. Janet Helms, *Black and White Racial Identity: Theory, Research, and Practice* (New York: Greenwood Press, 1990).

11. Markus and Kitayama, "Culture and the Self."

14

Beyond the Missionary Position:
Student Activism from the Bottom Up

ERIC C. WAT

Two summers ago, a student expressed interest in taking my "Asian Pacific American Leadership Development Project" (APALDP) course and asked me what he could expect to get out of the class. Only two weeks into my new position as the assistant coordinator of Student/Community Projects (S/CP) and as the instructor of APALDP, I was at a loss for words. I showed him the syllabus from the previous year. However, that syllabus is only a reflection of the emphasis and biases of my predecessors, a guide to how *they* would teach and had taught the class. The class predated me, and I had not had a chance to shape it in the way that I wanted to teach it. So as I was reading the "course objectives" and the "course description" to the student, it became obvious to him that I was mouthing someone else's words.

There were, of course, certain given principles on which APALDP operates. First of all, like all other projects of S/CP[1], APALDP stems from the idea that Asian American studies is about our communities and ourselves and that Asian American studies is an instrument of progressive social change. Inherent in these ideas is the notion that Asian American studies students have a particular role and mission in the communities. By making linkages between students and the communities, S/CP is the Center's mechanism through which these changes can be brought about. More specifically, as a for-credit course, APALDP is an institutionalized training ground for potential leaders in our communities in the future.

Secondly, leadership development with an Asian and Pacific Islander focus must go beyond the practical know-hows, such as team building and community mobilization. After all, one cannot mobilize a community effectively without knowing the community. Therefore, in order for anyone to assume leadership roles in the Asian and Pacific Islander communities, one must understand their internal dynamics and their connections to other communities of color as well as to the mainstream

American society. In its first quarter, APALDP explores different leadership styles and models of collectives. In addition, we address pan-ethnic assumptions,[2] inter-generational dynamics,[3] and the intersection of sexism, racism, classism and anti-immigrant "sentiments."[4]

The last principle stresses the importance of student activism. Here I define activism as any action an individual performs in a group setting with the intention of creating change for a more just society. Helping students develop a sense and need to bring changes to our society is, I believe, an essential priority of higher education. Therefore, such activities are not *extra*curricular, but *co*curricular. Academic research has consistently shown that cocurricular experiences have a major impact on a student's personal growth, moral development, and leadership skills. Furthermore, student development theory has suggested that student involvement enhances satisfaction of other aspects of one's educational experience. More importantly, other studies have indicated that "out-of-class radicalizing experiences do not wear off, but continue to shape a person's life long after they occur."[5]

Therefore, during the second quarter, students of APALDP are expected to complete an internship with community-based organizations in the Asian and Pacific Islander communities. For many of the students, the internship will be the first time they will have any interaction with a particular segment of the Asian and Pacific Islander constituencies, see how real-life politicking can affect decision making and how their contributions can have an impact—positive and negative—on real people's lives. Through the internship experience, the students can see the responsibility that comes with a commitment to the communities.

The idea is, of course, to get the students to take what they have learned in the first quarter about the communities and apply that knowledge to a working situation—that is, a merging of theory and practice. The two are interdependent of each other: theory informs practice, and practice refines theory. Both are needed. To simplify Paulo Freire, theory without practice is just words, and practice without theory is just thoughtless action. This simplification, however, overshadows the enormous difficulty of the task of student leadership development.

In fact, while I hold myself to these important principles and ideals, my experiences with the students in APALDP this past year have taught me that the picture is not always as tidy and neat. My assumptions of both the students and the communities have been so romanticized to the point that sometimes I was unprepared or unable to deal effectively with complications and obstacles as they arose. For example—just as the students need to understand the dynamics of the communities to assume leadership roles—in order to move the students, I have to be sensitive to the different locations they have already occupied, especially in terms of identity issues and political ideology. My messages, then, need to be fine-tuned to reflect these different locations. Otherwise, they will fall on deaf ears.

This paper, then, is a summation of the lessons I have learned. Realizing that each campus differs in political climate, geographical locations, student and community demographics, and financial and personnel resources, I do not intend this paper to be a comprehensive guide to student leadership development. Nonetheless, I hope that it can begin discussion and stimulate more insightful thoughts on similar issues.

Asian Pacific American Leadership Development Project

I have tried to model APALDP after one of the most important missions of Asian American studies as it was established in the late sixties. Specifically, I want the students to take the knowledge they have accumulated through this and other Asian American studies courses about our history and contemporary issues and apply it to our communities. This, however, has become an increasingly difficult task to accomplish. It is difficult because, I believe, Asian American Studies appears to be evolving into a "traditional" academic discipline. This trend includes a transformation by which academic discourse is made inaccessible to people outside and sometimes even inside the Ivory Tower and by which community issues become less and less relevant. For example, a friend of mine was surprised that the staff of the Asian American Studies Center had recently endorsed a political campaign against Proposition 187, an anti-immigrant ballot initiative in California. A few months later, the Center also stood in solidarity with our graduate employees when their campaign to unionize was not recognized by the university administration. The Center staff wrote a letter to the chancellor and closed down for two days in response to the graduate employee union's call for a campuswide walkout. In fact, it is not uncommon that our staff work side by side with students in political campaigns on campus and in the communities. Nevertheless, to my friend, these decisions were atypical because he couldn't see other academic departments doing the same thing. I think his was an important distinction because it brought in the question "Who owns Asian American studies?"

Indeed, the perception that Asian American studies is no different from other traditional disciplines is shared by both people in the community and students alike. Some community folks want to work with us only because we have access to a large pool of volunteers—i.e., students. A few significant exceptions aside, there have not really been too many attempts to include the students in decision-making and organizing efforts.

On the other hand, even those students in Asian American studies usually do not expect to incorporate the Asian and Pacific Islander communities in their course work. Consequently, when students do go out to the communities, they often end up doing the kind of "missionary" work that comes to characterize most community service. That is, it is very one way: Students "give" to the communities only, but they do not become a part of them. This in turn reinforces the separation of the two.

Furthermore, the changing background and ideologies of students who are taking Asian American studies today are also what made teaching community activism more difficult than I have anticipated. As I stated earlier, I have tried to put everything in the context of the mission of Asian American studies as it was established, and slowly I was beginning to realize the obvious fact that we are not in the sixties anymore.

The students who took APALDP that first year was of a different breed. They were ideologically diverse, which, frankly, was a surprise to me. With an emphasis on community activism, I thought the course would attract students who were already knowledgeable of, committed to, and/or passionate about community issues. Instead, the class was polarized by small factions of progressive students and self-identified conservatives. Both groups tended to dominate most class discussions. The majority of the students, however, were either "middle-of-the-road" or apolitical, who generally remained silent.[6]

In spite of political differences, an overwhelming majority of students knew somehow that the communities need help, but were unwilling to ask the tough questions, i.e., Why do they need help? How do the present conditions of the communities represent a legacy of racist and classist oppression that still persists to this day? Uncritical involvement in the communities is like a bandage that only covers the wound and cannot stop the pain. It might be benevolent, but it is still missionary.

Since I emphasized labor issues, most of the students became really resistant to a few ideas presented in class, while others adopted slogans and became champions of the working class without much critical analysis. What was distressing to me also was how classroom discussions had at times been reduced to simplistic labeling and name calling. For instance, when we engaged in an exercise dealing with class differences and dynamics, it was immediately branded as "socialist." When a vocal student raised her hand to make a comment, others who usually disagreed with her on other topics would make faces or tune out. I myself had been accused of trying to "convert law-school-bound undergraduates into leftist union organizers." We eventually sorted out many of these misconceptions and managed to have a very productive second quarter. However, the classroom dynamics were very different from what I had anticipated in the beginning.

Again, my inability to react effectively to these different viewpoints has to do with my romanticization of both the communities and, especially, the students. My assumption that the students would readily agree to one version of what the communities need could not be more false. Eventually, I have found that, while I need to be clear where I want my students to be, it is just as important, if not more, for me to understand where they are at.

For example, for the first quarter in APALDP, students were put into different groups to organize a campus event in order to learn about collective processes. The groups that I created were meant to reflect some semblance of gender, ethnic, and political diversity. The last would be inevitable even if the groups were chosen randomly. Some of the progressive students often complained that other group members were too mainstream and conservative. Though all of these progressive students had been active on campus or in the communities, they had managed to avoid working with people with vastly different ideologies—until now. Some of them expressed impatience and were ready to give up on them. One particular student became depressed once because she hit someone on the shoulder in the heat of an argument. It wasn't anything serious, she assured me, but she never thought she would resort to violence. In many ways, their frustrations were similar to mine. We had been racking our brains trying to get these "mainstream" and "conservative" students to see things our way, to get them to move from their locations to ours. However, we had been doing it without thinking about and trying to understand where it was exactly that they were coming from.

It was very easy to label people. What was worse, though, was when the progressive students perceived people they labeled "conservative" as enemies or obstacles in their struggles, instead of allies that could be won over. Any kind of consciousness can take years to acquire, and behavior often takes longer to change. The Los Angeles uprisings of 1992, for example, have turned many Asian American students, particularly of Korean descent, into activists, some of whom were taking APALDP. However, many of them forgot that at one time they were not too different from their fellow students in the class and that many personal battles of values are internal and invisible on the surface.

Similarly, I strongly believe that many conservative students, however steadfast they seem in their publicly expressed opinions, fight internal battles of their own. I am reminded of a journal entry a conservative student wrote for my class reflecting on a community event that he attended. He wrote:

> One particular piece [of the performance] I liked was done by a Japanese American. It started with him complaining about all the F.O.B.s ["Fresh

Off the Boat"] and how they are making life hard for the Americanized Asians with their accents. He talked about how he used to yell at his Mom for speaking Japanese in public and he never realized why until now. He yelled at her because all the times others made fun of him, he was taking it out on his Mom. Throughout the entire play, I was thinking this person is exactly like me. A mirror image. Everything he spoke about I went through. I too separated myself from the FOB's in high school and yelled at my Mom for speaking Chinese in public. I never realized why until this past weekend.

When I look back on my life, it is strange to see how much I have changed in a short period of four years. The person I was back in high school seemed so different from the person I am today. Although many would still characterize my ideology as mainstream and conservative, to me, I know I have come a long way. However, the process of "understanding" and "realization" has often been muddled and confusing. I guess that is why I keep taking these damn Asian American [studies] classes.

From talking with other students and professors, I gathered that the students who took my class were representative of the general population that is taking Asian American studies right now, at least at UCLA. They self-identify as Asian Americans without realizing the political implications of the term[7]; it is only a convenient tool to assert one's cultural pride. This is an important, and even necessary, first step to activism. However, when we stop at that, we, in Karin Aguilar-San Juan's words, "make the dangerous mistake of equating the process of acquainting ourselves with our ethnic, linguistic, religious, or historic roots with activism against racism."[8] To these students, their "Asian-ness" is asserted "often without a larger context in which they might see connections to other issues, and other communities."[9] This is both unfortunate and problematic because more substantive issues of racism and class oppression are shunned for the sake of forming a personal identity. But, I ask, have we become so self-involved that we actually think it is possible to form one's identity apart from others' struggles?

To help them overcome this egocentric activism, I must first understand where they are coming from. Regardless of economic status and political ideology, all Asian and Pacific Islander students have at least encountered "name-calling" racism. When they are pulled over by the police, it is likely that they would be asked whether or not they speak English, and it makes little difference that they have just finished their 180-page senior thesis on the virtues of Reaganomics. When angry Asian students demonstrate in a rally, there would be a few people telling them to "go back to where you came from," and it makes little difference that they and their parents and their grandparents were born here. Furthermore, most college-educated Asian Americans are also preoccupied with job discrimination, especially in the professional sector. Therefore, when qualified professors whom they respect can be denied tenure, they know they too will hit the glass ceiling some day when they are trying to realize their lofty aspirations.

Recognizing their difference from the mainstream often motivates them to take Asian American studies, but it is not enough to make a connection to the daily race and class oppressions of our communities. That needs to be worked on in a more sophisticated way. One example is the Garment Workers Justice Campaign, which is a case study I use in APALDP to illustrate the intersection of racism, classism, and sexism, and the exploitation of immigrants in this country. In the garment industry, the powerful manufacturers are not legally held responsible for the horrible working conditions of the seamstresses. The subcontractors serve as an insulation between the most powerful capitalists and the disenfranchised immigrant workers. Many APALDP students came from a law-and-order background, and they did not quite understand the rationale behind the campaign's focus on targeting the manufacturers, who have not broken any law. Therefore, we had to go into a discussion of who makes the laws, if laws are always just, who has power and influence in this society, etc. This discussion brought questions to many beliefs that some students had long held and helped the class move beyond an impasse.

Similarly, when I showed *The Fall of the I-Hotel*, a 1983 film by Curtis Choy about the eviction of *manongs* (first generation Filipino immigrants, who typically came to the United States in the 1920s and 1930s) living in San Francisco, many students in class could not identify. I asked them to think of "home" not as a geographical and physical reality, but as a mental and emotional sense of belonging. Then I asked them how many times they had been asked to evacuate their "home" for others' convenience.[10] I reminded them that the reason marginalized peoples were exploited time and time again is because they were often disenfranchised and unorganized, which led the powerful to believe that they could exploit them and get away with it. No matter how much they believe material success on an individual basis can protect them from the ugliness of hatred and oppression, when they are just individuals, it is just as easy for those who took everything away from the manongs to do the same to them. This is so because, as long as they remain mere individuals, they are not challenging the way race and class are translated into power and powerlessness. We can't afford to throw anyone away.

Though a surprise, that many of these students were taking APALDP was what made this class such a learning experience for me. It challenged the way I thought about students in Asian American studies. They were there voluntarily because there was already an interest in working in the Asian and Pacific Islander communities. But only when I figured out where they were coming from was I able to keep them interested enough to stay. Only then could I move them further by linking issues, making connections and eventually entrenching ideologies. To do the last, I had to be willing to challenge long-held beliefs, show their contradictions and offer alternatives—and must do so in this order. I had to use whatever got them here in the first place to move them further. Although all of them knew of my leftist inclinations, I don't think I would be as effective if I were to take the direct approach of simply lecturing on Marxist thinking, for example. They were not blank slates, but thinking human beings with critical abilities. Again, to get them where I wanted them to be, I had to start where they would start. Hopefully, once they filled up enough gaps themselves, they would be able to see the larger picture.

When it comes to missing the larger picture, the progressive students, in spite of their politically correct rhetoric, are not exempted. A lot of them see their academic responsibilities as obstacles in their activism. Consequently, many of them develop a disdain for their course work. In APALDP, that translated into a disdain for deadlines. When their grades suffer, they often rationalize it by thinking the classroom is less important than the "real world." What these students overlook is that they could be a unique asset to their communities because of their access to Asian American studies. Asian American college students are "virtually the only sector in our community today able to enjoy the benefits of Asian American Studies." This emerging power, writes Glenn Omatsu, "also carries with it a new responsibility: the need for students to share their knowledge and resource with others in the Asian American community."[11]

Meg Thornton, my coworker and coordinator of S/CP, also "sees the privileges and power of today's students in relation to the needs of the poor and the working poor." Asian American studies provides a source of self-knowledge and self-empowerment for the students. While "the vast majority of Asian Americans, especially adult immigrants, will never be able to take such classes in their lifetimes . . . students, she believes, can fill this vacuum by sharing their resources."[12] Because access to higher education is denied to recent immigrants and the working poor of our communities, many of our brothers and sisters are not aware of the racist history of this country. Consequently, they only see attacks on the poor and the people-of-color communities as isolated incidents, not the legacy of racism that predates the birth of this nation. Before Proposition 187, for example, I would have a difficult time explaining to my family— recent Chinese immigrants from Hong Kong—the relevance of the Chinese Exclusion Act in our lives. But as attacks on immigrants and immigration "reforms" become more ferocious and meanspirited, they are beginning to see the connection. This is only possible because I was willing to engage them in such discourse throughout the years, despite ridicule and condescension. Now when new anti-immigrant bills make their appearance in our local media, my family turns to me for my analysis. I know many of our students have experienced this transformation of their family in the last few years as well. And it is precisely because we are willing to take what we learn in Asian American studies and other classes back to our people that we are able to elevate the discussion in our communities. Disdain for academics does not automatically translate into better organizers.

Furthermore, sometimes students are so caught up with the logistics of activism that they forget movements are for real people who lead real lives. To broaden their concern with self-empowerment, one question we constantly have to ask the students is "Who is the movement for?" For example, in an action of the Garment Workers Justice Campaign, the students decided to send a targeted manufacturer, Jessica McClintock, a human-sized Valentine's card. On this card, students would write messages to demonstrate their support for the exploited garment workers. However, students wrote words like "bitch" and "white devil," which reflect more of their own frustrations than the actual struggle of the workers. An internship supervisor reminded me once that internship projects affect real lives and are more than just a grade. Students need to be sensitive to that, and we need to hold them accountable.

So in linking the students with the communities, we often have to remind them of the larger picture. But to be in a position to hold them accountable, we have to be out in the trenches with them, which sometimes means working with the students on the campaigns. I have found that the most productive time spent with students is sometimes in the communities. Given the fact that I am a novice in this field, my presence in the communities has given me credibility among the students. It also affirms what they are doing as important. One student has actually told me that, while most professors encourage their students to visit their offices to talk about their classes, they have no idea how much more of an encouragement it would be for her if their time together was spent in the communities, rather than just sitting in an office far removed from everyone else.

To prevent crisis and burnout, we need to be sensitive also to the limitations of being a student. For example, some students are so caught up with community activism that their academic work is neglected. Some encounter resistance to their involvement from their family and friends. Working in the communities often propels students to question their ideologies; the struggle to make better sense of the world often causes confusion. And increasingly, when the word "higher" in higher education refers to the cost rather than actual learning, many students have difficulties juggling school, work, and activism. Accessibility is the key here.

We have to be there to encourage them, and help them prioritize and sort out issues. It is important to realize that we cannot solve every problem for them and should not try to. But simply lending a sympathetic ear can be a most supportive thing that one can do to a depressed student.

While students need to be pushed to assume equal partnership in the communities, the communities often are just as blind to the potential resources inherent in students. One of the major complaints we received from APALDP students doing internships in the communities was that their field supervisors did not know how to work well with them. They had a difficult time distinguishing a student intern from a volunteer. Sometimes, students were treated with condescension. One student related to me an experience he encountered once in a community function, where someone actually terminated a conversation with him when that person found out he was "only a student" and had no business card to trade with him.

Students are not considered important and worth dealing with. Very often, they are relegated only to menial, clerical tasks. To be sure, no one is above the nitty-gritty work, definitely not in community-based organizations with a staff of one or two. However, when students are excluded from the decision-making process, when community leaders do not provide them with a context under which their organizations operate, both the students and the communities lose out. It reinforces the same sort of "missionary" attitude that needs to be adjusted. While we spent half the time reminding the students how much they can realistically accomplish with an internship, we spent the other half helping the supervisors to come up with concrete and creative ways they can engage the students in their work, instead of just having them as spectators.

Korean Immigrant Workers Advocates (KIWA), I think, provides one of the best examples of students working with the community. Even before the organization was established, Roy Hong, KIWA's cofounder and current executive director, consulted students on the need for an organization focusing on labor and workers' rights. There is presently a student on its board of directors, and students feel just at home in their office as they do in mine. One of the reasons why their boycott campaign against Jessica McClintock has been so strong is because they have successfully tapped into the resources of college students. They claim co-ownership of the campaign and compose the majority of the people who devise strategies, complete preparation work, and demonstrate in the rallies. Students have been able to do a lot of outreach and recruitment on their own campus as well as others, something that KIWA, lacking an adequate staff, cannot do on its own. From their involvement, students not only became educated about labor issues in the communities, but they also fortified their leadership and analytical skills, their commitment to the communities, and their self-confidence. To be able to act on behalf of the communities to change the relations of power, to no longer remain silent but to recognize and use the strength of one's voice: that is empowerment.

S/CP strongly believes that students in Asian American studies and the Asian and Pacific Islander communities exist in a symbiotic relationship. Not entrenched in the normalized ways of the communities, students sometimes provide fresh perspectives and challenges to the status quo. In communities bolstered by post-1965 immigration, people often lack a sense of history and analysis in this country, especially when it comes to people-of-color resistance. This is a vacuum that students, armed with Asian American studies, can fill. Working in the communities provides an opportunity for students as well, to ground their knowledge in day-to-day living, to synthesize the mind with the heart, the past with the present and the future, and to move beyond the missionary position.

There Ain't No Borders No More . . . Are There?

I first presented the initial version of this paper at the national meetings of the Association for Asian American Studies (AAAS), held in 1994 at the University of Michigan, Ann Arbor.

The theme of the 1994 AAAS conference was "Border/Crossings." I was fascinated by the slash mark between the two words, meaning a line situated at the border that gives us a space to decide whether or not to cross it, which implies there is a choice. This is interesting to me as a Queer Asian man because crossing borders for me is at once an option and an obligation. But as I and two other graduate students were going into Ann Arbor for the first time, we had this conversation with our white cab driver who had always wanted to live in Los Angeles. "But I would stay out of Compton, if you know what I mean," he offered. I didn't know if I should construe this as a racist remark from a white man who considers himself a liberal. Lost in my own confusion and unable to respond, one of the graduate students replied, "It's not just Compton anymore; it's everywhere."

That was the truth, and the truth always gets me thinking. "There ain't no borders no more," I agreed. The Korean merchants in Los Angeles know it. So do the Chinese couple selling burritos in downtown, telling jokes in Spanish to their Chicano customers. And I am beginning to discover that, whenever I come out to my friends and family, I am pulling them into my world: they *have* to deal with my sexuality. There ain't no borders no more.

But just when I was getting ecstatic with my new discovery, I ran into a wall on the first day of the conference—not a border, mind you, but a wall. It was towards the end of the first plenary session when both scheduled speakers, Richard Fung and Trinity Ordona, had concluded their presentations about Queer APIs. The majority of the audience immediately left their seats. They headed for the reception at the back of the auditorium, even though Dr. Lane Hirabayashi was introducing Ms. Michelle Tamotsu Trevino, a counselor from the Cultural Unity Student Center at the University of Colorado at Boulder, who would tell us the new developments of Amendment 2. This antiqueer amendment was passed a year before in Colorado and is appearing in different forms across the country. (Incidentally, the conference was moved from Boulder, Colorado, to Ann Arbor, Michigan, because of the passage of Amendment 2.) People continued to abandon the presentation for the back of the room, all the while talking to one another and ignoring what was happening on stage. They talked louder and louder, even after AAAS President Kenyon Chan took the microphone from Dr. Hirabayashi and issued a warning, even after the speaker from Colorado was greeted by scattered applause from the few people who had any sense of decency and respect. Although Michelle struggled to talk over the noise in the auditorium, it became obvious that she and the few people left in the audience were distracted.

I was very offended. Perhaps I shouldn't make this singular incident a manifestation of something larger, but I couldn't help but think this is what is wrong with Asian American studies today. We can intellectualize sexuality, we can talk about border/crossing, but when it comes down to real issues of oppression, people opt for free food. There was this wall I saw before me, and it was a wall erected by academics around themselves. Asian American studies marked the beginning of a social movement for progressive change for our communities, but I would think twice before entrusting the Asian American movement now to most of the people in the auditorium that day. They may be able to subvert the language in many different ways, throwing punctuation marks here and there as if slashes and parentheses were mass-produced by transnational capitalists. But are they truly subverting the power structure?

After twenty-five years, I thought to myself, the integration of students and the communities remains to be one of the greatest challenges of Asian American studies. I hope more of us will pick up the gauntlet.

Notes

1. Student/Community Projects (S/CP) is one of five units with the Asian American Studies Center at UCLA. Other S/CP projects and functions include:

(a) the annual Research Roundtable, a conference that brings academics and community leaders/activists together to talk about research relevant to the communities; (b) *Asian and Pacific Islander Community Directory*, a compilation of Asian and Pacific Islander community organizations to facilitate networking among and access to the Asian and Pacific Islander communities; (c) advising on student programming for organizations sponsored by the Center, including the Asian Pacific Coalition, a coalition of more than twenty Asian and Pacific Islander student organizations at UCLA; and (d) independent study with individual students or a group of students who want to become involved in the Asian and Pacific Islander communities, conduct more in-depth research of the communities, or develop courses not taught by the Center or on issues neglected by Asian American studies in general.

2. Is "Asian American" a biological fact or a socio-political construct? How do more recent immigrants and underrepresented APIs (e.g., Queers, Pacific Islanders, etc.) challenge the notion of an Asian pan-ethnicity?

3. How and why are cultural values propagated and transformed? What happens when traditional values become barriers, rather than assets, for APIs, especially for those of us who are women or Queer (or both)? How do differences between generations in terms of degree of acculturation create conflicts in our communities? How are our cultural values being manipulated by the mainstream society against us (e.g., the model minority myth)? What impact does it have on public policies, legislation, and popular sentiments?

4. The Justice for Garment Workers Campaign and the mobilization against Proposition 187, an anti-immigrant initiative in California, serve as good examples of how these oppressions are interconnected. They illustrate that the struggles of people of color and the working class are often a common one.

5. Tony Chambers and Christine E. Phelps, "Student Activism as a Form of Leadership and Student Development," *NASPA Journal* 31, no.1 (1993): 19–29.

6. "Progressive," "conservative," "middle-of-the-road," and "apolitical" are actual words that students used to describe themselves and each other in the class, in private conversations, as well as in written assignments. My own definition and analysis of API "conservatives" are influenced by my conversations with Glenn Omatsu and his article, "The 'Four Prisons' and the Movements of Liberation: Asian American Activism from the 1960s to the 1990s," which appears most recently in *The State of Asian America: Activism and Resistance in the 1990s*, Karin Aguilar-San Juan, ed. (Boston: South End Press, 1994), 19–69. Particularly helpful is a section within the essay entitled, "Strange and New Political Animals: Asian American Neo-Conservatives."

7. Yen Le Espiritu's analysis of the political development of the term "Asian American" (and the community) is particularly useful. See *Asian American Panethnicity: Building Institutions and Identities*, (Philadelphia: Temple University Press, 1992), 1–52.

8. Karin Aguilar-San Juan, "Linking the Issues: From Identity to Activism," *The State of Asian America*, Aguilar-San Juan, 8.

9. Aguilar-San Juan, "Linking the Issues," 9.

10. Anna Devere Smith of "Twilight: Los Angeles 1992," once said in an in-

terview that, as people of color in America, we all come from a place of "home-lessness": the idea that people who have more than one identity, and have more than one home, yet at the same time they cannot claim any of them as fully theirs.

11. Glenn Omatsu, "Asian Americans: 'From Margin to Center'?" *Amerasia Journal* 19, no. 3 (1993): 197–98.

12. Ibid., 198.

15

Vietnamese American Studies: Notes toward a New Paradigm

CHUNG HOANG CHUONG

Vietnamese American Studies: Here to Stay

In 1995, the community celebrated the twentieth anniversary of Vietnamese migration to America. Twenty years are indeed short if we compare to the migration history of other Asian American groups, yet it is an important point in the American experience of the Vietnamese American community. The second generation are now entering college in large numbers at many higher learning institutions. From the initial challenge of learning English to the issue of intergenerational differences, the community has gone through many changes. There were moments of glory with remarkable educational achievements among the youth and there were also moments of crisis with infighting among community leaders. One thing is for sure: the Vietnamese American community is here to stay. Gone were the arguments that there will be a massive return exodus predicted by conservative elements. Instead, there were many return visits (but not many opted for a plan for reintegration to the old society). More and more, the second generation feels at home in America. They have become part of this multicultural society.

Concomitantly, Vietnamese American studies has taken off in the 1990s. It has established a place in Ethnic Studies programs, Asian American studies (AAS) departments in California as well as other parts of the country, and in colleges and universities which have experienced large enrollments of Southeast Asian Americans. As one of the first to have developed and taught an ethnic-specific course along these lines,[1] I no longer feel alone in navigating the new waters of Vietnamese American studies. At San Francisco State, in the fall of 1996, Vietnamese American courses, such as AAS 370, 372, and 375, filled up fast after a few days of preregistration. University of Massachusetts at Boston, San Jose State University, the Universities of California at Berkeley, Los Angeles, and

Davis; De Anza College, and San Francisco City College, all have one or more courses on the Southeast Asian experience.[2] Many of my colleagues have done extremely well at each of these institutions. We have grown to a sizable enough group to warrant several panels in Ethnic Studies and Asian American studies conferences.

There are many questions and topics for discussion that I would like to address in this chapter. How do we approach this subject area of Vietnamese American studies? What are the current models in application? What is our main focus or changing focus given the changes in the population? What textbooks do we use? What emphasis do we put in the introductory course? How do we go about developing new courses? This volume is indeed a wonderful opportunity to share and discuss pedagogically and philosophically the topic of Southeast Asian Americans. I hope this is an auspicious beginning for an ongoing discussion, and even perhaps some of us will take on the initiative of organizing panels and workshops around this topic in upcoming Asian American studies conferences.[3]

Establishing the Bases

The courses on the Vietnamese American experience which I developed at the University of California, Berkeley, in the early 1980s were among the first such offerings in the United States.[4] As I recall, even with two courses on Vietnamese Americans at Berkeley, there were many important issues that we could only cover superficially. Every semester, new materials are added and discussed in the context of changing resettlement patterns and postresettlement issues within the Southeast Asian community.

Subsequently, colleagues such as Hien Duc Do and Katharya Um provided new angles of analysis by presenting the Southeast Asian experience from their own respective discipline as sociologist and political scientist. Collaboration and joint research work with other Asian Americanists brought out issues such as the "scatter approach" applied to the Southeast Asian refugees in sending them across the fifty states. The approach was very similar to the policy adopted by the U.S. government in the aftermath of World War II when more than 100,000 Japanese Americans were unjustly incarcerated. Japanese American internees were also forced to disperse after their release from the camps.[5]

With the increase in the number of Vietnamese students in many of the campuses in the California State University system, there is definitely a need to offer more courses in Vietnamese American studies. The question here is: should we follow other Asian American studies models? At San

Francisco State, for example, Asian American studies offers three courses on the Chinese in America. AAS 310 discusses the experience of Chinese Americans in general. AAS 315 looks at the Chinese American personality, and AAS 322 focuses on the Chinese American cultural identity as expressed in the language and literature. In looking at the available and increasing literature on Vietnamese Americans, I have to say that we can safely follow the existing approach. Naturally, there must be some variations in the subtopics as well as the contents of each of the courses. For example, in AAS 370, which covers topics on Vietnamese American creative expression, we should devote a great deal of time covering the richness of Vietnamese American literature written and published in Vietnamese.

In the fall of 1996, we began to offer two new courses on Vietnamese American studies here at San Francisco State University (SFSU). These new courses will be instrumental in exploring and bringing forward the new issues that have been overlooked or, due to their controversial character within the community, remained largely untouched. I am referring to the political changes in Vietnam as well as the reaction of the overseas community with respect to these changes. There are an increasing number of leaders who feel that it's time for conciliatory feelings toward the home country (although there are still, of course, a few who continue to think that the war is not over). Other such issues are: what is our stance concerning the affirmative action debate? Should we be joining other minority groups in combating a new rise in anti-immigrant sentiments? How do we approach broad-based coalitions? The issue of welfare reform will hit the Vietnamese community hard. How do we prepare for this? Those are indeed important issues that must be included and addressed in Vietnamese American studies courses.

New Directions

Currently, most of my topics for the semester-long AAS 370 course address contemporary changes in the community. Issues such as identity, intergenerational differences, discrimination, and youth problems associated with growing up in America with a different home culture are examined and discussed. Not surprisingly, we come across more materials debating this new Vietnamese American identity by younger writers. Along with these essays and articles, there are also writings of many Vietnamese who returned to their homeland for a visit and who felt that the reconnecting experience was truly eyeopening and inspiring amidst protests and concerns from their parents and relatives who still harbor hostile feelings due to their refugee experience. Those are among the many issues associated with the changes in perspectives within the community and between generations.

Indeed, after keeping the same focus for several semesters—with an examination of the Vietnam/American War, the aftermath, the refugee movement with its respective demographic characteristics, and the challenges of the resettlement process—my Asian American studies 370 course includes extensive materials and discussion on two other important aspects of this migration: 1) the resettlement programs and their characteristics at the three levels: federal, state, and local; and 2) the impact of such policies, government programs, and services on different refugee communities at selected geographical concentrations and times of arrivals. In fact, there are new studies that compare and contrast the government service recipients' reactions from their point of view.[6] As active participants in the various programs, how do they cope or adjust to these policies with different sets of personal strategies? In other words, in addition to their intent, what is the actual outcome of "planned" refugee policies? We also need to look at the differences between specific states' refugee policies: for example, why did California attract far more Vietnamese than the rest of the country? What are the factors that have facilitated secondary migration there? At least at this stage, and in terms of examining colleagues' courses outlines, I found the same focus and approach, with some variations that reflect the local context of resettlement and community issues.

Other important topics included in the course revolve around discussions about forced migration—what is a refugee? What is the official definition of a refugee based on the research of Kunz, Loescher, and Zucker and Zucker, all of which acquaint students with the concepts of unplanned population movement, political asylum, and the effects of massive refugee movements across international borders.[7] As a resettlement country, what are U.S. policies on specific groups of refugees and the "quality of mercy" organized by the international relief organizations?[8] Life in the refugee camps is also covered with special attention given to the countries of asylum, such as Thailand, Malaysia, and Hong Kong. How did these countries cope with unwanted and sudden population influxes? What happened to these policies vis-à-vis the change of heart of the world community, when "compassion fatigue" took over? These are new course topics that help students to understand the changes both in the United States and Southeast Asia.

Finally the last third of the course involves an in-depth examination of the resettlement process in the United States which covers a number of issues in regard to adjustment. The situation in California is examined closely because it is the state with the largest concentration of Southeast Asians. Quickly, I found out that a fifteen-week course would not do justice to the many issues and challenges that confront the Vietnamese American community. With the arrival of the second generation, the political changes in the home country, the warming up of relations between two former enemies, we have to bring up new issues that must be included and discussed in class. Yet, I found myself quickly running out of time.

The Future of Vietnamese American Studies

It is not too early to think of new courses that cut across ethnic groups and experiences. The notion of pan ethnicity can be introduced along with cross-generational issues.[9] Topics such as educational issues, community politics, and public policy issues can span across Asian American groups. Recently, the issue of youth violence became very prominent in the community, with increasing attention by the mainstream press. Yet, within the community, few ethnic newspapers dare to tackle the issue or at least provide a forum to discuss the problems openly. On the other hand, when a call published in Vietnamese newspapers by the FBI encouraging Vietnamese Americans to report so-called communist activities, some leaders quickly took side without allowing time for possible dialogue and discussion in assessing the effects of such police and surveillance action within the community. There was definitely a split between younger Vietnamese American reactions and older individual leaders on this important issue when law enforcement tactics were perceived by the younger group as divisive and creating an atmosphere of fear and mistrust within the community. As always, it is all too easy to get sidetracked by emotional issues.

So far, with a good ten years of Vietnamese American studies, we have fulfilled the first phase of developing a component of Asian American studies. Looking at the next step, there are indeed a wide range of issues and tasks. How do we "export" this area of Asian American studies to other campuses with large Vietnamese student populations? How do we develop new scholars in this field? What is our research agenda for the 1990s and the next millennium? How do we obtain the full support of the community? Where can we find resources? How do we create a partnership with the community for long-term projects?

In addition, what are our priorities for the next ten years? What are the newly emerging issues in the postresettlement era? What are the psychological changes that could affect the Vietnamese American family? What constitutes Vietnamese American identity? How do we go about empowering the community? What is the most efficient way to engage in mainstream political processes? What kind of opportunities as well as issues could emerge when the United States and Vietnam get closer? What are the current political and economic changes in Vietnam that could affect the community abroad? Finally, how do we build a broad coalition with other Asian American and minority groups in the midst of this conservative climate and anti-immigrant feelings?

SFSU's Vietnamese American Studies Center

As of this writing, in response to these questions, San Francisco State University is establishing a new Vietnamese American Studies Center. The last two years saw an increase in joint academic activities and exchanges between San Francisco State University and many institutions in Vietnam. Several SFSU delegations went to Vietnam, including one headed by our president, Dr. Robert Corrigan. Vietnamese academics in return scheduled a San Francisco stop in their itinerary. Asian American studies at San Francisco State University is connecting with the Southeast Asian studies program at the Vietnam National University in Ho Chi Minh City in regard to a number of different research projects. Other SFSU colleges and departments are exploring various areas of exchanges and research. So far, the Vietnamese American Studies Center has prepared the groundwork for the following activities:

1. Opportunities will be created for SFSU students to study and engage in research projects in Vietnam. Vietnamese American students in particular will benefit from such educational exchange programs.
2. Students will have opportunities to learn Vietnamese, Vietnamese history and culture as these courses will be available by way of faculty exchanges and joint research projects. Preliminary inquiries indicate that there are needs and interests among the Asian American student population.
3. Both the SFSU and Vietnam universities will engage in extensive research and publication projects. Currently, we are planning an international conference on urban changes and development in Vietnam in 1997 with the participation of SFSU faculty, researchers from the Social Science Committee of Ho Chi Minh City, the department of Southeast Asian Studies, Vietnam National University of Ho Chi Minh City, Can Tho University, and the National Institute of Agricultural Planning and Projection in Hanoi.

Needless to say, there will be obvious psychological gains from the point of view of the Vietnamese American students who will be able to reconnect with their roots, understand postwar issues in Vietnam, and the challenges related to the development of a new era of relations between this country and Vietnam. Furthermore, the generation gap will be narrowed when the American-born and the 1.5 youth (i.e., those children who were born in Vietnam but raised in the United States) better understand the experiences and the differences that have kept countries and generations apart for so long.

Vietnamese American studies is growing. At one time it was hard to find materials dealing with the refugee experience. Now, the list of Vietnamese entries is getting longer in the yearly update of our Asian American bibliography. To maintain this level of commitment, we still need to encourage our own Vietnamese American students to look seriously at this area of specialization simply because they are the best at examining, studying, and presenting the issue from their own vantage points. There are opportunities both within the community and in the academy. It took quite a few years of struggle and hard work for Asian American studies to get to this stage since the first two voluminous anthologies *Roots* and *Counterpoint* were published back in 1971 and 1976, respectively.[10] Vietnamese American studies has benefited from this precedence and we must follow this lead, only at a faster pace this time. For example, a glance at the available literature can assure the Vietnamese American studies specialists that they can indeed choose from many new reading materials for their classes.[11]

It took longer than a quarter of a century or more than a generation for the Chinese Americans to reconnect with their homeland. Indeed it was not until the late seventies that Chinese Americans made the return trip to visit their birthplaces. For Japanese Americans, the war and the internment experience have shaped the community in such a way that it took many years to come to terms with this particular experience via the redress movement engineered by the Sansei generation. For the Vietnamese Americans, it took less than twenty years to reconnect with the homeland. In fact, within one generation, the Vietnamese Americans were able to reunify with their families as well as return to Vietnam for visits. With the emerging ease of traveling and the new relationship between the two countries, how do we approach the teaching of Vietnamese American studies in the year 2000? What should be included in the new course outline? In fact, diaspora studies have been looked at seriously by many institutions.

Within the last few years, with frequent interaction and exchanges between the diasporic community and the homeland, we have to look at what this relationship means and the possible act of reconciliation. What are the steps and what kind of problems do we foresee? A new psychological situation emerges as the second generation feels very differently about the war and the place their parents once called home. They do not have the same hostility and the same hatred that their parents, even today, find difficult to forget and to forgive. Many have returned and felt instantly attracted to villages, landscapes, and city streets they only remember vaguely. Many returned to help, and others got involved in education and health projects. These actions are based on genuine feelings. Given these perceived changes, what is the future role of the Vietnamese American community with respect to Vietnam? What are the divergent views on this issue of reconciliation and reconnection with the homeland?

Thus, it is important to look at a new paradigm for the teaching of Vietnamese American studies based on these rapid changes that happen within the community, in America, and in Vietnam. The pattern has shifted from a community facing survival problems to a community that begins to engage in the political process. Increased voter registration and a local candidate expressing interest in a government office show a different community agenda. A younger and more vocal leadership is taking the helm in building the capacity of the community. In the midst of these changes, other social issues emerge quickly: gambling, the youth issue, the rising divorce rate, the question of language maintenance, life and opportunities in various Vietnamese enclaves, and the new Amerasian arrivals. They must certainly be addressed with studies and given possible solutions.

Toward a Culture of Diversity

No formula carved in stone can offer a specific paradigm for Vietnamese American studies. Only sensitivity and flexibility will allow us to appreciate conditions in a changing community. From courses aimed at introducing the refugee experience and looking primarily at migration's impact on the local community, Vietnamese American studies courses must now look at the postresettlement stage after the first movement in 1975. Political changes from both sides of the Pacific Ocean require some rethinking. Vietnamese American studies cannot rely on the cold war theory to explain the causes of the Vietnamese migration; rather, we need to look at the new transnational exchanges and population movements from a global economic perspective. Increasingly, migratory labor movements within Asia are comprised of mostly women. No one can deny their new economic role. The new Asian world order comprised of tigers and dragons in Southeast Asia challenges the older migration theories. The directions of these population movements have also shifted dramatically with new opportunities in Asia. America is not the only choice as final destination but only one of the choices or simply a stopover. The movement back across the Pacific has already taken place in this day and age of transnationalism.

If this will be reality in the not too distant future, can we then establish a relationship between Vietnamese American studies and Vietnamese studies or Asian studies? From my own point of view, this could be very beneficial to both disciplines. Can students major in one and minor in the other? With such a background, graduates would be in a better position to take full advantage of the opportunities here at home and abroad.

Closer to home and straight ahead, the Vietnamese Americans experiencing discrimination and many other problems in their resettlement realize that they cannot stand alone to face the dismantling of programs and services. Increasing anti-immigrant feelings with the passage of proposition 187 and 209 threaten community survival. It is not true that Asian immigrants and refugees will not be affected as legal entrants as some of the leaders tend to portray. The Vietnamese American community cannot stand alone in this struggle. We need to reach out and form new alliances and solidarity that Yen Le Espiritu found to be important and essential in the protection of the rights and interests of the less powerful groups.[12] The growth of Vietnamese American studies is inevitably linked to the survival and development of Asian American studies as well as Ethnic Studies.

Vietnamese American studies has made the first important step. The tasks ahead for current and future Vietnamese American specialists are crucially important. We must always readjust and rethink in facing new challenges. The second generation is now entering college in large numbers. This group is very different in terms of thinking, needs, and aspirations. Will the second generation of these immigrants and refugees be any different from those of the other Asian American immigrant groups? When and how will Vietnamese become an integral part of Asian America and treated as equals? Responding to these many questions, Hanh Thanh Cao, a young Vietnamese American wrote: "Our time has come, our challenge to redefine 'mainstream,' and our vision of a culture where the dominant element is diversity. The Vietnamese American is now part of that element. It is necessary that we must identify with that element for it means our own survival in America."[13]

Notes

1. In spring 1981, I taught the very first course on Southeast Asian American studies at the University of California, Berkeley. I had almost thirty students the majority of whom were Vietnamese immigrants. I had time to cover: the range of

demographics of the different refugee groups from Southeast Asia, the migration process, and some aspects of the resettlement. The emphasis, however, remained largely on the refugee experience and the concept of Vietnamese American identity which was quite new for the majority of my students who came from the very first Southeast Asian immigrant movement in 1975. The following semesters saw an increase of students from various ethnic groups. They made up almost half of the class roster. Asian American Studies 125 soon reached fifty to sixty students per semester at UC Berkeley.

2. I learned that my colleague, Professor Pham Cao Duong, was teaching the same course at UCLA and my friend, Professor Peter Kiang, is advancing very steadily along the same direction at the University of Massachusetts at Boston. In ethnic studies, Professor Yen Le Espiritu at UC San Diego and Hien Duc Do at San Jose State University are active in contributing and expanding the field of Vietnamese American Studies. For us, it was a very rewarding moment when we had our very first panel at the annual Association for Asian American Studies Conference with an interested audience who shared in the discussion various perspectives and experiences from across the country. Along with these important academic activities, Vietnamese American students are increasingly active on their own campus with conferences, symposia, and annual meetings, bringing professors, students, and community members for discussions on issues in the local community. Conferences organized by Vietnamese American students at UC Berkeley, CU Boulder, UC Irvine are examples of such efforts. We witnessed the "coming of age" of Vietnamese American studies.

3. This is definitely a first attempt to generate future dialogue and hopefully this exchange and sharing of ideas will continue with many more colleagues joining in the conversation through face-to-face meetings or in the wide world of cyberspace. (The idea of setting up a web site to enhance and facilitate this exchange and dialogue would not be too difficult to implement.)

4. Several semesters of AAS 125, which I described above, with increasing enrollments led to the preparation for a new course, AAS 126, that looks specifically into the various refugee policies and the effects of these policies on the overall resettlement process.

5. See, for example, Roger Daniels, *Prisoners Without Trial* (New York: Hill and Wang, 1993), and Harry H. L. Kitano, *Japanese Americans: The Evolution of a Subculture* (Englewood Cliff, N.J.: Prentice Hall, 1976).

6. Steven Gold and Nazli Kibria, "Vietnamese Refugees and Blocked Mobility," *Asian and Pacific Migration Journal* 2, no. 1 (1993): 32.

7. See Egon F. Kunz, "The Refugee in Flight: Kinetic Models and Forms of Displacement," *International Migration Review* 7, no. 3 (1973): 53 Gil Loescher and John A. Scanlan, *Calculated Kindness* (New York: The Free Press, 1986); and Norman L. Zucker and Naomi Zucker, *The Guarded Gate* (San Diego: Harcourt Brace Jovanovich Publishers, 1987).

8. Peter Rose, *Working with the Refugees* (New York: Center for Migration Studies, 1986).

9. Yen Le Espiritu, *Asian American Panethnicity* (Philadelphia: Temple University Press, 1992).

10. Amy Tachiki, et al, eds. *Roots: An Asian American Reader* (Los Angeles: UCLA Asian American Studies Center, 1971); Emma Gee, et al., eds. *Counterpoint: Perspectives on Asian America* (Los Angeles: UCLA Asian American Studies Center, 1976).

11. In this new emerging area of Vietnamese American expression and specifically in the literature, *The Other Side of Heaven* and *Once Upon a Dream* can be a good survey of the Vietnamese American writings. Lely Hayslip's *When Heaven and Earth Change Places* (New York: Doubleday, 1991) and Nguyen Qui Duc's *Where the Ashes Are* (Addison Wesley Publishing Company, 1993), provide two examples of contemporary Vietnamese autobiography. Wendy Duong's "From Madame Butterfly to the Statue of the Awaiting Wife in Northern Viet Nam: Feminity Between Two Worlds," *The Ky* 21 (1994) and Qui Phiet Tran, "Contemporary Vietnamese American Feminine Writing: Exile and Home," *Amerasia Journal* 19, no. 3 (1993) give a us a good look at the Vietnamese woman's experience and the exile literature produced in the native language. In a number of *Amerasia Journal* articles, essays, and reports, authors introduce the emergence of Vietnamese American voices, sociopsychological issues, and patterns of settlement. Those who would like to address the issue of identity and personality can indeed refer to James Freeman's *Hearts of Sorrow* (Stanford: Stanford University Press, 1992), alongside the work of Gold and Kibria, and other articles from a wide range of sources: *Amerasia Journal, Journal of Ethnic Studies, Journal of Refugee Resettlement, International Migration Review, Diaspora, Journal of Refugee Studies*, and from Australia, the *Journal of Vietnamese Studies*. The Vietnamese experience in Canada and Australia can indeed be added to the reading list with published works by Nancy Viviani, *The Long Journey* (Melbourne: Melbourne University Press, 1984) and Louis J. Dorais, Lise Pilon Le, and Huy Nguyen, "Exile in a Cold Land," *Lac Viet Series, No. 6* (Boston: University of Massachusetts, William Joiner Center and Yale Center for International and Area Studies, 1987).

The materials contained in those books focus on the psychological effect of forced migration, the refugee experience, and the consequences of internal population movements, known as secondary migration. From the refugee status to the new Vietnamese American identity, these materials can be the basis for a course that addresses the various problems that an incoming Vietnamese immigrant has to face. Complex issues such as the changing role of the Vietnamese woman, the intergenerational differences, and the issue of communication or lack of communication within the family can be examined in depth. Comparing to the available materials in Japanese American studies and Chinese American studies, it seems that we have much less. However, there are also new sources such as newspaper reports, Vietnamese ethnic magazines, and other articles that bring out important current issues.

12. Le Espiritu, *Asian American Panethnicity.*

13. Hanh Thanh Cao, "Vietnamese Identity as a Fortress: The Case of Andrea," *Horizons* 1, no. 2 (1992).

16

Empowering the *Bayanihan* Spirit: Teaching Filipina/o American Studies

EMILY PORCINCULA LAWSIN

Diaspora and the Studies

Filipino studies is constantly evolving, just like Asian American studies. We now have scholars who study Filipinos in the "diaspora" all over the world, not just in the United States.[1] These new perspectives, revolving around transnational movements and migrations, have clearly produced significant data as well as global vantage points. Both, in turn, allow us to place locally-framed representations into a broader comparative context, which is of undeniable value.

As an equally significant contribution, Asian American studies can offer the means to reconnect that same diaspora to the heritage of struggle and accomplishments that characterize the history of Filipinas and Filipinos in the United States. In this sense, historical knowledge can continue to serve each generation as a source of strength and pride. And, as I indicate below, in regard to Filipina/o American studies, strength and pride are the key resources that enable our students to reach out to others in solidarity.

The Filipina/o American Experience

In my few years as a college instructor, I have been fortunate to have taught and tutored many subjects, from such broad topics as Introduction to Asian American Studies, Introduction to Women's Studies, and Developmental Reading and Writing, to more specific topics in Asian American Literature and the Filipino American Experience. Of all of these, teaching "Filipino American Experience" courses has probably been the most rewarding, challenging, and important in my own development as a scholar and as a Filipina American.

187

When I moved from Seattle to Los Angeles, I was rather intrigued by the denotation in UCLA's course catalog of a course entitled "Pilipino American Experience."[2] Experience? How could one teach someone the whole "experience" of a people? Surely in a ten-week quarter (six weeks during summer session), some "experiences" would be privileged over others. What "experiences" would or could those be? Who is to say that their experience as a Filipino American is (or isn't) more worthy than others? Why not simply place the course under the rubric of "Filipino American History," if that is what the majority of the readings pertain to? After enrolling and sitting in on numerous Filipino classes taught by various scholars, I can understand UCLA's denotation now: it is quite an "experience."[3]

The students in Filipino American Experience courses don't just learn historical facts, dates, and figures; we interact with numerous community members (not just "leaders"). We study each other's families; we engage in transnational debates; we visit community sites; we learn about culture and history through living, reliving, reading, reciting, revisiting, remembering, and relating, using various common languages: food, emotion, and devotion to a *bayanihan*—community—spirit. Romanticism aside, these are the bases on which we can construct a pedagogy for teaching the Filipina/o American experience. And when I say "we," I mean it as both a former student and as a current instructor because each party to the pedagogical transaction is constantly learning and continually working to expand the field of Filipino American studies.

Bayanihan Spirit: Back to the Barangay

In his path-breaking book *Pasyon and Revolution*, Philippine historian Reynaldo Ileto examines popular movements in the Philippines by looking at what he calls "history from below;" that is to say, investigating history from the common people's perspective, in indigenous languages, rather than through the colonizer's lens.[4] This is a prevailing concept in the Filipino American Experience course as well. Although we may not read entire texts written in Filipino languages, we do read extensive oral histories and journal entries written by Filipino Americans. By doing this, students get a firsthand account of what community life was actually like in the past.

Many students have particularly enjoyed readings by lesser-known authors as much as those that have become more popular. For example, in light of the supposed dearth of information on Filipinas, I weave readings on women through every week of the course. The most compelling for students has been a compilation of diary excerpts written by Angeles

Monrayo Raymundo from 1924 to 1927.[5] Raymundo, a second-generation Filipina, documents her daily life as a twelve-year-old growing up in
a "strike camp" led by the famous Pablo Manlapit in Oahu, Hawaii,[6]
and her family's subsequent move to agricultural camps in San Lorenzo
and San Ramon, California. Coupled with more in-depth studies, Raymundo's diaries give voice to the people whose lives were affected by
such historical events. Students then respond and relate to the events in
creative ways, sometimes even acting out Raymundo's stories during discussions. They then compare her diary to the oral histories and photographs contained in their main textbook, *Filipinos: Forgotten Asian
Americans*, by Fred Cordova.[7] The discussion remains as a constant
point of reference and carries over weeks later in the semester when we
discuss their other texts, films, and guest speakers, whether they deal
with "Pinay Power"—Filipina American Women's issues—or more contemporary youth issues, or the mainland's migrant labor force.

By constantly engaging Ileto's concept of learning "history from
below," rather than just from the mouths of infamous leaders, we create
a learning environment that reflects the spirit of indigenous Philippine
culture and social organization. During the introduction to the course,
we spend a few sessions discussing the history of the Philippines, in relation to its colonization by Spain and the United States. By doing this, we
not only learn about the concepts of colonialism, racism, capitalism, and
imperialism, but we also set a foundation for employing indigenous concepts of a communal society, a *barangay*. The students learn that barangays were, at the most basic level, small, egalitarian, Pre-Spanish
communities based on kinship, common economic interests, and shared
rituals.[8] They identify with this concept and agree to treat our classroom
as a barangay where we practice a collaborative approach to education,
rather than reinforce the practice of individualistic competition for
grades.

From Principles to Praxis I

These principles are then carried out in numerous ways throughout the
semester: through class discussions, community participation, and term
projects. Each student is expected to contribute something to the barangay. Each week, discussions are led by a group of students who sign up
for topics from the syllabus that correspond with their interests. Each
group is encouraged to use creative techniques in their discussion and
asked not to preach or lecture, remembering their goal of cooperative
learning.

A portion of each student's final grade also involves participation in the local Filipino American community. Since we are learning about different communities, each student is expected to "experience" some aspect of the larger community. They can do this by participating in educational conferences, forums, or even rallies, or by attending a community tour of "Filipino Town" and other areas that were once known as "Little Manila" in Los Angeles. The tour is usually the high point and most memorable part of the course.

In Los Angeles, the community tour has become popularized by Professor Royal Morales, better known as "Uncle Roy," who used it as a way for students to earn extra credit in the Pilipino American Experience course that he taught at UCLA. In doing so, he made the course a truly multidimensional one, by employing different teaching strategies and hands-on techniques. Since his retirement from teaching in 1996, Uncle Roy still leads tours for numerous campuses and organizations. The tour is usually led and narrated by him, other Filipinos who grew up in the area, and/or myself. In buses borrowed from the university or the City Council, the students and their invited guests visit historical sites, social service agencies, businesses, churches, the Filipino library, a community garden managed by senior citizens that is also home to a historical mural, a Filipino arts and crafts store, and of course, a Filipino restaurant. They not only see places and meet people they've read about, but also engage in discussions with old-timers and community workers, thereby learning how institutions and networks are at the core of a territorially based ethnic community. At the same time, they find a space outside of the classroom where they can bond together as friends and members of their own barangay—one of spirit, mutual regard, and cooperative endeavor—that can also persist irrespective of such territorial boundaries.

The major portion of the course involves a term project that the students can carry out individually or in a small group. They can opt to write a traditional paper based on an oral history interview, or volunteer with a community organization for the semester. Whatever option they choose, it must contribute something "new" to the barangay, in this sense, to the field of Filipino American studies. If they choose to do an oral history, they are given a multitude of options regarding how they choose to present the interviews, either via an artistic presentation like a video or photo display, or a play or short story, or via a more traditional format like an expository essay. Many of the students choose to write an essay and create accompanying photo exhibits, including color laser photocopies of their interviewee's artifacts, using excerpts from their interviews as captions. Each semester, the projects I receive get more and more elaborate. In fact, one semester, based on a suggestion from the department chair and the university archivist, the entire class erected an exhibit in the lobby of the campus library. The exhibit continues to be displayed at different events and locations. In this fashion, over the course of the semester and beyond, these students become multimedia educators as well.

From Principles to Practice II

In the past, a few students have chosen to intern or volunteer with a community organization as their term project. Like the exhibit exercise, this option demands much more intense administration and creativity by the student, the host organization, and the instructor. The organization must be a local Filipino one or an agency that somehow serves the needs of Filipinos. The few students who have chosen this option have been individuals who feel that they have either written too many oral history papers for their other classes and/or that an internship would help them become more involved with the larger community.

In the first few placements, I learned that the way we set up these internships determines their value and usefulness. The usual procedure is that the intern meets with me more often than other students; we discuss their interests and career aspirations. I then suggest a couple of places that may match their interests in some way. For example, one student who wanted to go into medicine or public health interned with a local clinic that serves many Filipino elderly and teens. Another student who wanted to be a filmmaker worked with the director of the local Asian American media archive on a five-minute video montage. Depending on their dedication, these internships can enhance the students' access to related opportunities. In these two cases, the first student got a job at the clinic the next semester and the second is now helping to produce a Filipino American film.

Initially, the most difficult part of an internship project is coordinating the placements and finding an organization willing to work with a student for such a short period of time. The placements have generally been with people whom I know personally through my own work in the community. They graciously take on the student as a favor to a friend, rather than as a slave for their organization. Fortunately, I haven't run out of friends yet, but this is clearly not the best way to set up the positions because they can be sporadic and few. Subsequently, difficulties can arise when some expectation is not fulfilled, either by the student, or in the context of the internship itself.

Lack of time and direction can also complicate the situation. The project that the students work on at the site must be manageable enough to complete within a few weeks. In addition, the fact that the site is usually off campus and that the course is not solely "field" based, makes more work for the instructor. Coordinating such placements may be easier if done through a campus internship program that regularly handles such procedures. Such programs are rare on most campuses, much less one administered by an Asian American studies advisor.[9] A more effective procedure may be to set up the parameters of a few internships before the semester starts and then offer those options to the students who may want them, or to offer it as the sole option to the entire class. This may limit students' choices somewhat because the positions will be less individually based, but it does provide more direction in the long run. When everything goes well, the results are gratifying. An example of one of the most effective internship projects, initiated in this case by a small team, was to bring Filipino high school and community college students onto campus for a weekly discussion about issues affecting them and the community. It was effective because the students designed it in conjunction with the community service that they did for their Filipino American Students Association (FASA). Now FASA plans to continue the program as a recruitment and retention mechanism, thereby enlarging our barangay on campus.

All of these kinds of collaborative pedagogies reinforce our principles for creating a maximally effective learning environment for Filipino American students: fostering a community spirit while simultaneously promoting creativity, critical thinking, and engagement. Each type of project serves a twofold purpose: it reinforces students' sense of identity, while they also serve the community. Most of the students usually donate their tapes, exhibits, papers, and other materials to the local chapter of the Filipino American National Historical Society, the Pilipino American Reading Room and Library, and/or the Asian American Studies Reading Room for other students, scholars, and community members to view. In doing so, they make a contribution to and investment in the re-creation of barangay in the spirit of bayanihan.

The Validity of Ethnic Specificity

When I was still in graduate school, I was insulted by one senior Asian American studies professor's interrogation of such ethnic-specific courses, when he said to me and others, "What purpose do they serve in advancing a pan-Asian community?" My response was both personal and professional: it is such courses that attract underrepresented students who then, in turn, re-energize and re-create the very notion of community.

In my sophomore year of college, I was flunking calculus and chemistry, so I was getting pretty bored with my pre-engineering courses. As a dutiful daughter, I was studying to be an engineer to complete my father's educational dreams that were disrupted by the onset of World War II in the Philippines. Fortunately, an insightful and caring Asian academic counselor recommended I take a few courses that would really interest and inspire me. "Emily, why don't you take some Asian American studies classes? With your extracurricular activities, I think you may enjoy them," she said, referring to my many years with the Filipino Youth Activities organization of Seattle.

"What's that? I don't want to study Asians. I'm Filipino," I said.

"Filipinos are considered Asians. They study Filipinos in the course too."

"I don't know," I said, convinced that the elective credits would be a waste of money. At the time, I was putting myself through school, so every class counted.

"O.K., well, there's another course on Filipinos taught in the same department. Maybe you would like to try that one. You are supposed to take a prerequisite course, but talk to the professor and see if he'll let you in anyway," she said.

Little did I know how much that short conversation would change my entire life. I think of that moment every time I design a new course, change some part of my curriculum, or meet despondent students. At the beginning of each school year, I tell a new generation that story, and it's as if I'm looking in a mirror. These students tell me that they do not feel an affinity towards learning about "other" Asian Americans until after they have learned more about themselves. Nonetheless, in the course that I teach, we take a comparative stance, examining similar and different histories of other Asian ethnic groups, in order to build a deeper understanding of the commonalties that people of Asian descent in the United States share. So, in the final analysis, ethnic-specific courses are key to Asian American studies if we are to expand the field of scholarship about underrepresented groups that is available. Students in these courses can and do play a central role in developing cutting-edge research and disseminating it to wider audiences.

Recent Developments at California State University, Northridge

I have had an opportunity to implement these same pedagogical principles at California State University, Northridge (CSUN). By way of background, although there have long been Filipina/o Americans in the San Fernando Valley and on this campus, there were no Filipina/o course offerings until after I was hired. Now, three years later, the students who have taken the Filipino American Experience course have consciously taken up "the struggle" for recognition and retention of Filipinos. These students, Filipino and non-Filipino alike, have organized amongst themselves, on their own, with little or no guidance from faculty or staff, to bring Filipino American scholars, community workers, and performers to campus. These activities exceed the requirements of the course. More recently, a group of them have founded a committee they call "SPAHM" (not to be confused with the luncheon meat delicacy) which they proudly translate as, "Students for a Pilipino American History Month." In their first year of organizing, the SPAHM committee was able to obtain funding from the Associated Students governing body to have a series of ten different educational events during the month of October.[10] As a committee of FASA, they also brought other speakers to campus later on in the year. FASA then went on to win a record of four awards from CSUN's Associated Students, including "Best Student Group" and "Best Student Programming," a remarkable feat considering that the previous year the campus newspaper refused to recognize their efforts. Their efforts are inspiring and invigorating, for the programs they have produced have been avenues for them to showcase what they each have learned about Filipino American history. They have, in essence, mastered the idea of "putting your education to work," a goal to which all of Asian American studies should aspire.

Promises and Agendas

Because it was so underemphasized in earlier years, there are solid reasons to prioritize the diasporic dimension to the contemporary Filipino American experience as we approach the turn of the century. However, this cannot and should not blind us to serious, ongoing issues that face us in the United States. It is no secret that there are far too few Filipino professors teaching Asian American studies. By offering the kind of course I've outlined here, we hope to see our numbers on campus reach parity with our larger population, both at the chalkboard and behind the desk. With Filipinos being the fastest growing Asian immigrant group in the United States, the second largest Asian group in the nation, with roots that stretch back to the year 1587,[11] one would think that Filipino American studies would be the most advanced topic within the field of Asian American studies, but it is not.

In his reflective essay entitled "Pilipino American Studies: A Promise and an Unfinished Agenda," Royal Morales describes the 1970s as a "decade of promise" for our field and the 1980s as a "time of retreat and retrenchment," when institutional cutbacks and attacks on affirmative action and Ethnic Studies began to surface.[12] In that 1987 article, Morales ponders the future, specifically, whether the promises made (that

Pilipino American studies would flourish), will be fulfilled. Now, more than ten years later, Morales, query is still unresolved, and sadly, the struggle has been made even more difficult in light of passed anti-immigrant and anti–affirmative action legislation.

Uncle Roy goes on to delineate three demands we need to make in order to expand Pilipino American studies' future in American academia: 1) we must demand funding to improve and expand the curriculum, 2) we should demand more teachers who will be sensitive to Filipino community issues, and 3) we must strengthen campus and community ties. By offering Filipino studies courses, we are indeed expanding the curriculum and hopefully continuing to strengthen campus and community connections. In addition, we now have many more Filipino scholars seeking and securing their masters and doctoral degrees, as well as tenure-track jobs. However, it is also no secret that some of our *kababay-ans*—our compatriots—have also been passed over, have had positions promised to them taken away, have been denied tenure, or are stuck in part-time lectureships with little or no job security.

Our message to those in the higher echelons of academia and Asian American studies is: "We are in the academic pipeline, now let our people flow!" Clearly, our demands will not be fulfilled without a political sensibility that revolves around community solidarity and activism. By teaching Filipino American studies and other ethnic-specific courses, we provide a mechanism which can keep academia accountable to the growing community and vice versa, while enlarging the base of students who continue to take other Asian American studies courses.

Notes

Author's note. My deepest thanks to Lane Hirabayashi for his patient editorial advice; to Joseph Mahony and Marvin Rosete for their technical assistance with this chapter; and to Don Nakanishi, Enrique de la Cruz, and Kenyon Chan, for allowing me to implement these strategies on their campuses. Many thanks also to Scott Kurashige and teaching assistants Allan Aquino, Louie Ulanday, Lisa Casabar, and Zita Diamante-Nguyen, for enduring my unending trials.

1. Two examples of this literature are Vicente L. Rafael, ed., *Discrepant Histories: Translocal Essays on Filipino Cultures* (Philadelphia: Temple University Press, 1995); and Linda Basch, et al., *Nations Unbound: Transnational Projects, Postcolonial Predicaments, and Deterritorialized Nation-States* (Langhorne, Penn.: Gordon and Breach, 1994).

2. The spelling of Pilipino with a "P" rather than with an "F," as in Filipino, is used in UCLA's course catalogues and student census, in recognition of the shift in political identity in the 1960s social movement for self-determination. Other California campuses have also used the "P" designation; however, the use

of the "F" has been more widely used in course descriptions nationwide. In a similar vein, Professor Dorothy Fujita-Rony and other scholars have been advocating more recently for the use of "Filipina/o," to emphasize the inclusion of the more-neglected histories of Filipina women into the field of study, much like the movement of Chicano studies to "Chicana/o" or "Chicana and Chicano studies."

The spelling choices can become confusing in the classroom, where more than one student wrote throughout their essays: "P/Filipina/o Americans," to which I responded with bold-faced circles: "CHOOSE ONE." Since then, I have made it a point to spend extended time in class discussing the issue of naming and colonization through a section that Professor Royal Morales cleverly titled "To P or Not to P," essays, cartoons, and journal articles that I've compiled on the heritage of Pinoy—Filipino American—words, which discuss not only their spelling, but their historical origins.

3. As we do not learn in a vacuum, I thank veteran Filipino and Filipino American studies professors Dorothy Laigo Cordova, Fred Cordova, Peter Bacho, Linda Revilla, Royal Morales, N.V.M. Gonzalez, Steffi San Buenaventura, Michael Salman, and Enrique de la Cruz for welcoming me into their classrooms and their homes. I also thank professors Tania Azores, Arleen G. de Vera, Jon Cruz, James Sobredo, Eric Reyes, Leny Strobel, Oscar Campomanes, and Joan May T. Cordova for sharing their insights, syllabi, and friendship throughout the years.

4. Reynaldo Clemeña Ileto, *Pasyon and Revolution: Popular Movements in the Philippines, 1840–1910* (Quezon City, Philippines: Ateneo de Manila University Press, 1989), 1–27.

5. Angeles Monrayo Raymundo, "Excerpts from the Diary of Angeles Monrayo Raymundo, 1924," *Lost Generation: Filipino Journal* 1 (1991): 31–41; and Angeles Monrayo Raymundo, "Diary Excerpts of Angeles Monrayo Raymundo, 1927," *Generation Insights, Reflected Memories: Filipino Journal* 2, no. 2 (1992): 3–13. Both excerpts are from the journal published by the Santa Clara Valley chapter of the Filipino American National Historical Society.

6. For other readings on Filipinos in Hawaii, see for example, Miriam Sharma, "Labor Migration and Class Formation among the Filipinos in Hawaii, 1906–1946," in *Labor Immigration Under Capitalism: Asian Workers in the United States Before World War II*, Lucie Cheng and Edna Bonacich, eds. (Berkeley: University of California Press, 1984), 579–615; or *Social Process in Hawaii* 33 (1991), a special issue on "The Filipino American Experience in Hawai'i, in Commemoration of the 85th Anniversary of Filipino Immigration to Hawai'i," Jonathan Y. Okamura, Amefil R. Agbayani, and Melinda Tria Kerkvliet, eds. This volume also includes a bibliography on the topic, compiled by Alice W. Mak.

7. See Fred Cordova, *Filipinos: Forgotten Asian Americans* (Dubuque, Iowa: Kendall/Hunt Publishing, 1983). For a life history comparison, we also read Craig Scharlin and Lilia V. Villanueva, *Philip Vera Cruz: A Personal History of Filipino Immigrants and the Farmworkers Movement* (Los Angeles: UCLA Labor Center, Institute of Industrial Relations & UCLA Asian American Studies Center, 1992), as well as over five hundred pages of photocopied articles.

8. See Renato Constantino, "Baranganic Societies," in *The Philippines: A Past Revisited* (Quezon City, Philippines: Tala Publishing Services, 1975), 24–39, for more details. Naturally, this move entails a creative re-appropriation of tradition. Open-ended discussion is useful here, in order to point out the positive and negative aspects of barangays, including class and gender differentials, which need not be adapted wholesale.

9. At UCLA, the Asian American Studies Center has a "Student-Community Projects" unit that can help with such advising, but not all campuses do. *Maraming salamat* (many thanks) to Meg Thornton for her support in implementing such projects.

10. Since 1991, the Filipino American National Historical Society has deemed each October as "Filipino American History Month" in commemoration of the first documented landing of Filipinos in what is now known as the continental United States in October 1587.

11. For more on the first Filipinos in what is now the continental United States, see Lorraine Jacobs Crouchett, *Filipinos in California, from the Days of the Galleons to the Present* (El Cerrito, Calif.: Downey Place Publishers, 1982), 5–17; Marina E. Espina, *Filipinos in Louisiana* (New Orleans: A. F. Laborde & Sons, 1988); and Eloisa Gomez-Borah, "Filipinos in Unamuno's California Expedition of 1587," *Amerasia Journal* 21, no. 3 (Winter 1995/1996): 175–83.

12. Royal Morales, "Pilipino American Studies: A Promise and an Unfinished Agenda," *Amerasia Journal* 13, no. 1 (1986–87): 119–24.

17

Building Community Spirit: A Writing Course on the Indian American Experience

ROSANE ROCHER

Nothing I have done as a scholar or as a teacher ever led me to reflect on the nature, authority, and purpose of knowledge as much as offering for the first time a writing course that challenged students to explore their experiences as members of a first generation born of Indian immigrants to be raised in the United States. These students turned their collective experience into a shared knowledge that can be of service to themselves and their community. In such a student-centered course my function was not that of an authority-endowed teacher but that of a midwife helping knowledge that demanded to be born. For students parturition was at once painful and exhilarating. Only after the first edition of the course was over did I read Kenneth A. Bruffee's book on collaborative learning.[1] Like Bruffee when struggling to organize freshmen composition courses for large numbers of ill-prepared students, like Lane R. Hirabayashi when faced with a different student population for his courses in Asian American studies (AAS) when he moved from California to Colorado, I responded intuitively to feeling less than adequate for the task at hand by empowering students.[2] I will henceforth turn into a purposeful method a technique that was born of necessity.

Since the reasons why I felt less than adequate and why the course was a necessity are the very grounds on which my method was developed, I must start with some personal and institutional background.

I am not a specialist in Indian American studies (IAS), nor even in AAS; I am an Indologist with principal expertises in classical Sanskrit and in the Indian-British intellectual encounter in the late eighteenth and early nineteenth centuries. I am not IA, nor even AA; I am a member of the class of the 1966 "brain-drain" immigrants from Belgium—the "brain" was that of my husband; I was at that time wifely baggage, unempowered

199

by my one-year-old Ph.D. Although I am a veteran of wars against sexism and tokenism in and out of the academy, I have not had to endure
racism. While I lack the characteristics featured in the last three letters of
the WASP acronym, I am undeniably W, and I am constantly reminded
of the oppressive character of that congenital trait when IA students who
have been raised and educated in the United States and do not have a
trace of an accent treat my foreign-born, -raised, -educated, -accented
self as more "American" than they are. Why, with these disabilities, I
was impelled to offer a course on the IA experience was a matter of
institutional necessity.

In recent years the University of Pennsylvania (Penn) has attracted an
increasing number of IA students and of AA students generally. In the fall
of 1993 the proportion of AAs in the full-time undergraduate student body
was 17 percent and growing.[3] Among these, students of South Asian descent constitute one of the three largest groups.[4] Undergraduate classes
offered by the Department of South Asia Regional Studies, including language classes, have become populated by a majority of IA students.[5] Faculty used to seeing as their primary function the "deparochialization" of
the curriculum and the indoctrination of mostly European Americans in
the importance of Asia, and of South Asia in particular, have had to assume a new role, that of providing for South Asian ethnics the fundamen-
tals of cultural recovery.[6] I have gone a long step further. Student need has
turned me into a campus lobbyist for the creation of an AAS program and
for the improvement of support services for AA students. I have also been
impelled to introduce a writing course on the IA experience.

The proximate cause for initiating a course on the IA experience was
nonetheless a push from a different quarter, Penn's introducing a writing
requirement to take effect with the entering freshmen class of 1993.[7]
Prompted by the deparochializing rationale that students should not
write exclusively about Western topics, I undertook to transform into a
full-fledged writing course the writing-intensive freshmen seminar I had
taught for the prior five years on "India in Western Eyes" and which
aimed at exposing the cliches and stereotypes about India that are ram-
pant in Western writings.[8] Convinced that students write best about what
they are most interested in, and since my old course consistently attracted
a majority of IA students, I resolved to make IA students' concerns central to my writing course. I knew the urgency of these concerns from
papers with recurrent titles such as "Who am I?", "Self-hatred," and
"Growing up a Coconut" which students had turned in, even though
they were only tangentially related to my old course.[9]

When I realized that I was engaging on the path of IAS with the handicap of not being IA, or even AA, I tested the waters with leaders of the

South Asia Society (SAS), several of whom had taken my old course. Not only did they give me a green light, they also became enthusiastic partners in the development of the course. Besides holding several planning sessions in my office in May 1993, during which we drew up a list of issues of major concern to young IAs, I budgeted some of the monies my department received as an incentive to sponsor a writing course for us to attend at the Association for Asian American Studies meeting in Ithaca, New York, in June 1993. It so happened that Sucheta Mazumdar was paving the way of SAS leaders to attend that conference so that they could report on the active role they had played during the federal trial of alleged perpetrators of a hate crime against an IA doctor in New Jersey.[10] At night, as my student friends and I huddled, we discussed at length the reluctance they had met in their community to face up to anti-Indian racism of a more violent kind than the commonly acknowledged glass-ceiling problem and to resort to concerted community action for redress. I was as prepared as I could be to meet a like resistance on the part of students in my writing class.

Setting aside the research project I had planned to work on, I spent the summer of 1993 preparing a syllabus for a writing course on the IA experience. Reading up on IAS and AAS through the summer alleviated my lack of knowledge, but, however comforting, the endorsement of the SAS leadership did nothing to solve the congenital problem that I was not of optimal ethnicity for an IAS course. It was crucial that I not appear to be a teacher or a judge, but that students be engaged in a collaborative voyage of self-discovery. Course process needed to be addressed even before course contents.

I took a series of principled steps to remove myself as a teacher and to appear only in the role of a facilitator. There would be no lectures, of course, but only discussions of assigned readings and of the students' own writings. In order to counter students' propensity to write for a readership of one, their teacher, I set up tasks in such a way that they would write for specific groups of peers: the SAS leadership, the editorial board of *Mosaic: Penn's Asian American Literary Arts Magazine*, and readers of the campus newspaper *The Daily Pennsylvanian*. Students were also told that, since documentation on the post-1965 IA experience is at present limited to that of the immigrant generation and to the concerns expressed by that generation about their offspring, theirs are new, precious voices. They were asked to write their papers as documents about the concerns, problems, choices, and aspirations of their generation, and I vowed to preserve them for the collective memory of future IA generations and for the use of scholars. They responded to these tasks with waxing confidence and pride.

For the purpose of peer review, which is recommended for good writing, students were divided into groups of five, in which they commented extensively on the first drafts of their teammates' papers.[11] I unfortunately neglected to provide for a crucial step, reading aloud and discussing revised versions in the entire class. In their wisdom, students found ways to return to their and their peers' papers for full discussions. Providing systematically for periods in which all short papers are read and longer papers presented in abbreviated version—which I had planned only for their final papers—would have contributed to removing myself even further as the sole recipient of their work.[12] It would also have allowed students to better gauge the quality of their written work relative to that of others in the class, and it might have made them less anxious to be formally graded during the course of the term.[13] A decision that served me in good stead was not to prepare a firm syllabus. I had perforce to choose a set of readings before the beginning of the semester, but I decided to assign work in successive handouts, so as to reserve opportunities to look into my students' faces, to listen to their voices, and to steer my course accordingly. Most risks I took panned out; mistakes were mostly on the side of caution.

Since most IA students at Penn come from post-1965 immigrant, professional, suburban families, who have not lived in closely knit communities and who see nothing wrong, at first, in being labeled a model minority, I thought that it might be prudent to begin the course reading parts of the Helwegs' book, *An Immigrant Success Story*,[14] and to alternate sets of texts that I had assembled in a reader and that offered contrary points of view. Students were, however, more sophisticated than I expected them to be in criticizing the book for focusing too narrowly on the most successful segment of their community, and they were so taken with the texts collected in the reader, which offered them novel perspectives, that we cut short reading the book, which I know now need not be assigned for the next edition of the course.

First Paper

For their first essay, assigned to be written in the first person singular, students were asked to feature a defining moment in their identity. Since I was concerned that they might not be prepared this early in the course to lay bare their feelings for reading and discussion by peers who were still strangers, they had the option of writing about issues other than ethnicity—"defining moment" was the key. Yet the models with which they were provided and which were discussed in class were short pieces that Penn students, most of Korean ethnicity, had published in *Mosaic*,[15] and students were asked to write their papers for possible submission to that AA magazine. All but one chose to write about defining moments of ethnic identity and/or cultural recovery; the one student who did not wrote about the most traumatic experience that had shaped her.[16] Hiding feelings was obviously not a concern.[17] Students gave eloquent expression to feelings of pain, shame, confusion, insecurity, isolation, alienation, loss of culture, severance from grandparents back in India, resentment at being perceived as Indians in America and as Americans in India, and anger at cruel jokes and other forms of verbal harassment. In a general discussion which they initiated and which took on the characteristics of a collective catharsis, young people who had grown up deprived of IA peers or who confessed to having, in the past, avoided associating with other IAs, marveled at, and bonded over, their shared experiences. Yet they resisted interpreting repeated instances of insults and slights as evidence of a pattern of racial prejudice on the part of the majority community, but insisted on viewing them as isolated episodes to be dismissed as the lapses of an "ignorant" few. More progress might have been made if the discussion had been planned and if the papers had been read to the entire class, as will be done in the next edition of the course. Yet it was evident from these first papers that what IA students yearned for—and claimed to have achieved—was a sense of triumph at having overcome obstacles, or, as one student put it, a restoration of "pride, joy, and dignity."[18]

Second Paper

Unlike the first essay, which was intended to express personal feelings, the second paper, assigned to be written in the third person plural, required students to act as detached observers and describers of the behavior of others. Students were asked to attend a social, cultural, religious, or political gathering of IAs and to write a report that focused on the behavior of the younger generation in attendance. The putative readership for their reports was that of the campus newspaper, *The Daily Pennsylvanian*. In preparation, students read and animatedly discussed in class two scholarly pieces devoted to their generation.[19] With a few notable exceptions,[20] papers focused on what students termed the generation gap, and more specifically on poor communication between immigrant parents and their American-raised children. Paper after paper described functions in which groups of parents and children sit apart, eat different foods, and do and talk about different things and in different languages. Students reported amply about tactics developed by teenagers to get around their parents' ban on dating and described an atmosphere in which all are conscious of what goes on, yet maintain a cloak of ignorance and obfuscation. Though they demonstrated an acute awareness of how treasured and nurtured IA children are, in the general discussion many expressed sorrow at their inability to talk about topics other than school with one or either of their parents. They also fretted that, in what they took to be their parents' struggle to establish themselves financially, there had been little time to impart to them an understanding of their cultural and religious heritage, which they saw only as empty rituals and phrases in an inaccessible language which youngsters avoid participating in or sit through under duress. Under these circumstances, several expressed pessimism about the likelihood that Indian culture will be maintained in the United States. It is this hunger for cultural recovery that impels IAs in droves to take courses on Indian culture when they enter college; it also makes the Hindus among them vulnerable to transnational right-wing organizations that take on benevolent hues for diasporic populations that are eager, yet uncertain of how best, to preserve and transmit their cultural and religious traditions.[21]

Third (Midterm) Paper

For their third and longer paper, which was assigned at midterm, students were given a choice between a research paper, a bibliographical essay—an option that none took—and a critical essay based on literary texts. All options required students to make use of library resources. A special session was arranged for a reference librarian to introduce them to database searches and other efficient uses of a large research library.[22] In addition to being technically informative, the library session was a booster for students, in that it demonstrated that the IA experience—and the AA experience generally—is the subject of sustained and library-enshrined literary production and scholarly inquiry.[23] In reinforcement, a library assignment challenged students to identify the several locations in which fieldwork was conducted for a number of books, and a prize was promised to the student who, in the judgment of his/her peers, made the best nutshell oral report on a book of his/her choice.[24] Preparation for the paper also included three sets of readings.

The first set of preparatory readings, buttressed by the videotape *The New Puritans: The Sikhs of Yuba City*, featured pre-1965, mostly West-Coast, rural-labor immigration and the impact of Asian exclusion laws.[25] The discussion of these documents revealed that students in the class had no prior knowledge of, yet were thrilled to learn about, this part of their community's history. Students registered little anger at the discovery of past legally mandated discrimination, which they chose to view as a chapter of an ancient history that no longer cast shadows on the present, and they focused their comments on the pride they took in the way pioneer generations had overcome adverse conditions. I resolved not to drive the point, but to let the collocation of this set of readings with the next speak for itself.

The second set of preparatory readings offered gripping testimonies and a scholarly analysis of contemporary anti-Indian racism.[26] Even though I anticipated that students might be reluctant to acknowledge the reality and occasionally violent character of anti-Indian racism, I was nevertheless taken aback by their attempted denial. Till then, they had heard only muted echoes of hate crimes perpetrated by "Dotbusters" even in nearby locales.[27] Although they readily admitted the existence of color prejudice within their community, they took pains to recast racial attacks against IAs as resentment by displaced groups against the success that immigrants from India have had in taking over failing businesses and making them profitable. When asked to formulate steps for future action, they did not call for social, political, or legal redress, but only suggested ways to make besieged IA communities less clustered and less visible. Several students sought to discredit the testimonies of victims by describing them as "exaggerated," and some pointed to the immigrants' prejudices against American culture and to their unwillingness to assimilate as the proximate causes of their problems. I was able to redirect some of the discussion by reacting to statements such as "This is like living with the KKK! That's not America!" with an "OK, let's discuss the KKK and its place in America." I brought in the parallel of rape victims to suggest that "some might say" that victims are sometimes blamed for the perpetrators' crimes—a point that seemed to register at least with women in the class. Yet the resistance was overwhelming.[28] In this session it became almost unbearable for me to refrain from thrusting my views upon students. The European American student apparently felt likewise, since it was the only occasion on which he was prompted to blurt out an admonition, "Listen, you guys, you've got to face it. There are a lot of closet racists out there. You've just got to face it!" Yet the class failed to come to a satisfying closure. As we left, battered, bruised, exhausted, and distraught, I asked students to give some more thought to the issue and to write up further insights during what happened to be the midterm break.[29] In their written comments they admitted that the evidence with which they had been confronted was "upsetting," "disturbing," and "shocking," and that it made them "angry," even "furious"—sentiments the expression of which they had repressed or directed at other targets during the discussion. The culture in which they were brought up has taught them that voicing anger is both impolite and an admission of failure to resolve problems, but anxiety and resentment simmered under a lid they labored to keep tight. Reading their comments made me realize that the unsatisfactory discussion we had had was due to a mix of sheer terror and of a resolve not to voice anger on the students' part.[30] Three students chose to conduct further research on issues of anti-Indian racism for their midterm papers.[31]

During the mid-term break students read Bharati Mukherjee's novel *Wife*, which they found disconcerting since its title made them expect a traditional tale of a long-suffering, self-abnegating wife such is encapsulated in the mythological model of Sita. Not surprisingly, those who commented positively on it—some of the women and the EA male—gave it a feminist reading. Most reacted negatively to the novel on the grounds that it might reflect poorly on the IA community; they judged it a book that was all right for IAs to read, but that they did not wish other Americans would read. Several students struggled to shape their views and returned to this reading assignment in successive additions to and revisions of their reading logs.[32] Three chose to devote their midterm papers to a critical analysis of female protagonists in Mukherjee's fiction.

Most students chose to write research papers on the issue of family relations, which was their primary concern and to which the remainder of the course was devoted.[33]

Fourth Paper

For their fourth paper, assigned to be written in the first person plural, students were asked to address an open letter to the South Asia Society for possible publication in *The Lotus*, the SAS newsletter. They could define as they wished the "we" who addressed SAS, and whether to write to the SAS leadership or membership. In preparation, they read an opinion piece by Bharati Mukherjee and a report on a campus roundtable discussion of AA pan-ethnicity.[34] I hoped that they would enter the debate that is rife among upperclassmen about whether SAS should be a strictly social and cultural association or whether it should engage in ethnic and political activism. Most chose to argue for an intensification of the big-brother/big-sister program that SAS has instituted for entering freshmen of South Asian ethnicity. They also pleaded for an active program of cultural and religious—primarily Hindu—recovery and for a concerted effort to educate the student population at large about Indian culture. In this and other instances, IA students positioned themselves primarily in relation to other IAs and to the majority community; none chose to follow up on the issue of AA pan-ethnicity. Discussions allowed me to introduce again the possibility of common action with other AA groups, which they readily embraced, but which, in spite of the preparatory readings, none had thought of on his/her own or during the peer review. SAS was given copies of these papers, stripped of their authors' names.

Fifth Paper

For their final paper students were asked to interview a cohort of ten to twelve young IAs at Penn or elsewhere on a topic of their choice—students in the class were ruled out as potential interviewees. Preparation for the paper included two sets of readings. Case studies in the realm of clinical psychology showed students how to use personal narratives and gave them a better appreciation of the trials of migration.[35] Articles on matrimony, and particularly on arranged marriages, provided a basis for reflection on and discussion of an issue that often opposes immigrant parents and their children.[36] This was the topic that, throughout the course, students most wished to discuss and to which they found ways to return in a variety of contexts.[37] Drafts of the students' proposed questionnaires were discussed in class. The loaded way in which students initially formulated their questions showed that they expected all their interviewees to feel about issues the same way they did—or thought they did. They were surprised to discover a range of opinions and dimensions that had not occurred to them or that they were still groping for. In almost all cases, their conclusions differed significantly from their expectations. Though students were warned against the temptation to draw too general a conclusion from too small a sample, they were challenged to formulate working hypotheses that participants in future editions of the course or scholars anywhere might wish to test and document further. They responded to this task with enthusiasm, pride, and a sense of responsibility, like pioneers on the cutting edge of scholarship or founders of a field of sustained enquiry and relevance.

Eight of the papers were devoted to family issues. With the exception of paper #3, they drew a hopeful picture in which, past an initial chafing at poor communication and strict disciplinarian rules, interviewees expressed appreciation for their parents' role and a firm commitment to the preservation of strong family ties. Even on the sore subject of arranged marriages, though initial rhetoric was shrill, prolonged interviews documented trust in parental good intentions and sound judgment, and an eagerness to reach accommodation rather than confrontation. IAs were overwhelmingly identified as prospective partners of choice.

The other six papers were devoted to issues of cultural and ethnic identity. Though the likelihood that Indian culture will be preserved in the United States continued to be viewed with pessimism, respondents were consistently described as having traveled toward a positive ethnic identity. Most collectively affirming was the correlation that was documented between a positive identity and community size. For many respondents from suburban and other areas who had had little opportunity to live in an IA community and to enjoy cultural reinforcement prior to entering college, Penn was what one described as "a dream come true" (quoted in paper #13).

Since papers were presented to, and discussed in, the full class, students became better aware of the commonality, yet of the multiple shadings, of their experiences, and of a variety of available options, when they had often thought of themselves as trapped in situations that allow them no elbow room. The testimonies they collectively gathered gave them a less Pollyannish view of American society and a better understanding of their parents' situation. They reached a common conclusion that what they had thought of as isolated problems were pervasive in their families and communities, and that concerted family and community action was needed to address them.

Perhaps even more affirming than conclusions reached was the process of collecting testimonies from an IA community. Though many students did not find it easy to identify ten to twelve fellow students who would sit for interviews with them during the last weeks of the semester, they reported that the interviews were often longer and more expansive than they had expected or planned.[38] The effect of the course spilled over to others in the IA community of Penn students and in students' home-towns. Several students conducted interviews in their own communities and discussed their projects with their families and friends during the Thanksgiving recess. For them this final paper represented more than a course assignment; it developed into a quest for answers that they wished to obtain for themselves personally and collectively.

Final Comments

In a retrospective on the course, students remarked that it took them on paths that they did not expect. They anticipated that it "would only en-tail writing about the hackneyed topic of maintaining the Indian identity in America and preserving the culture."[39] They found it disconcerting at first to be challenged to develop resonant, assertive voices, and to con-front broad social issues. They have been inured to suffering alone and in silence, to ignoring taunts, denying problems, and resorting to avoidance tactics; working collaboratively toward developing a collective social conscience and facing the prospect of assuming positions of service and leadership in their community is a slow, painful, but stirringly empower-ing process for them.

For me, the experience of challenging students to take charge of their learning process was stirring as well. I am now so persuaded of the intrinsic benefits of a nonfoundational teaching method and of a collectively empowering approach to learning that I would wish to pursue this pedagogical stance as a matter of preference, not just of necessity.

APPENDIX

Student Profiles

#1–7: female Hindu Indian Americans; ##8–10: male Hindu Indian Americans; #11: male Sikh Indian American; #12: male mixed Indian-Christian and Russian-Jewish American; #13: male Irish American raised around the world; #14: female Christian Indian raised in the United Arab Emirates. All students were first-semester students, except #14, a sophomore.

First Paper

#1: A Religious Revelation; #2: Who Am I? #3: Acknowledge the Intention; #4: Christmas: Celebrating It Indian Style; #5: The Man in the Glass; #6: Lost in a Crowd; #7: Exchanging Roots; #8: Hate Becomes Pride; #9: Identity; #10: Diwali, Taking Pride in the Light; #11: Insulted; #12: Misfit; #13: Philippines; #14: A Turning Point at a Traffic Light.

Second Paper

#1: Generation Gap; #2: Where Has It All Gone? #3: Media Stereotypes Questioned; #4: Pooja: A Documentation of Conversations; #5: Letting Loose; #6: Generation Gap; #7: An Indian Wedding under Fireworks; #8: Children in the Temple; #9: Indian Americans in North Philadelphia; #10: Youth "Dating" and Dancing at an Indian Festival; #11: The Birthday Boy; #12: An Indian Wedding in an American Church; #13: A Visit to a Japanese Church; #14: A Diwali Cultural Show.

Third Paper

#1: Relations in Indian American Families; #2: Hinduism and America; #3: The Land of Opportunity . . . Sometimes; #4: College Admissions: Discrimination against Asian Americans? #5: Immigrant Women in the Works of Bharati Mukherjee; #6: The Double Standard;

#7: Parental Expectations and the Identity Crisis of Second-Generation Indian Americans; #8: East Indian Children in North America: A Comparison between Socialization Patterns; #9: A Disadvantaged Minority Status for Indian Americans?; #10: Racism and Discrimination against Indian Americans; #11: The Sikh Immigrant and Second-Generation Experience in North America; #12: The Disintegration of the Traditional Indian Immigrant Family; #13: Female Characters in the Works of Mukherjee; #14: Disillusionment of the Female Indian Immigrant: A Critical Analysis of Bharati Mukherjee's Works.

Fourth Paper

Open Letter to the South Asia Society.

Fifth Paper

#1: Cultural Community Involvement of Young Indian Americans; #2: Arranged Marriage: Second-Generation Indian Americans and their Future; #3: If Honesty Is the Best Policy . . . ; #4: Are Young South Asian Americans Secure about Their South Asian Identity? #5: Are Arranged Marriages a Passing Phenomenon? An Attitudinal Profile of Indian Americans; #6: The Role of Indian Parents in the Lives of Their Children; #7: The Second-Generation Indian-American Woman; #8: Parents and Children: A Study of Parental Influences on Educational and Career Decisions of Indian American Children; #9: Indian Americans Involved in the India Earthquake Relief Effort at the University of Pennsylvania; #10: Survival of Indian Culture and Religion in America; #11: Parents Just Don't Understand—Or Do They? #12: A Study of the Changing Face of the Traditional Indian American Family; #13: Prejudice in the United States: South Asian Experiences with Racism; #14: Young Indian Americans' Emotional Ties to India: Running Hot and Cold.

Notes

1. *Collaborative Learning: Higher Education, Interdependence, and the Authority of Knowledge* (Baltimore: Johns Hopkins University Press, 1993).
2. See the genesis of Bruffee's method in chapter 1 of *Collaborative Learning* and Lane Ryo Hirabayashi and Malcolm Collier's account, "Embracing Diversity: A Pedagogy for Introductory Asian American Studies Courses," in *ReViewing Asian America*, Wendy Ng, et al., eds. (Pullman: Washington State University Press, 1995), 15–31.
3. This figure, provided by Penn's office of Planning and Analysis, Institute for Research in Higher Education, is based on self-identification by American

citizens and permanent residents. By the rules under which the survey operates, students who do not identify their ethnicity are counted as non-Hispanic whites. International students, many of whom are from Asia, are not included in this figure. Like other elite institutions, Penn has been shown to admit fewer Asian American students than the qualifications of applicants would warrant (Richard M. Lee, "Asian American Applicants and Elite Undergraduate Admissions: A Case Study of the University of Pennsylvania, 1978–1989," paper read at the Association for Asian American Studies meeting, Ann Arbor, Michigan, April 1994. This point was first made internally by Samuel Z. Klausner, "The Power to Sculpt University Admissions is the Power to Be Unjust," [Penn's] *Almanac*, 19 September 1989.

4. No official figures are available. According to Joseph Sun, interim director of Penn's Greenfield Intercultural Center, the three largest ethnic groups, in roughly equal numbers, are Chinese, Korean, and South Asian. Other Asian ethnicities are represented in much smaller numbers.

5. Besides classical Sanskrit, Penn offers classes in Hindi, Urdu, Gujarati, Panjabi, Bengali, and Tamil on a regular basis. Since Penn attempts to accommodate any group of at least six students who register for a first-year course in any language, Pashto, Sindhi, Marathi, and Malayalam have also been taught in recent years. The largest undergraduate class in South Asia Regional Studies, Ludo Rocher's "Legacy of India," a lecture course on the cultural history of South Asia, broke the two hundred enrollees' mark for the first time in its latest edition, in spring 1994. Seventy-one percent of the students in that class were of Asian ethnicity (48 percent South Asian, 23 percent other Asian).

6. This task is made even more complex by the fact that the student clientele includes Indian Americans (IAs) who are issued from "twice-migrant" families, i.e., families of Indian ethnicity that were settled for one or more generations in, and later displaced from, East Africa and other former parts of the British Empire, and international students of Indian descent whose families live in Hongkong, Singapore, the Gulf states, and other diasporic locations.

7. The writing requirement can be fulfilled by taking either a course in English composition or a writing course sponsored by a department other than English and supported by the Writing Across The University (WATU) program, or two courses that include a WATU-supported larger-than-average writing component. WATU emphasizes the drafting and revising of papers and, among other services and to the extent possible, provides faculty across the university with modest stipends to hire graduate students as writing tutors whom WATU trains to help undergrads with the revising process.

8. The experience of this course suggests that Indian American students are more, not less, likely to have absorbed these stereotypes. Unlike most European Americans, who have not read or thought much about India before they entered college and who come to this course pretty much as blank slates, many Indian Americans need to unlearn what Western literature and journalism have taught them about their ethnic home.

9. The coconut is the Indian American equivalent of other food-based (oreo cookie, banana) images for ethnic Americans who struggle with problems of identity.

10. This is "alleged," since the brutal assault was ruled not to have been ra-

cially motivated. Penn's South Asia Society (SAS), which maintained a constant presence at the trial, organized a candlelight protest demonstration on campus after the verdict was announced. SAS leaders reported on their efforts in panel 1.9 "Roundtable: South Asians in New Jersey and New York: Community Violence and Coalition Building," Tenth National Conference of the Association for Asian American Studies, Ithaca, New York. Sucheta Mazumdar first met leaders of SAS when she visited Penn as a member of an external advisory panel invited by the dean of the School of Arts and Sciences to make recommendations about initiating AAS at Penn.

11. Students watched the videotape *Student Writing Groups: Demonstrating the Process*, produced by Connie J. Smith and Susan Wyche-Smith (2nd ed., Wordshop Productions, 1988). Contrary to the recommended procedure, however, papers were not read aloud and commented on immediately. With IA students, many of whom are quiet, reluctant to make snap judgments, and polite to a fault, comments increase in volume and in quality when they are arrived at by reading the texts at home and jotting down suggestions before discussing the papers in groups. I chose the first teams for gender and other diversity. For later papers students took charge of rotating group membership so that, in the end, all had worked with all.

12. On the utility of reconvening smaller groups into plenary sessions, see chapter 2 in Bruffee's *Collaborative Learning*.

13. I had resolved not to grade papers during the term, but to grade only the final portfolios, to which students were asked to add a cover letter that assessed their strengths, weaknesses, and progress. Students became so anxious, however, that I ultimately gave in to their demands and provided provisional "grade estimates" for their papers.

14. Arthur W. Helweg and Usha M. Helweg, *An Immigrant Success Story: East Indians in America* (Philadelphia: University of Pennsylvania Press, 1990).

15. "Chink" by Helen Hyun; "Jackal" and "A Reminder" by Sharon Kim; "How Could I Be Crying?" by Sheela Athreya—who will serve as writing tutor for the next edition of the course—and "The Ticking" by Michele Poly, *Mosaic: Penn's Asian American Literary Arts Magazine* 1, no. 1 (1993): 12; 37; 40–41.

16. Student #5 wrote about how her resolve to abstain from drinking stemmed from the death of her closest friend in a drunk-driving accident. Even the lone European American student in the class (#13) wrote about racial prejudice. See a log of student profiles and the titles of their several papers in an appendix to this article.

17. One student volunteered the comment that this was the first time that he had been allowed to write about feelings.

18. Student #10. The writer whose closure was in the most sober vein was the lone student of mixed parentage (#12), who concluded "I do not try to contradict anyone, for these labels are only a small reflection of who I am."

19. S. Parvez Wakil, C. M. Siddique, and F. A. Wakil, "Between Two Cultures: A Study in the Socialization of Children of Immigrants," *Journal of Marriage and the Family* 43 (1981): 929–40; and chapter 5, "The Second Generation," in John Y. Fenton's *Transplanting Religious Traditions: Asian Indians in America* (New York: Praeger, 1988).

20. A suburbanite writer (#9) wrote a startled—and startling—report on what he witnessed during a weekend spent cruising through a tough inner-city neighborhood with an Indian American gang. One student (#5) described the release and bonding that women across generations experienced at a festival at which no males were present. Other papers that did not focus on generational issues featured campus events. Student #3 reported on a meeting organized by South Asia Society disccuss with the comedic group "Mask and Wig" a skit that was offensive to IA students and to review clips of TV programs, which were found to be consistently derogatory. The lone international student, a Christian Indian raised in the Arab Emirates (#14), reported with pride on a cultural show that was held in celebration of a Hindu holiday.

21. The North American branch of the Vishwa Hindu Parishat (i.e., Global Hindu Association)—an organization that has been officially banned in India since the destruction of the Ayodhya mosque by a Hindu mob in December 1992—organizes summer camps for youths in which the emphasis is on cultural and religious traditions. Some of the students in the class had attended such camps, to which one returned as a counselor.

22. Subject to adequate notice, sessions are scheduled at specific times and on specific topics requested by teachers. Reference librarian Debra Rill, to whom I gave a list of the reading assignments for the course, conducted preliminary searches to familiarize herself with relevant issues before meeting with the class.

23. As one student commented in awe, "I had no idea that so much had been written about us!"

24. In the list that was given to students locations were deleted. The books were: Maxine P. Fisher, *The Indians of New York City: A Study of Immigrants from India* (New Delhi: Heritage, 1980); Usha R. Jain, *The Gujaratis of San Francisco* (New York: AMS Press, 1989); Bruce La Brack, *The Sikhs of Northern California 1940–1975* (New York: AMS Press, 1988); Karen I. Leonard, *Making Ethnic Choices: California's Punjabi Mexican Americans* (Philadelphia: Temple University Press, 1992); Iftikhar H. Malik, *Pakistanis in Michigan: A Study of Third Culture and Acculturation* (New York: AMS Press, 1989); James G. Chadney, *The Sikhs of Vancouver* (New York: AMS Press, 1984); Sathi S. Dasgupta, *On the Trail of an Uncertain Dream: Indian Immigrant Experience in America* [New Jersey] (New York: AMS Press, 1989); John Y. Fenton, *Transplanting Religious Traditions: Asian Indians in America* [Atlanta] (New York: Praeger, 1988); Parmatma Saran, *The Asian Indian Experience in the United States* [Madison, Wis.] (Cambridge, Mass.: Schenkman, 1985); Parmatma Saran and Edwin Eames, ed., *The New Ethnics: Asian Indians in the United States* [New York] (New York: Praeger, 1980); Proshanta K. Nandi, *The Quality of Life of Asian Americans: An Exploratory Study in a Middle Size Community* [Springfield, Ill.] (New York: Praeger, 1980); and Margaret A. Gibson, *Accommodation without Assimilation: Sikh Immigrants in an American High School* [rural northern California] (Ithaca: Cornell University Press, 1988). Students declined awarding the prize and declared that all had done an excellent job.

25. Chapter 8, "The Tide of Turbans," in Ronald T. Takaki's *Strangers from a Different Shore: A History of Asian Americans* (Boston: Little, Brown, 1988);

Bruce La Brack, "Evolution of Sikh Family Form and Values in Rural California: Continuity and Change 1904–1980," *Journal of Comparative Family Studies* 19, no. 2 (1988): 287–309; Marcelle Williams, "Ladies on the Line: Punjabi Cannery Workers in Central California," in *Making Waves: An Anthology of Writings by and about Asian American Women*, Asian Women United of California, eds. (Boston: Beacon Press, 1989), 148–59; *The New Puritans: The Sikhs of Yuba City*, directed by Ritu Sarin and Tenzing Sonam (Cross Current Media, 1985). The student of Sikh background (#11) chose to investigate this topic further for his midterm paper.

26. The testimonies "Being Indian in Jersey City" by Hardayal Singh, "Racial Hatred" by Madhu S. Chawla, and "Different by Choice" by Sudershan S. Chawla in *Asian American Experiences in the United States: Oral Histories*, Joann Faung Jean Lee, ed. (Jefferson, N.C.: McFarland, 1991), 112–20; a letter sent by "Dotbusters" to the *Jersey Journal* on 5 August 1987; and Sucheta Mazumdar's "Race and Racism: South Asians in the United States," in *Frontiers of Asian American Studies: Writing, Research, and Commentary*, Gail M. Nomura et al., eds. (Pullman: Washington State University Press, 1989), 25–38.

27. Student #2 commented, "I remember that during these incidents, my parents told us that we were not going to go to the *Puja* [i.e., worship] in Jersey City that year because it was too dangerous. I didn't understand at the time how serious it was. Now . . . I am truly shocked."

28. Rita Chaudhry Sethi's since published "Smells like Racism: A Plan for Mobilizing against Anti-Asian Bias," in *The State of Asian America: Activism and Resistance in the 1990s*, Karin Aguilar-San Juan, ed. (Boston: South End Press, 1994), which discusses anti-Indian incidents in New Jersey and which will be one of the texts added to the reader for the next edition of the course, should be helpful.

29. Students were required to keep a journal in which they recorded their reactions to readings, but they were given the option of turning these in or keeping them until the end of the term. Our understanding was that I would read any piece of writing that they would turn in and that I would return it to them with my comments within a week.

30. Another circumstance in which students reacted with visible fright was the discussion that followed viewing a tape of the TV program "The Patels: Owners of the Tenderloin" produced by David Rathod (*On Express*, KQED TV, San Francisco, 30 March 1988). Perhaps because I failed to prepare students adequately, they paled when, in an attempt to introduce the concept of middleman minority, I brought in the parallel of Korean American merchants in South Central Los Angeles.

31. Students #3, 9, and 10. The paper of student #4 on discriminatory practices in college admissions was the result of prior concerns.

32. One student (#8) reached a closure only after a joint campus appearance by David Henry Hwang, Bharati Mukherjee, and Ronald Takaki: "Many members of our class thought that it was not appropriate for Mukherjee to write about an Indian woman who is not representative of her ethnic group. However, after listening to David Henry Hwang speak, I disagree with them. The author

does not have an obligation to portray a member of a minority group as a heroine or villain. Simply, the author should make the character seem human. I believe that Mukherjee accomplished this."

33. One (#2) wrote about the maintenance and proselytization of Hinduism in America.

34. Bharati Mukherjee, "Immigrant Writing: Give Us Your Maximalists," *The New York Times Book Review*, 28 August 1988; "A Roundtable Discussion on Asian American Identity," *Mosaic* 1, no. 1 (1993): 28–29.

35. Prakash N. Desai and George V. Coelho, "Indian Immigrants in America: Some Cultural Aspects of Psychological Adaptation," in *The New Ethnics: Asian Indians in the United States*, Parmatma Saran and Edwin Eames, eds. (New York: Praeger, 1980), 363–86; and chapter 6, "The Indian Self: Reflections in the Mirror of the American Life Style," in Alan Roland's *In Search of Self in India and Japan: Toward a Cross-Cultural Psychology* (Princeton: Princeton University Press, 1988).

36. Rashmi Luthra, "Matchmaking in the Classifieds of the Immigrant Indian Press," in *Making Waves*, Asian Women United of California, eds. (Boston: Beacon Press, 1989), 337–44; Ramdas Menon, "Arranged Marriages among South Asian Immigrants," *Sociology and Social Research* 73 (1989): 180–81; and Gura Bhargava, "Seeking Immigration through Matrimonial Alliance: A Study of Advertisements in an Ethnic Weekly," *Journal of Comparative Family Studies* 19, no. 2 (1988): 245–59. Students were also asked to select a matrimonial ad in the ethnic weekly *India Abroad* and to present an oral analysis of it in class.

37. Career choice becomes contested mostly for upperclassmen. Penn's culture of low departmental and school boundaries and of customized degree programs allows Indian American students to mitigate or to postpone what might be a contentious decision in that it affords them the possibility of earning a combination of major and minor, double majors (i.e., majors in more than one department or program within one of Penn's schools) or dual degrees (i.e., degrees in departments or programs in more than one of Penn's schools) with relative ease, albeit with purposeful planning. An increasing number of Indian Americans pursue minors in South Asia Societies; most who major in South Asia Society do so as a second major or degree.

38. In many cases, they said, "we ended up talking for hours."

39. Shweta Parmar, "SARS 009.301: Writing about the Indian American Experience," *The Lotus*, 7 February 1994.

18

Teaching the Asian American Experience through Film

JUN XING

The Recognition of Asian American Filmmaking

The last few years represented a landmark in Asian American filmmaking. "As if at the wave of a magic wand," in the words of *A Magazine*, Asian American films have suddenly been transformed into marketable products. Making three times its production cost, Wayne Wang's *The Joy Luck Club* (1993) became the first commercial success for Asian American cinema. Ang Lee's *The Wedding Banquet* was nominated for the Academy Award in 1993, and won the prestigious Golden Bear Grand prize at the Berlin Film Festival. Hawaiian-born and New York-based Japanese American director Kayo Hatta's *Picture Bride* (1994) was the winner of the Audience Award at the 1995 Sundance Film Festival. Freida Lee Mock and Jessica Yu won two Oscars for their *Maya Lin: A Strong Clear Vision* (1995) and *Breathing Lessons* (1996). *Time* magazine dubbed this critical success of Asian American films "China Chic," and *Cinevue*, newsletter of Asian CineVision, the largest Asian American media center in the nation, proclaimed that finally "Asian American cinema has arrived."

This recent Asian American cinematic breakthrough represents exciting opportunities for teachers and scholars in Asian American studies. Over the last three decades Asian American film and video artists have produced hundreds of social-issue documentaries, dramas, and experimental films dealing with various aspects of the Asian American experience. The growing ranks of independent films have addressed significant issues of racial representation, countered old and new stereotypes, challenged the universal mainstream standards of art, and established an intertextual dialogue with Hollywood films. Together with other forms of Asian American art, they have become a powerful pedagogical tool for teaching the Asian American experience. Scholars have already recog-

217

nized the important work that filmmakers are doing. Sucheng Chan, for example, provided a list of documentary films (alongside the usual bibliography) suitable for classroom use in her two history textbooks. Roger Daniels and Harry Kitano have likewise listed films in the second edition of their widely adopted textbook on Asian Americans.

Despite these achievements and the public's recognition of them, there is nonetheless a great deal of confusion regarding what constitutes an Asian American film. For example, how should we define Asian American films? Does the term, "Asian American," refer to the ethnicity of the filmmakers or the topic of the films, regardless of who makes them? Where do we draw the boundaries? Are films with a clear Asian American theme, but shot by a multiracial crew, such as Oliver Stone's *Heaven and Earth*, considered Asian American? Are formal and technical properties equally, if not more, important defining characteristics? In other words, is there such a thing as an Asian American film genre, as Thomas Cripps described black films? If so, what are its thematic and structural conventions? How does this Asian American film genre, as in the case of the slave narrative in literature, come to define the structure of subsequent works on the subject? How, in short, do Asian American films differ from Hollywood movies?

These questions served as the starting point in my developing an experimental course on "Asian American Identities and Popular Culture." Even though popular culture is in the title, the course focused primarily on the smaller universe of motion pictures.[1] Using race and ethnicity as primary frames of analysis, the course attempted to introduce students to the booming field of Asian American cinema. Moving beyond a simple survey of Asian American screen images, the course sought to examine ethnicity as a force both in front of and behind the camera, exploring the nature of the ongoing negotiations between mainstream Hollywood culture and the subcultures of Asian Americans. In this paper, I would like to discuss the potentials as well as problems I experienced in teaching this course. First, I will detail the approach and outline the specific themes pursued each week during the semester. Because of its experimental nature, the course was heavily discussion-oriented. At the same time, I hope to address some of the theoretical and pedagogical challenges I encountered in designing the course.

An Initial Conceptual Framework

Though the focus of the course was the study and analysis of Asian American independent films, we spent the first half of the semester reading and exploring critical concepts such as "image," "identity," and "representation," while screening a selective group of Hollywood films. Since Asian American independent cinema has come largely as a result of Hollywood's long history of abusive Asian and Asian American portrayals, I hope to provide students with the intertextual framework needed to understand the Asian American productions screened in the second half of the semester.

The first two weeks focused on defining ethnic stereotyping and introducing students to the basic film language necessary for the course. Marlon Riggs' *Ethnic Notions* (1987) was screened in its entirety to generate discussions on some key sets of questions: the relationship between imagery and reality, or rather the origins of those racial stereotypes; the interaction between the images of others and self-images; and the relationship between societies or groups that produce the films and the societies or groups created in the films?[2] Since film is a medium based on a certain level of literacy and the course used films as its primary texts, students were also assigned a chapter on visual language from John O'Connor's *Image As Artifact*.[3] The reading offered students, the majority of whom were undergraduates, some rudimentary knowledge of film language, especially the four primary film techniques: mise-en-scène, cinematography, editing or montage, and sound.

With this background in place, we spent the next five weeks scrutinizing Hollywood representation. Carlos E. Cortes' essay, "What is Maria? What is Juan? Dilemmas of Analyzing the Chicano Image in U.S. Feature Films," provided the conceptual framework.[4] According to Cortes, there were three main areas of research in the history of ethnic film images: content analysis—analysis of films as visual texts; control analysis—analysis of the process of filmmaking; and impact analysis—analysis of the influence of films over the audience and vice versa.[5] To showcase Asian film images, I chose Cecil B. D'Mille's silent masterpiece *The Cheat* (1915) for class screening in week three.[6] Sumiko Higashi's essay "Ethnicity, Class, and Gender in the Film 'The Cheat,' "[7] and Gina Marchetti's introductory chapter from *Romance and the "Yellow Peril": Race, Sex, and Discursive Strategies in Hollywood Fiction*[8] were assigned as common readings. While Higashi's essay focused on the historical dimension for the production of the film, Marchetti's is a nuanced analysis of what she called the motif of rape fantasy. To equip students with some analytical tools, two chapters from Edward Said's book *Orientalism*[9] were assigned in the following week. Said's powerful concept of Orientalism brought class discussion to the theoretical level, especially about the question of power and systems of representation.

To move the discussion from film image to what Stuart Hall has called the "politics of representation," week five focused on a reading from Eugene Wong's *On Visual Media Racism: Asians in American Motion*

Pictures.[10] Wong argued that although the motion picture industry's racism against Asians had its definitive individual and cultural proponents, it was the institutionalized nature of the industry's racism against Asians that was particularly humiliating.[11] Specifically, he had identified three industrywide racist practices: role segregation (yellow face), role stratification, and role delimitation.

Finally, the class examined the relationship between media stereotypes and their social impact during week six. Pam Tom's black-and-white narrative film *Two Lies* (1990) was screened with Eugenia Kaw's essay "Medicalization of Racial Features: Asian American Women and Cosmetic Surgery."[12] Tom's featurette provided a disturbing and eerie look into identity crises from the perspective of a Chinese-American teenager as a result of her mother's cosmetic eye surgery. A perfect companion piece, Kaw's well-documented case study of the popular types of cosmetic surgery among Bay Area Asian American women (eyelid restructuring, nose bridge buildup, and nose tip altering) suggested that these women had internalized not only a gender ideology like other women, but also a racial ideology that associated their natural features with negative connotations. To add a different perspective, the class also screened Deborah Gee's *Slaying the Dragon* (1987), a film exposing how race and sexuality were intimately intertwined in the exploitation of Asian women in Hollywood cinema.

In the subsequent week, the class summarized the three related ways in which stereotyping functioned as means of social control: justification of the status quo; internalization of dominant values by racial minorities; and the development of cognitive associations between race and aesthetics. At this point, I felt it was good timing to introduce my students to the increasing body of literature in the feminist film criticism. Two essays, "Visual Pleasure and Narrative Cinema" by Laura Mulvey and "White Privilege and Looking Relations: Race and Gender in Feminist Film Theory" by Jane Gaines, were assigned to set up the class for a meaningful dialogue. While the value of Mulvey's groundbreaking essay was that it raised provocative questions about the source and function of male visual pleasure, making the important shift from women images to the signifying practices of the film medium itself, Jane Gaines called our attention to its serious limitations.

By the end of the first seven weeks, it was clear to the students that Asian American independent filmmakers have been operating against Hollywood's deeply entrenched historical, stereotypical, ideological, and institutional practices. The filmmakers not only have to confront the daunting task of dismantling and creating critical alternatives to Hollywood screen images, but also to find ways to work around established conventions in the industry. With this understanding, the class was ready to move on to Asian American cinema through careful discussions of each of the three basic types: social documentaries, family dramas, and experimental films.

Independent Filmmaking

Following the midterm in week eight, the class began examining Asian American independent filmmaking. *Claiming A Voice* (1990) on the history of Visual Communications was viewed as an introduction. Students were both surprised and inspired to learn about the VC story. They were amazed by the productivity and tenacity of this early Asian American underground film industry. During our postscreening discussion, one particular topic generated some really interesting conversation: the lack of recognition for Asian American films and the relative popularity of Asian American literature in the last twenty years. Opinions diverged and no agreement was reached by the end of the class. The following is a summary of the three major perspectives.

One perspective was that the media of film and literature belonged to two separate realms, the literary being very different from the visual. Traditionally, Asians were disembodied in American culture. Asians could be intelligent, but not physically viable. We saw a lot of Asian doctors and engineers in the media, but we rarely saw Asian sports stars and fashion models. Asians had the brains, so to speak, but not the bodies.

Another point was that independent films needed an audience to support. Unlike African Americans, who made up almost 32 percent of the moviegoing population in the country, Asians simply did not have that numerical weight. Historically, race movies, for example, were made specifically for the black audience, never intended to be viewed by the white audience. Black filmmakers had a strong tradition behind them, while Asian Americans did not. In comparison, it would be easier for Asian American literature to cross over to mainstream readers.

Third, the students observed that the difference between Asian American fiction and film was largely due to their content. *Woman Warrior* and *The Joy Luck Club*, for example, were heavily embedded in traditional Chinese themes. Both books appealed to the mainstream readers partly because of the Chinese mythologies, from the legend of Fa Mulan to the myth of the Moon Lady. In contrast, Asian American films, especially the documentaries, focused on identity issues, history, family and everyday immigrant lives in the United States. They did not carry that selling point of exotica.

Before class, the students had all read two essays: "A History in Progress: Asian American Media Arts Centers, 1970–1990" by Stephen Gong, and "Moving the Image: Asian American Independent Filmmaking, 1970–1990" by Renee Tajima, both from *Moving the Image: Asian Pacific American Independent Media Arts*.[13] In his essay, Gong distinguished media arts from the media industry. "The Asian American media arts movement," he said, "from its inception was an alternative movement developed in opposition to mainstream strategies and structures in the film and television industries."[14] In our follow-up discussion, class members tried to identify the major differences between this so-called alternative media and Hollywood. Renee Tajima's essay, on the other hand, was a detailed introduction to the different productions, from the documentaries to the dramas.

Documentaries

In the following week, we focused our attention on the documentary, the earliest and predominant element in the Asian American genre. Together, the class viewed clips from three films: Christine Choy's Oscar-nominated *Who Killed Vincent Chin* (1989); her earlier film, *Mississippi Triangle* (1984); and Loni Ding's *Nisei Soldier* (1989). Luis Francia's article "Asian and Asian American Cinema" and Loni Ding's "Strategies of an Asian American Filmmaker" provided the basis for class discussions. Francia's thesis, "In Asian American cinema the documentary has become the logical antithesis to the . . . mainstream view of Asian American culture and history," became the focus of our early discussion. Students seemed to agree that the predominance of documentaries was the result of limited funding and resources, but we could not agree to what extent it reflected a conscious ideological preference on the part of the filmmakers. While Francia's essay focused more on the genre, Ding's essay led our attention to the different strategies she had employed in her productions.

Learning about strategies, nothing seemed to be more meaningful than talking to an Asian American filmmaker. With this in mind, I invited Steve Wong, a Denver-based Chinese-American filmmaker into our classroom. Wong gave an inspiring lecture on his own documentary productions, followed by demonstrations from his latest film, *One, Two Man* (1995). Wong's guest lecture was very well received, and he made the course an even more meaningful learning experience for the students.

Asian American Family Dramas

We continued our examination of Asian American films by looking at Asian American family dramas in week ten. Wayne Wang's 1989 feature

Dim Sum was screened in class. The postscreening discussion was orga-nized around the following two themes. First, almost all the Asian-Ameri-can-directed independent features, from Wayne Wang's mother–daughter sagas *Dim Sum* (1984) and *The Joy Luck Club* (1989) to Ang Lee's "father knows best" trilogy *Pushing Hands* (1991), *The Wedding Banquet* (1993), and *Eat Drink Man Woman* (1994), could be broadly defined as family dramas. Unlike the popular martial arts and ghost-story genres, these fam-ily dramas were first and foremost family stories about the bond of strong kinship ties as well as domestic tensions across racial, gender, generation, and class lines. What was the significance of this mode of narrative for Asian American filmmakers? Was the popularity a result of Asian cultural traditions or an Asian American historical specificity? How did the special dynamics in Asian American family formation, mandated by the long-time exclusionist policies and racism, become the thematic focus for Asian American artists? Second, these dramas explored differences among and between Asian Americans and took the interrogation of an essentialized identity as their central themes. Critique of the fixed notions of Asian American racial, cultural, and sexual identities seemed to be the trademark of Asian American dramas. What were the major themes in this intratex-tual dialogue on race, ethnicity, and gender debated in these family genre films? How did these family stories subvert the notion of monolithic identi-ties by emphasizing the process of "becoming" rather than "being"?

Two essays provided the framework for our discussion on identity pol-itics. One was Stuart Hall's "Cultural Identity and Cinematic Represen-tation," where Stuart Hall challenged the primordial version of identity. Hall talked about an identity as a process of "becoming" rather than "being." "Cultural identity," as he remarked, "is a matter of 'becoming' as well as 'being.' It belongs to the future as much as to the past. It is not something which already exists, transcending place, time, history, and culture . . . like everything which is historical, they are subject to the continuous 'play' of history, culture and power."[15] Hall's argument sug-gested insightful, pertinent strategies for taking the question of Asian American identities beyond the essentialist position. Lisa Lowe's essay "Heterogeneity, Hybridity, Multiplicity: Marking Asian American Dif-ferences" made those issues closer to home, exploring how the politically negotiated and socially constructed identities were tackled in a series of Asian American films. Through the twist and turns of mother–daughter, father–son and generational, racial, and cultural tensions, Lowe demon-strated that ethnicity was not naturally given but invented, not linear but cyclical, not fixed but contingent as presented in those films.

In our final session in the week, the class identified three common themes from these family narratives:

1. The dramas all challenged the artificial category of Asian Americans as a hyphenated ethnicity and explicitly questioned limited and prescriptive boundaries of Asian American identities. These films portrayed contradictory identities that defied any dogmatic notion of purity. Viewers came to realize that identities did not have to be fixed in a single geographical or cultural space.
2. Identity was presented as a melange rather than in binary opposition. Asian immigrants in America faced two kinds of binarism: Asian or American, black and white. Historically, racial formation in America was basically black and white. The dramas boldly transgressed these boundaries. They addressed identity as a mixture of all different kinds of things put together.
3. The films helped to illustrate the processes and strategies by which Asian Americans constructed and articulated their personal choice of identities. No film seemed to possess a convenient closure of the matter. Identity politics were taken as a point of departure rather than one of closure. Identity was a constantly changing and flexible concept, not an essentialized notion.

Experimental Films

Among all Asian American independent productions, experimental films received the least critical attention. Our class spent the twelfth week on this Asian American avant-garde. I prefaced Trinh T. Minh-ha's *Surname Viet Given Name Nam* with a biography of the Vietnamese director and theorist and a handout of her interview with Judith Mayne. *Surname Viet* was an extremely complex film for undergraduate students, who expressed very different reactions to it. Some felt very frustrated, others lost interest within ten minutes of viewing and only a few found it thought-provoking. We started the discussion by talking about our own viewing experience. If we felt challenged by the screening situation, where did the discomfort come from? Several issues were brought up immediately. Some students were puzzled about the meaning or message of the film. They said they could not figure out the main story line. Some students complained about the English subtitles, which were sometimes too small to read and the larger-sized subtitles, which flowed too fast to follow. Some students even complained that the restless camera distracted their attention. Based on these reflections, I confronted students by questioning if these difficulties were the result of the filmmaker's technical incompetence or her deliberate use of experimental techniques. After some deliberations and debates, the class slowly came to the agreement that those were experimental techniques used to test the boundaries of conventional filmmaking. Building upon this agreement, I replayed some parts of the film, and the class picked up many specific examples this time. Almost everyone mentioned that the film challenged the fixed notions of time and space. In terms of time, flashback, backtracking, repetition, and other highly disjunctive ways of editing were cited. Experimental spacing techniques were also used to break the spatial logic. Negative/black/empty space, split-screen, out-of-focus shot, and superimposition were some of the more prominent examples.

Casting and Representations

Toward the end of the semester, in the thirteenth week, the class examined the recent debate over the Broadway play *Miss Saigon*. Students read Angela Pao's article "The Eyes of the Storm: Gender, Genre and Cross-Casting in *Miss Saigon*." "Yellow-facing" was not as pervasive now as before, but role stratification still persisted. For example, when Alan Parker's *Come See the Paradise* (1987) was first released, some Asian Americans accused Dennis Quaid, a white actor, of stealing the stardom. The movie was about the interment of Japanese Americans during World War II. Quaid played a guard who fell in love with a Nisei woman interned in the camp. Regardless of the intentions, the message conveyed was very clear to Asian Americans: a white lead was needed to make the movie acceptable for the mainstream audience. This perhaps was not unique for Asian Americans. Native American critics raised the same issue with *Dances With Wolves* (1992). A drastic departure from the old "noble salvage" image, the movie was a more sympathetic portrayal of Native American people. But Indian media activists raised a legitimate question: did they need a white guide into Native American culture and a white surrogate for acceptance from the mainstream audience? In the Broadway play *Miss Saigon*, by casting Jonathan Pryce, a white British actor, as the lead role of a Eurasian male character, the British producer Cameron Mackintosh literally practiced the same tradition of role segregation. Under the disguise of artistic freedom, his argument for color-blind casting could only serve to reinforce inequalities already in existence.

Angela Pao's critical essay added one interesting dimension to the debate. She called our attention to how cultural process worked in the case, specifically gender and race. She argued that color-blind casting was impossible in *Miss Saigon*. The producer's decision to cast an Asian woman and a Caucasian man was not accidental. It had something to do with the genre and the theatrical perimeters: East-West tragic romance. Like *Madame Butterfly* and *The South Pacific*, this Western maternal melodrama carried the following imperatives: the Asian prostitute, the "fallen woman"; the maternal devotion to the child and to the lover; the desertion; and inevitably, the suicide. Sticking to the genre imperatives decided that the Amerasian role had to be played by a white man.

What is an "Asian American" Film?

As a natural conclusion to this experimental course, the class spent its final two weeks on the thorny question: what films should be considered Asian American? Since we need to define our subject matter before we could really study it, the question came up time and again during the semester. Similar debate has been waged about black filmmaking. In March of 1994, New York University organized a panel on black films. The seven panelists, including filmmaker Spike Lee and writer Ishmael Reed, debated a similar set of questions: should only blacks make movies about blacks? Should black filmmakers be limited to black themes? Does having black-controlled films guarantee they are good movies? Who should see what movies or should blacks see films directed by non-blacks?

My lecture on the subject was designed to raise rather than answer questions. I introduced students to the two main definitions given by filmmakers and critics: the "ethnicity definition" and the "political definition." Writing on the history of Asian American media centers, Stephen Gong, a long-time Asian American media activist, emphasized that Asian American filmmaking was largely based on the assumption of a pan-Asian ethnicity, the belief that "being Asian American transcended the experience of being solely Chinese, Korean, or Japanese American."[16] This may imply that Asian American films were defined as films made by Asian Americans. In other words, the ethnic background of the filmmakers and their cultural knowledge were the deciding factors. For example, Daryl Chin, a Chinese-American playwright and cofounder of the Asian American International Film Festival, on various occasions, insisted on the primacy of filmmakers' ethnicity, "[If] an Asian American made the movie, but the movie did not have specific Asian American content, was it still an Asian American movie? My answer is yes."[17] Historically, this cultural essentialism was a direct result of the long-time frustration and anger among Asian Americans over the degradation of their images on the silver screen. To control the screen images, which defined so much of their lives, Asian Americans felt that they themselves had to be in control both in front of and behind the camera. Even more importantly, Hollywood's institutional racism, carefully documented by Eugene Wong, validated this essentialist point of view.

However, I highlighted several inherent contradictions in this definition. First, the imprecise nature of Asian American identities created problems. Who was an Asian American? Was there a pan-Asian identity or representation? In view of the recent literature on ethnic identity formation and development, more and more people are challenging the primordial version of identity. Secondly, it was a dubious assumption that the mere ethnic background of a filmmaker would guarantee a truer representation of Asian Americans. The current debate among Asian Americans surrounding *The Joy Luck Club* was a very good example. Despite the overwhelmingly positive reviews, the film was highly controversial within the Asian American communities. Furthermore, film production is a collaborative process, and it can hardly be controlled by one single ethnic group. To survive in the field, it might be necessary for Asian Americans to cross the racial and ethnic lines. In the production of *The Joy Luck Club*, for example, Wayne Wang did have complete creative control, but the project could be classified as a crossover production, since Amy Tan was joined by Ronald Bass, a Caucasian Academy Award-winning screenwriter, in writing the script. Similarly, both *M. Butterfly* and *Golden Gate* (1994) were based on Chinese American playwright David Henry Hwang's screenplays, but were directed by non-Asians. These kinds of crossover productions will certainly increase as more Asian Americans break into the studio system. Should we exclude those films?

As a direct outgrowth of the civil rights movement and political activism in the 1960s, Asian American cinema was a political and activist movement. Writing on the history of the media centers, Stephen Gong rightfully observed, "the Asian American media . . . is fundamentally a political (rather than a cultural or ethnic-based) movement." From the beginning, the pathbreakers tried to build a so-called triangular cinema of community, storyteller, and activist. Thus, many Asian American filmmakers insisted on a political definition: Asian American films were political, activist, and community-based films about Asian Americans. While indeed most of the works produced in the seventies or early eighties were struggling to define Asian American identities, reclaim untold stories, and fight racism, there seems to be thematic differences in more recent productions. Wayne Wang's *Smoke* (1995) was the most ready example. Some new artists who emerged fresh from film schools, for example, produced films that were not necessarily culturally introspective or linked to their ethnicity. Actually, there was growing resistance among Asian American filmmakers to confining their works to political filmmaking. Valerie Soe, a Chinese-American video maker, for example, argued that "it's more important not to pigeonhole Asian Pacific artists into only dealing with culture specific topics and themes . . ."[18]

This diversion in political filmmaking should be viewed in the context of the changes in the larger society as well as the Asian American communities. With the end of the cold war, the worldwide decline of communism disillusioned many so-called Asian American guerrilla filmmakers. The ideological mass appeal driven by third-world revolutions in the 1960s and '70s were very much lost by the late '80s. The demographics of Asian American communities had also undergone drastic changes. The new emergent communities had vastly different political and social agenda from the earlier better-established ones. For example, because of their war experience, the Southeast Asian refugees were very anti-Communist and could much more easily buy into the "melting-pot" ideology. It was reported that when Trinh Minh-ha's *Surname Viet* was screened in her own community, the audience missed the theme of decolonization and embraced it as an anti-Communist documentary. Further, the mass media coopted Asian Americans in their struggle with racial and ethnic conflicts in the society. The popularity of Asian American works in literature could have lent credibility to a sense of euphoria among some Asian Americans. Under these circumstances, there began a slow but definite shift from political filmmaking. The original political orientation was gradually changed in recent years. Some younger and film-school-trained filmmakers openly refused to link their works to their ethnicity.

As in the case of black filmmaking, the greatest challenge to Asian American filmmaking as alternative cinema came from its relationship with the Hollywood industry. Since moviemaking was such a capital-intensive and mass-audience-driven business, Asian American film practitioners had long been debating the pros and cons between the two strategies: seeking entry into the system in order to subvert the system from within or remaining independent and challenging the system from without. As Asian Americans began to have the clout that black filmmakers slowly acquired in Hollywood, it was no doubt that louder cries of sell-out were to be heard from within the Asian American communities.

A Genre Perspective

Throughout the course I had proposed what I called a genre approach. My hypothesis was that there existed a distinctive Asian American film genre and Asian American cinema should be appraised as a genre in its own right, in its unique cultural and discursive practices and in its complex dialectical relationship with both Hollywood narrative and other forms of Asian American art. Thomas Cripps argued years ago in *Black Film As Genre*[19] that black film must be seen as a genre for what it said and how it was said, rather than who was saying it. Among Asian Americans, Tajima was one of the earliest in calling for critical attention to

"Asian American aesthetic sensitivities." In an interview with Diane Mei Lin Mark, Wayne Wang asserted, "There's part of me that's very American, and I want to make movies that have no Asian characters. But my aesthetics, which is very much Chinese, would still come through."[20] Was there a distinctive Asian American film aesthetics? How were these Asian aesthetics, if there was one, reflected in their works of art? How did an Asian American film differ from Hollywood conventions structurally and formally? Or, to put it differently, had an Asian American film genre emerged?

There seemed to be two problems with the notion of an Asian American film aesthetics. First, Asian America is largely geographical and racial rather than a cultural concept. While we may speak of Asian American culture, paradoxically there is no such "thing" as an Asian American culture. Asian Americans in this country do not share a common cultural or linguistic heritage. As Tajima wrote, "The notion of plurality as the fabric of our own cultural identity contradicts our need for cohesion, our search for Asian American soul." Secondly, there was so much debate about the hyphen in the label of Asian Americans. Did we really need a hyphen between Asian and American. In other words, what is the essence of Asian American aesthetics, Asian, American or a combination of the two. As Daryl Chin was quoted as saying, ". . . any definition of Asian American (sic) aesthetics must be ipso facto partial, because the idea of Asian aesthetics must be pluralistic."[21] In view of these difficulties, I had come to the conclusion that the best way to define Asian American films should be through a careful analysis of each individual film, looking at its production process, its points of view and its formal styles.

Chan Is Missing: **A Paradigmatic Contribution**

In my lecture, I used Wayne Wang's early film *Chan Is Missing* as an example of this approach. Released in 1981, the movie was now considered an Asian American classic. First, thematically, Wang refused to exploit Chinatown as the exotic, dark, mysterious locale as it had traditionally been used in the mystery genre. The film offered an insider's perspective into the intricate conflicts and tangles of Chinatown life. The movie was an interesting character study that defused stereotypes. The characters were emotional, political, and fallible. They could laugh, cry, swear, and fight. They did not always keep their cool, stay on top of the situation, or succeed as do-no-wrong heroes. They were ordinary human beings. This intimate point of view functioned as an important corrective to the widely held stereotype of Asians and Asian Americans as stoic, emotionless people.

In terms of style, in sharp contrast to Hollywood's convention of glossy surface, continuity editing and "invisible style," the *Chan* film was noted for its various discursive innovations. The montage in the film, for example, was highly experimental. The film's ending was particularly symbolic. Toward the end of the film, Jo announced in a voice-over that "if this were a TV movie, an important clue would now pop up and clarify everything." No such clue appeared in the film. Instead, Jo explained that the search for such neat coherence was a Western trait. For those who could "think Chinese," what was not there became meaningful as what was. The open-ended plot seemed to be a direct contradiction to the Charlie Chan mode, where there was always a solution to the mystery.

Wayne Wang made an interesting comment on this point, "Asians tend to have a much higher tolerance for ambiguity, and have always historically been able to deal with ambiguity a lot more than so-called Caucasian minds, or Western minds."[22] Better still, the narrative sensitivities were supported by a significant use of mise-en-scène, which suggested a syncretic mix of Chinese rituals, music, and languages. Cinematographer Michael Chin revealed that he used the documentary-type shoot-from-the-hip format. His Chinatown mise-en-scène, in his own words, was filled not just with Asian "images," but with the visual and aural texture of Chinatown life, including music and language. As Diane Mei Lin Mark put it nicely, if language was a medium of culture, then we were brought to the heart of Chinese American cultural life. Our ears were initiated to Cantonese, Mandarin, and Chinese American English in black dialect, professional dialect, and Chinatown dialect. Equally important, it was Wang's deliberate decision to privilege the Asian audience that Chinese was not subtitled. Thus, I argued in class that *Chan Is Missing* could be loosely defined as an Asian American genre film and hopefully this film could serve as a model for the analysis of other films across a number of diverse styles, stories, and modes.

Notes

1. This course was taught first in the spring of 1992 at Carleton College, Northfield, Minnesota, then offered at Emory University, Atlanta, Georgia, and in the fall of 1995 it became a regular course under the auspices of the Center for the Applied Studies in American Ethnicity at Colorado State University, Fort Collins, Colorado.

2. I. C. Jarvie, *Movies and Society* (New York: Basic Books, 1970), 5.

3. John O'Connor, *Image As Fact: The Historical Analysis of Film and Television* (Malabar, Fla.: Robert T. Krieger Publishing Company, 1990), 302–24.

4. Carlos E. Cortez, "What is Maria? What is Juan? Dilemmas of Analyzing

the Chicano Image in U.S. Feature Films," *Chicano and Film: Essays on Chicano Representation and Resistance*, Chon A. Noriega, ed. (New York: Garland Publishing, Inc., 1992), 83–104.

5. Cortez, "What is Maria."

6. This film was only available on 16-mm format. I am aware of only two sources for the film, the Film Library in New York and University of Denver library.

7. Sumiko Higashi, "Ethnicity, Class, and Gender in Film 'The Cheat,' " in *Unspeakable Images: Ethnicity in the American Cinema*, Lester D. Friedman, ed. (Urbana: University of Illinois Press, 1991), 113–39.

8. Gina Marchetti, *Romance and the "Yellow Peril": Race, Sex, and Discursive Strategies in Hollywood Fiction* (Berkeley: University of California Press, 1993).

9. Edward Said, *Orientalism* (New York: Pantheon Books, 1979), 1–28.

10. Eugene Wong, *On Visual Media Racism: Asians in American Motion Pictures* (New York: Arno Press, 1978).

11. Wong, *On Visual Media Racism*, 1–55.

12. Eugenia Kaw, "Medicalization of Racial Features: Asian American Women and Cosmetic Surgery," *Medical Anthropology Quarterly* 7, no. 1 (March 1993).

13. Russell Leong, ed., *Moving the Image: Independent Asian Pacific American Media Arts* (Seattle: University of Washington Press, 1991).

14. Stephen Gong, "A History in Progress: Asian American Media Arts Centers 1970–1990," in *Moving the Image*, 1–9.

15. Stuart Hall, "Cultural Identity and Cinematic Representation," *Framework* 36 (1989): 70.

16. Gong, "A History in Progress," 1–2.

17. Daryl Chin, "After Ten Years: Some Notes on the Asian American International Film Festival Program" (New York: Asian CineVision, 1988), 16.

18. Valerie Soe, "On Experimental Video," *Moving the Image*, 238.

19. Thomas Cripps, *Black Film as Genre* (Bloomington: Indiana University Press, 1979).

20. Diane Mei Lin Mark, "Interview with Wayne Wang," from *Chan Is Missing* (Honolulu: Bamboo Ridge Press, 1984), 105.

21. Daryl Chin, "Film Forums: The Asian American Case," *CineVue* 1, no. 3 (New York: Asian CineVision, 1986), 9.

22. Mark, "Interview with Wayne Wang," 112.

19

Teaching Asian American Studies in Community Colleges

SUSIE LING

I remember a twenty-four-year-old Cambodian student who flunked his first Asian American history test. His academic preparation was not his only handicap. He had emotional difficulty with the class discussions about the early pioneers who worked so hard yet died as bachelors thousands of miles from their homeland. It reminded him that he too had lost his whole family when he was running through the mined jungles of Cambodia toward Thailand. He fought starvation by eating roots, somehow made it to America, and somehow survives. He wanted to try college, but he couldn't continue.

As an Asian American studies instructor at a community college, I have many fond memories of students especially of those who decided to major in Asian American studies. I keep mementos of such "successes"— letters of recommendation I submitted on their behalf, thank-you letters, postcards . . . But I also remember many of the students who dropped out or flunked. Their stories haunt and taunt me.

There was another student I chided for getting a "B" on a test when she had gotten an "A" on an earlier test. I lectured her about the need for commitment and the importance of education. She apologized but told me she had personal problems. I said that that was no excuse. She then explained that her sister was trying to commit suicide because her brother wanted to kill their parents. Most of me couldn't believe this story, but I knew it was true. She dropped the class.

Another student told me he felt that college was like another country although he was born and raised fifteen miles away. The language, customs, dress, and culture at the college were so different from his barrio neighborhood. Nobody in his family or neighborhood understood why he wanted to go to college. And nobody in college seemed to understand his background.

I teach Asian American studies at a community college in the Los

Angeles area. Students at the community college report the same academic and personal goals as students in four-year institutions, but they come from a much wider range of backgrounds. Some students remind me of the '49ers, Isseis, and manongs discussed in Asian American history. They are often the same age and same class background as the early Asian pioneers. Their faces and stories seem interchangeable. Is Asian American studies just another three hours per week on the college agenda of such students or does Asian American studies have a larger role to alleviate their sufferings and/or empower their future?

Is teaching Asian American studies at a community college pedagogically different from teaching Asian American studies at a four-year university? The student community seems different. The mission of community colleges is different from their four-year counterparts. Do community college instructors need to focus on a different set of goals and ideals? As an instructor, what can I do to prevent someone like that twenty-four-year-old Cambodian student from dropping? Should I do anything at all?

The Community Colleges' Impossible Dream

The 1960 Master Plan of Higher Education formalized a three-tiered system of public higher education in California. This pyramid begins with the campuses of the research-oriented Universities of California (UCs), followed by the California State University (CSUs or Cal States), with community colleges at the bottom. California's community colleges were charged with three major tasks: providing a two-year educational degree, providing vocational education (from auto mechanics to nursing), and providing the first two years of curriculum for transfer-eligible students. As the economic crisis in California's educational system worsens, the more cost-effective community college system is receiving more and more of the responsibility for educating the growing population. In 1993–94, the state of California spent about $18,000 per full-time student in the UC system as compared to about $3,000 per full-time student in the community college system. And yet the community colleges are supposed to transfer less-prepared students to the UC and CSU systems as "third" year students, rather than as "first" year students. It is a difficult task.

Community colleges were founded on the principle of open enrollment. Until the 1980s, California community colleges charged no tuition for resident students. For those over eighteen, admissions and enrollment is based on first come, first served. Regardless of a person's educational and personal background, they have the right to attempt education or more bluntly, "the right to flunk." In my classrooms, I've enjoyed the participation of an eighty-year-old grandmother who lived through the flapper era. Last semester, there was an immigrant from Mexico with four children, a third-grade education, and diagnosed learning disabilities. We inherit many of the "drop-downs" from the CSU and UC systems. While I have no numbers to cite, a significant number of CSU and UC graduates gained part of their higher education at community colleges. We also welcome the dropouts from the K–12 system and the drop ins or adults interested in personal development.

Each community college campus is unique. Some are urban and some are quite rural. As I have taught at Pasadena City College for over ten years, I will use it as a case study in this essay. Since I have had the privilege to teach at six other four-year campuses in the Southern California area as a part-timer, I have some basis for assessing the community college experience in a broader context.

Pasadena City College (PCC) is a suburban campus founded in 1924. It has a cherished reputation for high transfer rates. Current enrollment is 24,000, but only 27 percent are full-time students. Most of the student population is employed, some full time. I've seen my share of 8:00 a.m. students coming off an evening shift of work. A significant proportion of our students are parents and/or have other serious family responsibilities. PCC is a diverse campus, as the student body is made up of 34 percent Chicano/Latino, 33 percent Asian and Pacific Islander, 24 percent European American, 9 percent African American, and 1 percent American Indian. Almost 60 percent of the students are female. About 35 percent of the students are not citizens of the United States. While 38 percent of the student population is under twenty-one years of age, 30 percent are over 30 years of age. Faculty composition is 8 percent Asian American and 72 percent European American.

At Pasadena City College, classes are held from 7:00 a.m. to 10:00 p.m. with some courses meeting on Saturdays. Each class is taught as an ESL (English as a second language) class and each class has a sprinkling of students with disabilities from dyslexia to deafness. While instructors have few research responsibilities, we have heavy teaching loads: minimum of five courses a semester or about fifteen teaching hours per week with two or three different preparations. Faculty average about 200 to 250 students per semester. Instructors have administrative responsibilities as well as the obligation to engage in intensive one-to-one academic and personal counseling sessions with students. With little support staff and office equipment, we type our own exams, grade every paper, and often run the mimeograph machine ourselves.

Asian American Studies Alive and Sometimes Well in the Community Colleges

In 1994, I performed an informal survey of Asian American studies in the California community college system. (See Appendix #1.) My principle finding is that Asian American studies is alive and sometimes well in the community colleges. The 1960s struggle for Asian American studies from San Francisco State to UCLA impacted the community colleges. Many campuses were able to establish their own Asian American studies curriculum in the late 1960s and early 1970s, such as Merritt College (which actually had Asian American studies before UC Berkeley), San Francisco City College, Laney College, Cabrillo College, Santa Monica City College, East Los Angeles City College, and Los Angeles City College. Another wave of campuses is developing and/or reestablishing Asian American studies in the 1990s: Cerritos College, Fresno City College, Cypress College, and Ventura College. Mesa College in San Diego recently started Asian American studies at the behest of the campus administration rather than in response to the usual faculty and student interest. Mission College and Los Angeles City College no longer offer their previously existing Asian American studies courses. Of the 107 California community college campuses, I counted twenty-one with existing Asian American studies courses.

Of these twenty-one Asian American studies programs, San Francisco City College should be singled out. San Francisco City College actively teaches nine separate courses in their Department of Asian American Studies. They enroll nine hundred students per semester. In contrast, most other campuses teach one or two Asian American studies courses occasionally.

Pasadena City College is a campus that can boast of a twenty-year tradition in Asian American studies. Today it has the second largest Asian student population in the California community college system (second to San Francisco City College). Like other community colleges, the establishment of PCC's ethnic studies courses were the result of the faculty's diligent efforts. The three Asian American studies courses here—History 41 (History of Asian Pacific Americans), Sociology 41 (Contemporary Issues of Asian Pacific Americans) and Psychology 41 (Psychological Issues of Asian Pacific Americans)—were proposed by a counselor who was active with Japanese American Citizens League in the early 1970s. This curriculum series was established along with similar series in African American and Chicano/Latino studies. All of these courses are housed along with classes covering everything from anthropology to philosophy in the social sciences division. While ethnic studies is not recognized as a subdiscipline (for example, History 41 is considered a history course), there is an unofficial alliance between the faculty who teach ethnic-studies-related courses.

My assignment in the department is officially "Asian American Studies/History." I am the first and only full-time instructor at PCC with a designated Asian American studies assignment. Once in a while, part-timers may teach one of the Asian American studies courses. While I have been able to maintain about 60 percent of my work load directly in Asian American studies, I also teach U.S. history, women's studies, and world history. Other full-time community college instructors teaching Asian American studies also teach ethnic studies, Chicano history, U.S. history, Asian history, languages, sociology, etc. Other campuses use part-time instructors only in Asian American studies.

Should We or Do We Teach Asian American Studies Differently at Community Colleges?

I don't know. I asked this question of many of my Pasadena City College colleagues and Asian American studies colleagues in preparation for this self-assessment paper. One Asian American studies instructor from Cal State Long Beach suggested there was an ethical answer and a practical answer. He said that as most students at the Cal States were employed, it was not practical to expect the academic rigor he would expect from UC students. A UC Irvine professor pointed out that research skills and scholarship were very much emphasized in his Asian American studies courses as he was actually preparing students for graduate studies. UC Irvine's Asian student population is also immigrant and very diverse. I admit community colleges assign fewer readings and research papers.

Most of the PCC colleagues answered the same question bluntly. They said, "No." Some added that they had experience teaching at four-year institutions and they do not change either the content or the style of their courses. As PCC is expected to transfer students to the four-year institutions, it would be a great disservice to students to compromise academic standards. We are pledged to offer lower-division college courses and must stand up to rigorous articulation agreements.

However, PCC colleagues say there is more emphasis on teaching skills at the community colleges. Our lower-division courses have a student capacity of forty-five versus the auditoriums of two hundred at the UCs. One PCC professor suggested that "less than good" teaching cannot be tolerated at the community colleges. She suggested that PCC instructors make fewer assumptions about students' academic preparation and are more in tune with students' off-campus concerns. While the classroom instruction is the same, office-hour activities are significantly different.

Community college instructors offer more office hours to students and spend much energy on remedial activities and confidence-building pep talks.

Different Goal: Getting "Out" of the Community

An eighteen-year-old Vietnamese woman came to drop my class many years ago; she was going to quit school because her fiancé said it wasn't necessary for her to get an education. Despite empty threats, I failed to change her mind. Last week, a Taiwan Chinese twenty-one-year old told me she wanted to cram as many units as possible into her schedule, despite poor grades. She wanted to finish her education so she could get a job and stop being a financial burden on her mother. The mother was a housekeeper for a relative and deep in debt. The mother was also emotionally abusing her and wanted her to quit school. The student had not shown up for class all this week. An ex-Marine Pilipino's big dream was to go to San Jose State only because he had a cousin there. With a near 4.0 GPA (grade point average) but obviously a first-generation college student, he never thought of going to a UC. Teaching Asian American studies is my vehicle to encourage these students and others to get out of their community so that they have a chance to see other possibilities. As their teacher, I want to encourage them to end their relative isolation as well as their victimization.

After all that training in Asian American studies to "get into the community," now I spend so much energy trying to get Asian American students "out" of their community. It goes back to divergent definitions of "community." While we may want to encourage the UC students to cross the tracks and to get involved with those less fortunate, this is not the agenda for community college students. Community for them is their overcrowded home; community is their "less than minimum wage" workplace. PCC students and some of their parents want above all else to get out of this community. They want the American dream, which is not present in the ethnic ghetto. For both community college students and four-year university students, "community" does mean broadening their personal horizons and understanding their responsibilities to society. Asian American studies is a vehicle towards that end. Asian American studies is about questioning the status quo and about self- and group-empowerment.

While I may ethically and practically teach the Asian American studies at a community college similar to the way I would teach it in a UC setting, I hope the content of the course works different magic on its own. UC students may see Asian American studies as another history research project, another step towards graduate school, but community college students seem to identify more with the history itself. I hope that they are able to find survival techniques and ways to keep their personal Gold Mountain dream alive in the history of their ancestors. I hope their sufferings are alleviated when they realize there were others who endured as much before. I hope they are empowered by the stories of Philip Vera Cruz, Dr. Sammy Lee, and my mother-in-law who answered, "No" on the 1943 Loyalty Questionnaire. I hope they pay more attention when I point out Carlos Bulosan only had three years of formal education.

While teaching at four-year campuses, my main goal was to document a pattern of racial discrimination and economic exploitation. The hope is that Asian American students will recognize racism and fight these reoccurring patterns. At the community colleges, many Asian American students identify, not just empathize, with the Issei picture brides and the Pilipino manongs. Asian American studies is about previous immigrants who have worked hard and made contributions despite the racism. I don't care that much if today's students drop the course or if they flunk; I just hope they heard the messages from their ancestors. Hopefully, they understood the history lessons as lessons of the triumph of survival.

I love teaching at the community college. I live in the same community as the students and see them as the clerks at my market, as the teachers for my children's preschool, and washing their cars down my street. Working with classes of about forty students (rather than two hundred) means connecting with them more on a one-to-one basis. It means following their progress from exam to exam. It means almost being able to watch some of their minds blossom week by week right in front of me. It is part social work and part parenting. It is introducing history to young minds and broadening my own understanding of history. It is about "successes" and "failures"—plenty of both. Being a teacher of Asian American studies at the community college level is committing to community and investing in our future.

Appendix #1

The survey also solicited problems and concerns of teaching Asian American studies at community colleges. Although not based on a random sample, my experience suggests that it is fairly reliable. Here are some of the key findings:

Isolation. Many of the Asian American studies instructors at community colleges complain of isolation. It is especially difficult to stay up to date on new concepts and debates in the ethnic studies field. There is a dire need for more informative and supportive networking that does not entail much physical travel.

Cutbacks. Similar to our four-year counterparts, cutbacks are a serious concern. As it has been proven again and again, Asian American studies is often first to be dismantled in an economic crunch. That is partially why instructors like me try to protect ourselves by gaining seniority in another discipline: for example, U.S. history. Thus, I cannot afford to be recognized only as an Asian American studies specialist.

Curriculum Growth. On some campuses, Asian American studies is just happy to be existing. On other campuses, there can be some limited development of new curriculum. At Pasadena City College, we recently established Sociology 14: Introduction to Ethnic Studies. I would also like to begin an Asian American literature course, but our course offerings are very dependent on the programs of the four-year transfer campuses. If the local four-year campuses do not recognize Asian American studies as lower-division transfer units, community colleges cannot offer such courses. For example, because few four-year campuses offer "Asian American women" as a lower-division course, I do not know of a California community college that can gain approval for this course. If a nearby four-year campus establishes "diversity" courses as part of its general education requirements, the whole curriculum at Pasadena City College would have to be reviewed. When most four-year campuses review their own curriculum, there is very little thought given to the impact of their actions on neighboring community colleges.

Language Skills and Academic Preparation. In my Asian American studies classes, over 90 percent of the students are Asian and about 50 percent have immigrated in the last five years. English comprehension and writing skills are definitely inferior to Asian immigrant students from four-year institutions. Verbal class participation is difficult. Many spend hours translating the reading assignments and still report little comprehension. Students' analytical skills need development. I spend significant class time encouraging students to find "main ideas" and the author's thesis. Some students who are educated in Asia have never been asked to express and support their own opinions in an essay. Other students can't remember one thing they learned in U.S. history in high school. I often discuss "how to study" during office hours when students are pulled in to discuss failing grades.

Useful Resources. There is a dire need for basic, useful resources such as textbooks and films. While there is more selection for instructors in four-year campuses, community college instructors need basic tools. Unlike instructors in the four-year counterparts, I can only expect students to read one major text. This text must be accessible to students in ESL and students with limited experience in reading. I prefer class films to not exceed thirty minutes and they must be close captioned (for ESL and hearing disabled students).

Student Integrity. Like four-year campuses, there is concern about the integrity of student work. As we must depend more on multiple-choice testing (as writing skills may be limited and faculty's time to grade is limited), we must police for cheating and plagiarism.

20

The Politics of Teaching Asian American Literature amidst Middle-Class, Caucasian Students "East of California"

SHENG-MEI MA

Despite this so-called era of multiculturalism, it remained disheartening for college professors to introduce texts into the classroom that challenged the cultural hegemony of American society. I experienced such frustration in my attempt to integrate Asian American literature in my world literature course at a state university in Virginia where the bulk of the student body came from a white, middle-class, suburban background in Washington, D.C., and surrounding areas. During our class discussion on the travails of early Chinese immigrants and the white society's racism, I was shocked by the passionate defensiveness of a handful of students and was unnerved by the apathetic silence of the majority of students. Their response awaked in me a Foucauldian realization of power and knowledge. I came to see the amazing role politics—the search for and maintenance of power—had played, often in an implicit manner, in the acquisition of knowledge. This was borne out by the fact that whenever the vested interest of a dominant group appeared to be threatened, as my students no doubt felt faced with a version of American history from the eyes of Chinese coolies, the reaction was swift and decisive.

To teach ethnic pain in Asian American literature amidst middle-class, Caucasian college students "east of California," therefore, requires careful political considerations, lest the course degenerates into a series of confrontations. One way of avoiding clashes is to select "safe" texts, popular texts which have been accepted by the American sensibility. For instance, Maxine Hong Kingston's *The Woman Warrior*[1] is now a standard textbook in universities. The American readership finds the novel engaging and nonoffensive, for the depiction of ethnic experience at Gold Mountain (the Chinese name for San Francisco) never directly indicts the

243

host country as responsible for the misery of Chinese Americans. When Kingston's second novel, *China Men*,[2] begins to chronicle the dehuman-ization of Chinese coolies by white railroad builders as well as by dis-criminatory laws passed by the U.S. Congress, the public's enthusiasm dwindles visibly. A sense of unease on the part of white readers has pre-cluded a total acceptance of *China Men*. However, even a "safe" text like *The Woman Warrior* can be problematized if one contests the reader's reception. Why does one prefer *The Woman Warrior* to *China Men*? Is it because the first novel seems to have less bearing on the reader person-ally and hence poses less threat? This self-reflexive approach is predi-cated, nonetheless, on the willingness to reexamine one's own positions and to engage in serious debates over complex issues such as ethnicity and hegemony.

An instructor can also choose "unsafe" texts, works that openly ex-plore the injustice of the system and the anguish of Asian Americans. With a certain amount of reservation, I tried this approach. In my intro-ductory session to Asian American literature (as a module of my world literature class), I showed Genny Lim's play, *Paper Angels*,[3] and assigned Elaine Kim's critical essay, "Images of Asians in Anglo-American Litera-ture," which is the opening chapter to her *Asian American Literature: An Introduction to the Writings and Their Social Context*[4]. Lim records meticulously the horrible conditions and mistreatment of Chinese immi-grants detained at the immigration station on Angel Island in San Fran-cisco Bay in the early decades of this century. Kim amasses a great amount of materials, through which the unabashedly vicious or the thinly veiled racism of both low-brow and high-brow Anglo-American writers is exposed.

Students' response to both works was primarily one of silence. Some professed a deep sense of unfamiliarity (disbelief?) with this part of the Asian American experience; they were so disoriented by the film and the reading that they were lost for words. The blankness on students' faces bespoke the distance between white America and Asian America, as the suffering of the latter in the hands of the former went largely unregistered in history and in collective consciousness. However, the blankness was gradually replaced by tinges of annoyance and impatience as I began to probe into the historical facts and details in both works. And then a handful of die-hard students found their voices and prevailed over the silent majority. It is difficult for me to gauge whether or not or to what extent they were speaking on behalf of the entire class. I can only record the argument this "minority" advanced.

These students employed several tactics to refute Kim's essay on the disparaging images of Asian Americans, which in part led to the policies against Chinese immigrants portrayed by Lim. None of these arguments, to be sure, was terribly original, but the joint forces of such banalities swept through the classroom, constituting something an instructor must address and seek to redress. Their first line of reasoning was intentionality, or, more specifically, the absence of malice. They contended that Charlie Chan, Fu Manchu, and others whom Kim explicated were created for entertainment and comedy rather than the denigration of minorities and foreigners. But entertainment at whose expense? Several students defended, in the name of recreation, the following passage from Jack London's *The Star Rover* (1915) quoted in Kim's piece:

> They [Koreans] went down like tenpins, fell over each other in heaps. . . . I [an Englishman] made a mess of them and a muss and muck of their silks ere the multitude could return upon me. There were so many of them. They clogged my blows by the sheer numbers of them, those behind shoving the front ones upon me. And how I dropped them! Toward the end they were squirming three-deep under my feet.[5]

I compared this passage to the staple scene in Westerns with the "red savages" being cut down by the cavalry and with a hero like John Wayne, his six-shooter smoking, towering over masses of mutilated bodies. A few students objected to the suggestion of racist attitude in such films; they insisted, with a grin and a shrug, that Westerns were nothing but movies. They were, I assume, secretly appalled by the unenlightened nature of our discussion, or they were possibly outraged by what they perceived to be political correctness impinging upon them.

If popular culture were truly as harmless as these students alleged, then one should be able to write a script of an Asian hero slaughtering hordes of bestial Caucasians and be expected to win the hearts of millions of white moviegoers. This reversal of London's plot should not theoretically detract from the entertaining effect; after all, one merely switched races. But such an arrangement would never succeed in amusing the American public. Even recent Westerns such as "Dances with Wolves" and "The Last of the Mohicans" continued the practice of featuring Caucasian protagonists when the films supposedly centered on the life and demise of Native Americans. The audience identified with the white actor who in turn identified with Indians, a convenient way of not alienating the white' sensibility while allowing moviegoers to feel that the wrongs had somehow been righted. In sum, entertainment reflects and molds our culture, which infiltrates into every corner of our consciousness. Stereotypes of insectlike Asians and Godlike Caucasians are gradually internalized and shape our behavior accordingly.

The second argument was that these Anglo-American writers were ignorant, hence dismissing our scrutiny as superfluous. Yet Kim cited a number of major American authors, such as Jack London, Bret Harte, John Steinbeck, and Frank Norris, writers who, even today, remain canonized in American literature. The stature accorded these writers, following the students' rationalization, seems unwarranted in view of their uninformed and indeed despicable opinions on race. However, these beloved American novelists are in no danger of being expelled for this reason from the canon. We need to instead analyze their distorting representations of Asians in order to avoid perpetuating the same kind of *willed* ignorance.

The students' third strategy was to discredit Kim's account by pointing out the "antiquated" nature of her materials. Kim referred to writers around the turn of the century, from which students immediately concluded that prejudice against Asian Americans was a thing of the past. If indeed it were, then why should students become defensive? If indeed it were, we should be able to read Kim's writing disinterestedly, as it had no relevance to our lives whatsoever. It was clearly not the case. The fact that these students' reaction was marked by denial of any injustice perpetrated against "the Other" demonstrated that racial tensions exist today, perhaps in subtler forms than before. Moreover, this argument simply failed to recognize the persisting manifestations of damaging stereotypes of aliens, such as the ones found in the "Rambo" series with blood-thirsty Viet Congs and in the rush of Japan-bashing originating from the very top of the Reagan-Bush administration. A self-imposed blindness prevented these students from perceiving what loomed large in the society as well as what existed within their own mind.

The final tactic and perhaps the most insidious one was that discriminations happened everywhere, implying that bigotry here at home and in Anglo-American literature was somehow justified. One hesitates to dignify such apologists with a response.

Ethnic pain is a powerful thing. To hold in mind past afflictions creates affinity amongst those who identify with the minority but encounters resistance amongst those who identify with the party wielding power. The quick, edgy response to Kim from the small number of students stemmed in part from their white, middle-class, suburban background, a background which, in their subconscious at least, appeared to have linked them with the immigration laws operating on Angel Island and the Caucasian authors who stereotyped Asians. Even though they would most likely disclaim any specific political ties, the students' actions belied an allegiance to the cultural hegemony of this country. To whitewash the sufferings of Asian Americans enabled these students to deny collective guilt and responsibility, sentiments most gnawing to one's conscience and therefore vigorously rejected by all.

Yet nothing burns in ethnic memory more intensely than a mass catastrophe; nothing unites the oppressed more firmly than the remembrance of an affliction visited upon them. Jewish Americans, as a result, mourned the Holocaust; Afro-Americans slavery; Native Americans 1492 and Columbus. In the same vein, Japanese Americans chronicled the forced evacuation and internment during World War II; Chinese Americans recorded the fatal blows to their community in the wake of the 1882 Exclusion Act as well as the pattern of persecutions targeting "chinks." The minority is compelled to commemorate its sufferings, which generate, among other things, a heightened self-awareness and ethnic identity. It is critical, however, not to abuse ethnic memory by flaunting it as an excuse for present failings, which would only justify the majority's resentment. That is certainly far from my intention in using Lim and Kim, but the student response has taught me a valuable lesson: any successful pedagogy in relation to the presentation of ethnic pain "east of California" must take into consideration not only the veracity of the subject matter but the *feeling* of the constituency, not only how to sustain this pursuit for historical fact and justice but how not to alienate middle-class, Caucasian students who might feel that they are the prey.

Notes

1. Maxine Hong Kingston, *The Woman Warrior: Memoirs of a Girlhood among Ghosts* (New York: Knopf, 1976).

2. Maxine Hong Kingston, *China Men* (New York: Knopf, 1980).

3. Genny Lim, *Paper Angels*. Directed by John Lone. (*American Playhouse*: PBS, 1985).

4. Elaine H. Kim, *Asian American Literature: An Introduction to the Writings and Their Social Context* (Philadelphia: Temple University Press, 1982).

5. Jack London, *The Star Rover* (New York: Macmillan, 1915), 157.

Appendix

Resources for Innovation/Excellence in Teaching: A Select, Annotated Bibliography

MALCOLM COLLIER AND
LANE RYO HIRABAYASHI

In addition to the excellent references cited in the chapters above, the following bibliography features resources which we think are especially useful for promoting excellence and innovation in the classroom. It is also worth emphasizing that untenured faculty should attend to the selection by Peter Seldin (1991) before getting too experimental. Like it or not, poor teaching reviews can limit if not end the lecturer's/tenure-track professor's career—even if the intent behind innovations is well meant.

Banks, James A., and Cherry A. Banks, eds. *Handbook of Research on Multicultural Education*. New York: Macmillan, 1995. This comprehensive compendium is held in most university-level library reference collections. Entries offer a plethora of substantive and educational research-oriented overviews; the bibliographies following each article are also useful.

Davis, Barbara G. *Tools for Teaching*. San Francisco: Jossey Bass, 1993. Another compendium, Davis's volume is an especially well-organized guide to a host of practical and technical issues in teaching. Each chapter is followed by a short list of carefully selected citations for further reading. Similarly, Leo M. Lambert, et al., eds., *University Teaching: A Guide for Graduate Students* (Syracuse, N.Y.: Syracuse University Press, 1996) is a recent resource that one can cite or assign to graduate students who expect to become, or who are already working as, one's teaching assistants. Its up-to-date contents makes it useful introduction for beginning professors, too.

Ellsworth, Elizabeth, and Mariamne Whatley, eds. *The Ideology of Images in Educational Media: Hidden Curriculum in the Classroom*. New York: Teachers College Press, 1990. This is one of a few collections that examines pedagogical dimensions of teaching with video and film, critically. The authors' discussion of "hidden curriculum" in regard to educational media is especially intriguing.

hooks, bell. *Teaching to Transgress*. New York: Routledge, 1994. A collection of insightful essays on teaching and learning—as well as on how one, as a teacher, must combat traditional hierarchies of oppression in the classroom—from a black feminist critic.

Although written to assist preservice and in-service teachers—and thus more technically-pitched than hooks—a comprehensive resource is Theresa Mickey McCormick, *Creating the Nonsexist Classroom: A Multicultural Approach* (New York: Teachers College Press, 1994). McCormick states, "This book elaborates on ways that the culture in most schools helps reproduce sexism and racism, and it provides educators with strategies for creating a more equitable school culture and practice."

Luke, Carmen, and Jennifer Gore, eds. *Feminisms and Critical Pedagogy*. New York: Routledge, 1992. This collection has seminal articles by feminist educators, many of whom critique patriarchy in theories of pedagogy. Authors are deeply concerned with the construction of subjects, narratives, and authority in contemporary classrooms. Luke and Gore also present fascinating interrogations of the concept of student "empowerment."

McCarthy, Cameron, and Warren Crichlow, eds. *Race, Identity and Representation in Education*. New York: Routledge, 1993. The authors in this anthology draw their inspiration largely from cultural studies. Their examination of the intersections between race, class, and gender in the classroom are always thought provoking and sometimes inspiring.

Nakanishi, Don T., and Tina Y. Nishida, eds. *The Asian American Educational Experience: A Sourcebook for Teachers and Students*. New York: Routledge, 1995. This state-of-the-art collection presents some of the best available research on the educational issues pertaining to people of Asian descent in the United States, and includes a comprehensive bibliography.

Seldin, Peter. *Teaching Portfolio: A Practical Guide to Improved Performance and Promotion Tenure Decisions*. New York: Anker Publishing, 1991. The basic idea Seldin proposes is that professors should put together a "teaching portfolio" that includes items such as philosophy of curriculum design, drafts of syllabi, copies of handouts, assignments, examinations, as well as samples of student exams, papers, and letters. Such a portfolio is much more indicative of "teaching" skills and achievements, as opposed to simple "Faculty/Course Questionnaires" (or FCQs)—especially given that students sometimes respond to innovation in the classroom with negative course evaluations.

Sage Publications has a series, "Survival Skills for Scholars," which offers short monographs that offer useful, if somewhat conventional, resources for the working professor. Examples include Maryellen Weimer, *Improving Your Classroom Teaching* (Thousand Oaks, Calif.: Sage, 1993), and John C. Ory and Katherine E. Ryan, *Tips for Improving Testing and Grading* (Thousand Oaks, Calif.: Sage, 1993). Also, Jody D. Nyquist and Donald H. Wulff's *Working Effectively with Graduate Students* (Thousand Oaks, Calif.: Sage, 1996), is a useful resource which discusses both managerial and pedagogical dimensions, including how one can best teach graduate students to teach. A related resource in the same series is Marcia Lynn Whicher, et al., *Getting Tenure* (Thousand Oaks, Calif.: Sage, 1993). While this is a useful generic overview of the subject, especially for those who are in mainstream academic departments, its major limitation is that it is geared toward the status quo. (Perhaps its tacit message is: "if you want to get tenure, try to get along with your colleagues, keep your head down, and don't buck the system!") We clearly need more discussion of prejudice and discrimination in the academy, and how, as a professor, to resist institutional sexism/racism. For one example of what can be done, see the eight articles that make up the special section, "Power to the People! The Don Nakanishi Tenure Case at UCLA," in *Amerasia Journal* 16, no. 1 (1990): 63–169.

Finally, there are many journals which regularly present up-to-date resources that teachers, from neophytes to the semiretired, will find useful and inspiring. These journals include: *The Review of Education, Pedagogy, Cultural Studies; Harvard Educational Review; Anthropology & Education Quarterly; Teaching Sociology;* the "Textbooks and Teaching" section of *The Journal of American History;* the "Teaching Radical History" section of the *Radical History Review; Race, Sex and Class,* etc.

Index

activism, 161–74
Aeneas, 18
affirmative action, 82
Afghanistan, 116
African Americans, 140n13
Africans, Asians' kinship with, 30–31
agriculture, working in, 25, 28
Aguilar-San Juan, Karin, 166
Aiiieeeee!, 93–94, 101
Alarcón, Norma, 18
Alexander, Meena, 120
Althusser, Louis, 14–15
Amendment 2, 172
anti-Asian/American sentiment, 19, 25
anti-Chinese movement, 19th century, 28, 29
arts, 52
Asian Americans: connection to country of origin, 4, 119–20, 132, 135, 177, 180–82, 210; defining, 5, 37, 87n1, 88n3; depiction in the media, 139n12, 212n20, 219–21; diaspora of, 119–20, 181–82, 194–95, 211n6; discrimination against, 79, 83–84, 153, 166–67, 195, 205, 209, 210n3; diversity among, 27, 41, 53, 112–19, 132, 135; and domestic abuse, 79; effect of NAFTA and GATT on, 56–57; emergence of working class among, 52–54; as employers, 55–56, 133; identity of, 13, 18–20, 35–47, 151–60; inclu-

sion criteria, 111–22; as informants, 124–25; intergenerational differences, 144–45, 203–4, 209, 210; internal prejudice, 134; masculinity and, 99–101; 1965 Immigration Act and, 3, 29; occupational patterns of, 51–56; and paper sons, 19–20; psychology and, 151–60; recent arrivals vs American-born, 4; sexual and racial formation of, 19; South Asians as, 112–22; stereotypes of, 19, 83–84, 90n18, 117, 133; in U. S. history texts, 28; viewed as unimportant, 16, 22n9; as wedge group, 90n18; youth culture of, 9

Asian Americans: An Interpretive History, 29

Asian American studies: Asian Americans in movies, 139–40n12; in community colleges, 233–41; community studies in, 146–50, 163–71, 189–92; differing priorities in, 2–3, 6; east of California, 243–47; ethnic-specific courses, value of, 193; experimental course in, 61–72; extracurricular praxis, 137, 141n19; feminism and, 3, 86–87; Filipinos and Indian Americans in, 88n3; gay liberation and, 3; and global capitalist class structure, 51–58; impact on psychology, 152–57, 157–58;

About the Contributors

Jachinson W. Chan is an assistant professor in the Asian American studies department, University of California, Santa Barbara. He is working on his manuscript, tentatively titled, *Chinese American Masculinities: From Fu Manchu to Bruce Lee.*

Chung Hoang Chuong is currently associate professor and director of the Vietnamese Studies Center at San Francisco State University. Focusing on many issues in the Vietnamese Diaspora, in 1994 he coauthored a study on the Vietnamese Amerasians in California.

Malcolm Collier is a founding member of the Asian American studies department at San Francisco State University, with considerable experience in research and advocacy in the areas of education and community development. He is the coauthor of *Visual Anthropology: Photography as a Research Methods* (University of New Mexico Press, 1987) and the 1997–98 president of the Society for Visual Anthropology, a section of the American Anthropological Association.

David L. Eng is an assistant professor in English and comparative literature at Columbia University. He is coeditor with Alice Y. Hom of *Q & A: Queer in Asian America* (Temple University Press, forthcoming) and has published essays in *Amerasia Journal, Critical Mass: A Journal of Asian American Cultural Criticism, Camera Obscura,* and *Social Text.* He is currently completing a manuscript entitled *Racial Castration: Managing Masculinity in Asian America.*

Timothy P. Fong is currently an assistant professor of sociology at Holy Names College in Oakland, California. His book, *The First Suburban Chinatown: The Remaking of Monterey Park, California* (Temple University Press, 1994), received the 1995 National Book Award in Social Sciences from the Association of Asian American Studies.

Diane C. Fujino is assistant professor in the Department of Asian American Studies at the University of California, Santa Barbara. Her research examines race and gender issues in discrimination and coping among women of color and Asian American interracial relationships. Her latest project involves gathering oral histories of Asian American women activists, with a particular focus on the life and politics of Yuri Kochiyama.

Lane Ryo Hirabayashi is professor in the Department of Ethnic Studies at the University of Colorado, Boulder, where he also coordinates Asian American studies. He has published a book, *Cultural Capital: Mountain Zapotec Migrants in Mexico City* (1993), as well as a number of anthologies including, *Inside an American Concentration Camp: Japanese American Resistance at Poston, Arizona* (1995). His new book, *Fieldwork in an American Concentration Camp: Tamie Tsuchiyama and JERS* is forthcoming in 1999.

Laura Hyun Yi Kang is assistant professor of women's studies and English and comparative literature at the University of California, Irvine. She is also an affiliated faculty member of Asian American studies and African American studies. Her book, *Compositional Subjects: Enfiguring Asian/American Women*, is forthcoming from Duke University Press.

Madhulika S. Khandelwal is acting director of Asian/American Center at Queens College (CUNY), where she also teaches courses on urban neighborhoods and Asian American communities. She is currently preparing a book titled *Becoming Americans, Becoming Indians: Indian Immigrants in New York City, 1976–1996*.

Ben Kobashigawa is associate professor in the Asian American Studies Department, College of Ethnic Studies, San Francisco State University. He is the translator and editor of *History of the Okinawans in North America*, published by the Okinawa Club of America and the Asian American Studies Center, UCLA, in 1988.

Year of the Dragon Korean-born, Hawaiian-reared, California-educated, and New York City dweller **Robert Ji-Song Ku**, after several years of migrant teaching at the Borough of Manhattan Community College, Bard College, Columbia University, and New York University, is currently very happy to be teaching American literature and Asian American Studies full-time at Hunter College, the school of his dreams. His fiction, essays, and editorial work appear in *Amerasia Journal, Artsprial, KoreAm Journal, SEORO*, and other publications. He is on the board of the Asian American Arts Alliance in New York City and is excited to be curating the centennial Korean American literature exhibit for the Korean American Museum in Los Angeles in 2000, the Year of the Dragon.

Gary Y. Okihiro is a professor of History and director of the Asian American Studies Program at Cornell University. He is author and editor of several books in Asian American and ethnic studies, and is a past president of the Association for Asian American Studies.

Emily Porcincula Lawsin is on the board of trustees of the Filipino American National Historical Society (FANHS). She has taught in the Asian American Studies Department at California State University, Northridge, and at the University of California, Los Angeles. An oral historian and performance poet, her poetry and essays on war brides and students have been published in *Flippin': Filipinos on America, The FANHS Journal, Seattle Arts, The International Examiner, Forward Motion Magazine's Asians in Struggle, Homegrown 3,* and *The Seattle Times.*

Ramsay Leim is professor of psychology in the Department of Psychology at Boston College and codirector of the concentration in Asian American studies. His interests include cultural and community psychology. His article, "Shame and Guilt Among First- and Second-Generation Asian Americans and European Americans," was recently published in the *Journal of Cross Cultural Psychology* 28, no. 4 (1997).

Associate professor at Pasadena City College, **Susie Ling** teaches Asian American studies, U.S. history, and world history at the community-college level.

Sheng-mei Ma is assistant professor of American thought and language at Michigan State University. His book, *Immigrant Subjectivities in Asian American and Asian Diaspora Literatures,* is scheduled to be published by State University of New York Press in May 1998. His book in progress, *The Deathly Embrace: Orientalism and Asian American Ethnicity,* was awarded the Rockefeller Fellowship for 1997–98.

Keith Osajima is associate professor of education and director of the Race and Ethnic Studies program at the University of Redlands. He continues to write about critical pedagogy and enjoys spending time with his daughter, Avery.

Rosane Rocher is professor and undergraduate chair in the Department of South Asian Regional Studies, University of Pennsylvania, where she is also director of the Asian American studies program. Among her publications are several books and articles on aspects of the intellectual exchange and negotiations between British orientalists and Indian traditional scholars in the late eighteenth century. She has addressed the need to build South Asian American Studies in "Reconstituting South Asian Studies for a Diasporic Age" (1994) and with a working bibliography of South Asian American studies, 1975–94 (1995), both published in *Sagar*, the South Asian graduate research journal, at the University of Texas at Austin.

Patricia A. Sakurai is an assistant professor in the Ethnic Studies Department at Oregon State University. Her work also appears in *Privileging Positions: The Sites of Asian American Studies*, published by Washington State University Press. She is currently working on an essay addressing Asian American studies scholars and the academic job market.

Eric C. Wat recently left the Asian American Studies Center where he taught courses on contemporary community issues and leadership development. He now dedicates his life (or at least the next year or so) to waiting tables and organizing, facilitating, transcribing, and editing roundtable discussions. If his fingers are crossed tightly enough, he will begin soon an oral history project for his Master's thesis on the gay Asian community in Los Angeles during the 1970s.

Jun Xing is assistant professor in the Department of History, and the Center for Applied Studies in American Ethnicity, Colorado State University. His new book, *Baptized in the Fire of Revolution: The American Social Gospel and the YMCA in China, 1919–1937*, was published in 1996 by Lehigh University Press.